LESS CHAOS LESS NOISE

EFFECTIVE COMMUNICATIONS FOR AN EFFECTIVE CHURCH

KEM MEYER

Less Chaos. Less Noise.

Kem Meyer

ISBN: 978-0-9974274-0-0

Library of Congress Control Number: 2016905778

Revised and updated from *Less Clutter. Less Noise.*, originally published by Thirty:One Press and WiredChurches.com in 2009.

This book is manufactured in the United States of America.

Editor: Haley Walden; Anna Floit, The Peacock Quill
Cover Design: Josh Lowder, Wheelhouse Creative
Interior Design: Phil Herrold, Melissa Washburn
Author Photo: Julie Cannon

“Kem shows us how to target and connect rather than barrage and confuse.

...relevant strategies that are laser-focused and people-driven.

...a field guide for connecting with your community and transforming lives...

"The greatest message ought to be communicated in the most memorable ways. And, Kem Meyer will show you how to do it. This book is both inspirational and practical. A must-read for those who care about communicating the message of Christ in the most compelling way possible."

—Mark Batterson, *New York Times* bestselling author and Lead Pastor of National Community Church

"Practical, insightful, even breathtaking at times. If your communications are failing to communicate, this book is a fabulous place to start."

—Seth Godin, bestselling author

"With a 360-degree view of the author and application of this book's content, I find myself in a unique position. As Kem's pastor, I've watched her integrate the values and principles espoused in this book throughout the fabric of Granger Community Church. This stuff isn't just theory. I know it really works. Kem has made this extraordinary material available to you. Use it up."

—Mark Beeson, Senior Pastor, Granger Community Church

"Meyer takes a candid look at the stupid barriers that prevent progress and explains how to tear them down. By reading this book, evangelists in churches, nonprofits, and businesses can learn to connect with the head, heart and gut of their customers and employees and then change the world."

—Guy Kawasaki, Chief Evangelist of Canva, board of trustees of Wikimedia, and Mercedes Benz brand ambassador

"This book is a field guide for connecting with your community and transforming lives; it needs to be on every pastor's desk in America. Speaking from years of experience as an expert in corporate communications, Kem Meyer reminds us that the most effective communication tool is 'simplicity.' In today's multi-platform, complex media world, *Less Chaos. Less Noise.* is my reality check."

—Phil Cooke, filmmaker, media activist and author

"As a leader, communication is key. And since we all communicate on a regular basis, pick up this book immediately. Whether web strategy, traditional mail, brochures, or social media, you'll learn from a proven and effective leader in Kem Meyer. After years of experience in both the corporate and church world, she understands what it takes to effectively get your message across. This book provides the lessons that will help you incorporate proven and practical communication practices into your organization."

—Brad Lomenick, author of *H3 Leadership* & *The Catalyst Leader*

"Practical. Brilliant. Profound. Funny. These are just a few words that came to mind as I read *Less Chaos. Less Noise*. Kem Meyer has become the leading expert for church communications. There is something here for every church leader or pastor—regardless of the size of your church."

—Tim Stevens, author, *Fairness is Overrated*

"I've worked with hundreds of churches over the last several years. One of the common areas where churches get stuck is with communications. Whenever that challenge rises to the top, I always recommend Kem's practical and strategic resources. Now, you get them all in one easy-to-read book. Every church leader, whether you are a communications director or not, should read *Less Chaos. Less Noise.*"

—Tony Morgan, founder & Chief Strategic Officer of The Unstuck Group

"Those of us who communicate in local churches, seeking to inform and persuade, would be wise to pay attention to this book. Kem Meyer writes out of her own experience in a highly effective local church where she has learned what kinds of messages have the best shot at breaking through the clutter and compelling individuals to action. Thank you, Kem, for this extremely practical and helpful tool."

—Nancy Beach, Leadership Coach, Slingshot Group

"In the 21st century, how a church communicates is more important than ever. Beyond being clever, we have to cut through the clutter of a noisy and chaotic world to spread a message that matters. Kem Meyer has been a trusted advocate for helping churches communicate better for over a decade and has been a leading voice about how to be smart about the tools we use to do it. This book is a tremendous resource to anyone who wants to communicate more effectively and purposefully."

—Tim Schraeder, Social Media Strategist. Community Builder. Church Communications Reformer.

"In the business workshops I teach, people of all generations consistently complain they are buried in messages. Most people tell me they ignore half of their email—and it's addressed to them. They ignore most messages, but want better communication. New technologies have allowed churches to dramatically increase the number of messages they can send. And, in the process, they increase the likelihood people they want to help will tune them out. That's why I love this book. Kem shows us how to target and connect rather than barrage and confuse. I guarantee you will do the classic head slap when she shows examples of how much clearer and simpler we can make our church communications."

— Haydn Shaw, Senior Consultant at Franklin Covey and author of *Generational IQ: Christianity Isn't Dying, Millennials Are Not the Problem, and the Future Is Bright*

"What a thought…Our message should be designed to meet the needs of those we are trying to reach, instead of ourselves. Kem's unique experience and skill provide us with a much-needed reminder and insights that will transform the way we communicate, and thus relate, to others. This book caught my attention from the moment I picked it up, and offered relevant strategies that are laser-focused and people-driven. One thing is for sure, Kem's common sense approach and encouraging style will make a difference in how you lead."

—Larry Little, Ph.D, author, speaker, and CEO of Eagle Center for Leadership

"Kem covered probably the most undervalued asset in any creative space, being either a marketing agency or a local church: communication. Being able to relate to people and convey your ideas clearly doesn't come naturally to everyone, but Kem has definitely laid out a great groundwork here to follow. I read this and found so many great, refreshing points that I will use daily."

—Matt Hernandez, VP On-Air Design, CBS Network

TABLE OF CONTENTS

A NOTE TO READERS — NEW AND OLD

I published the first iteration of this collection of stories in 2009 in a book titled *Less Clutter. Less Noise: Beyond Bulletins, Brochures and Bake Sales.* A lot has changed since then. But, there's more that hasn't changed.

Churches are still looking for more ways to get more information out to more people, while more people are looking for relief from more. And, while we've got access to so many new tools to help us do our jobs faster or easier, it doesn't mean we're doing them better. **The most effective communications are rooted in the power of *less*. Less chaos. Less noise.**

So, I've taken some time to update the old content with new examples, answer new questions to new pressures people are facing and provided some fresh handles to foundational principles that never change. I've also added more helpful tools in the back of the book from a variety of churches and consultants I've worked with over the past couple of years.

This little book is designed to be a common sense steroid shot in the arm. An encouraging dose of best practice vitamins. A cold splash of reality water on the face. And, a quick reference toolbox of examples. By the end (which shouldn't take too long to reach at all), you will be walking taller, basking in what you already knew in your heart, but may have forgotten.

ENJOY!

Kem Meyer

INTRODUCTION

Life is hard and people are bombarded, used, abused and skeptical. They live day to day in a stressed-out, over-committed, over-extended survival mode—whether they go to church or not. They simply don't have the margin for more, but they are looking for answers that will make a real difference in their lives.

The church should make it easy to find those answers. Most of the time, unfortunately, that is not what happens. Too often, churches just add to the confusion.

BEST INTENTIONS WITH DISASTROUS RESULTS

Scrambling to keep up and looking for ways to get their message heard, churches are creating more videos, designing new logos, printing more inserts, sending more emails, launching new apps and websites, posting more social media updates and trying to write lots of captivating content.

Here's what happens. The people they are trying to reach move further away just to survive the onslaught. They shut down. Stop listening. Move on. Because, more is not better.

Every organization, including the church, has to face a changing culture. Part of that requires us to get over ourselves and recognize that effective communication is really about "releasing the right response." The way to do it is by creating great experiences, a seamless message and a few smart systems. Sound complicated? It doesn't have to be!

MAYBE THIS IS YOU

You are committed to helping people take steps in their spiritual lives. You may have even devoted your entire life to it. You know the local church can change hearts and lives, but you are struggling to make that connection with people in your community.

You really are trying to figure out how to get people to notice.

On the other hand, maybe you "get it." You have a few things in your toolbox that could break your church out of a rut, but you're having trouble getting buy-in from your staff, peers or leaders.

Navigating through this change can be frustrating and discouraging.

WHAT YOU NEED

Great communication strategies will make a noticeable difference, and many churches today are making efforts to get better at it by jumping into social media, hiring graphic artists and videographers, creating "storyteller" roles and more. In the best scenarios, these steps can help.

But, more often than not, all this increased activity just adds to the frenzy instead of making a connection with their desired audience. Even with an increased awareness of better "communications and creative efforts," few teams understand the core objectives of the tools they're using, and even fewer know how to manage it.

Just as many people look to you for inspiration and practical answers, you are looking for practical answers, too. Something to help you get out of survival mode.

You don't need to read an exhaustive textbook with heavy narrative and academic case studies to learn how to plan and run an effective communication strategy. What you do need is air. A fresh perspective. An encouraging nudge. A few "aha" moments. A simple example or two that helps you stop focusing on the output and start focusing on the outcome.

YOU DON'T KNOW ME

Or even if you do know me, you might ask yourself as you're reading, "Who does she think she is and why is she talking to me right now?" Good question—let's get acquainted.

I took two major tours of duty in my professional experience: fifteen years in corporate communications and digital strategy for a global organization, and a dozen years on the staff team for a multi-site church. On the first tour, I picked up the strategic best practices and absorbed blunt, real-life public opinion about ministry and not-for-profit communication tactics. The second tour showed me ministry and not-for-profit work is harder, and more important, than it looks.

Though my vocational experience started on the outside, I have been part of my local church since 1991. In the past twenty-five years, I've worn every hat and played every role on payroll and off—skeptical guest, defensive attendee, lukewarm member, volunteer leader, part-time staff and executive leadership team member. I have watched and participated one step at a time as we experienced explosive growth and as we've struggled to turn around a trending decline. And, while I'm no longer on the Granger Community Church staff, my family and I are still serving, growing and attending there. It's our community. It is worth the "price of admission," if you will. But, it hasn't always been that way.

The beginning of my story is common. As a young adult, I was chasing everything that might compensate for the feelings on the inside I didn't know what to do with. Feelings of fear, insecurity, lack of purpose, loneliness, individuality—I had them all, even if I didn't recognize them for what they were.

Things in culture—things of beauty, art, excitement, fun, adventure—clearly captured my attention; they were not hard to find. I tried to fill the void with a career, more stuff and an active social life. On the outside, I was fulfilled and successful. I had it going on, but on the inside, I was empty. Without a foundation in Christ, I lacked the filter to know which paths were empty facades, and which were paths that would bring real life.

I was looking for inspiration and real answers that would make a difference in my life, but nothing about the church captured my attention. Even when I sought answers at the church, I could not find my next step. The church was like another world—one where I could not find a handle to hold onto. It didn't match anything I knew, so I left bombarded and confused and continued to chase the wrong things. My lasting impression of the church? It was for weak, out-of-touch people who just needed to "get a life."

AN INSIDER WHO NEVER LOST THAT OUTSIDER'S PERSPECTIVE

Obviously, something happened along the way to change my mind. I was able to find real answers and see the tangible difference Jesus could play in my life. I was able to take steps and learn how God created me the way I am, and that he has a plan for me.

Whether you recognize it yet or not, your audience has an outsider's perspective, too. People know they need "something more," but have stopped turning to the church for answers because its methods and language are clumsy and difficult. Maybe in times of crisis, ceremonial traditions or for an hour a week, the church is the place to be. But, what about for inspiration and direction for normal, everyday life? Not so much.

Are you interested in how an institution can still capture someone's attention in the midst of all of the chaos and cultural momentum? Keep reading.

COMMON GROUND

I've spent the past ten years facilitating workshops, speaking at conferences and providing custom coaching and consulting for hundreds of churches. Over and over, I have listened to what leaders are saying and how they are dealing with pain. The common issues I see surfacing about understanding different worldviews and finding ways to remove the barriers that keep people from connecting with Christ—and each other—is what led me to write this book.

NOT JUST FOR CHURCHES

While this book was written from the vantage point and uses a lot of examples from the local church, the principles speak loudly to the schools, not-for-profits and small businesses I work with as well. Anyone struggling to get the word out to motivate their audience to action can, and should, tap into these pages for support. My heart and drive is to bridge the gap; both sectors have so much to learn from each other.

Currently, 78 percent of Americans describe themselves as "Christian, but beliefs and practices vary widely.[1]" Even with such a high percentage of adult U.S. citizens identifying themselves as Christian, there is an increasing number of religiously unaffiliated, a steady drop in church attendance and growing tension over religious freedoms across America. I ask you, what better organizational case study to learn from than the church?

HOW TO USE THIS BOOK

A little background will help you digest what's next. My goal is to serve you with an easy, quick-reference, short course on incorporating proven communication practices into your organization—regardless of size, style or location. This book does not follow the typical linear, A-Z outline. It caters to the short attention span (for my sake and yours). It is conversational. It bounces around. It uses real stories and practical examples. You can read a few pages here and a few pages there. Relax, have fun and enjoy each bite-size serving. Each chapter will contain a new idea or story that encourages or challenges you to look at how you talk to people; whether it's through your announcements, apps, Photoshop or Facebook.

Although I will reference a variety of sources along the way, I have thought of you as I've developed the content in this book to deliver new insights from a real-life perspective. I realize this is crucial as you try to apply practical principles in a not-so-practical reality. Use the examples and stories in this book to promote team discussions in your world, bridge the gap and help leverage the power that already exists in your environment. I'm setting the stage now; the only way to reveal fresh observations is to put an end to preconceived notions. Every page is designed to provide you the context for reinvention.

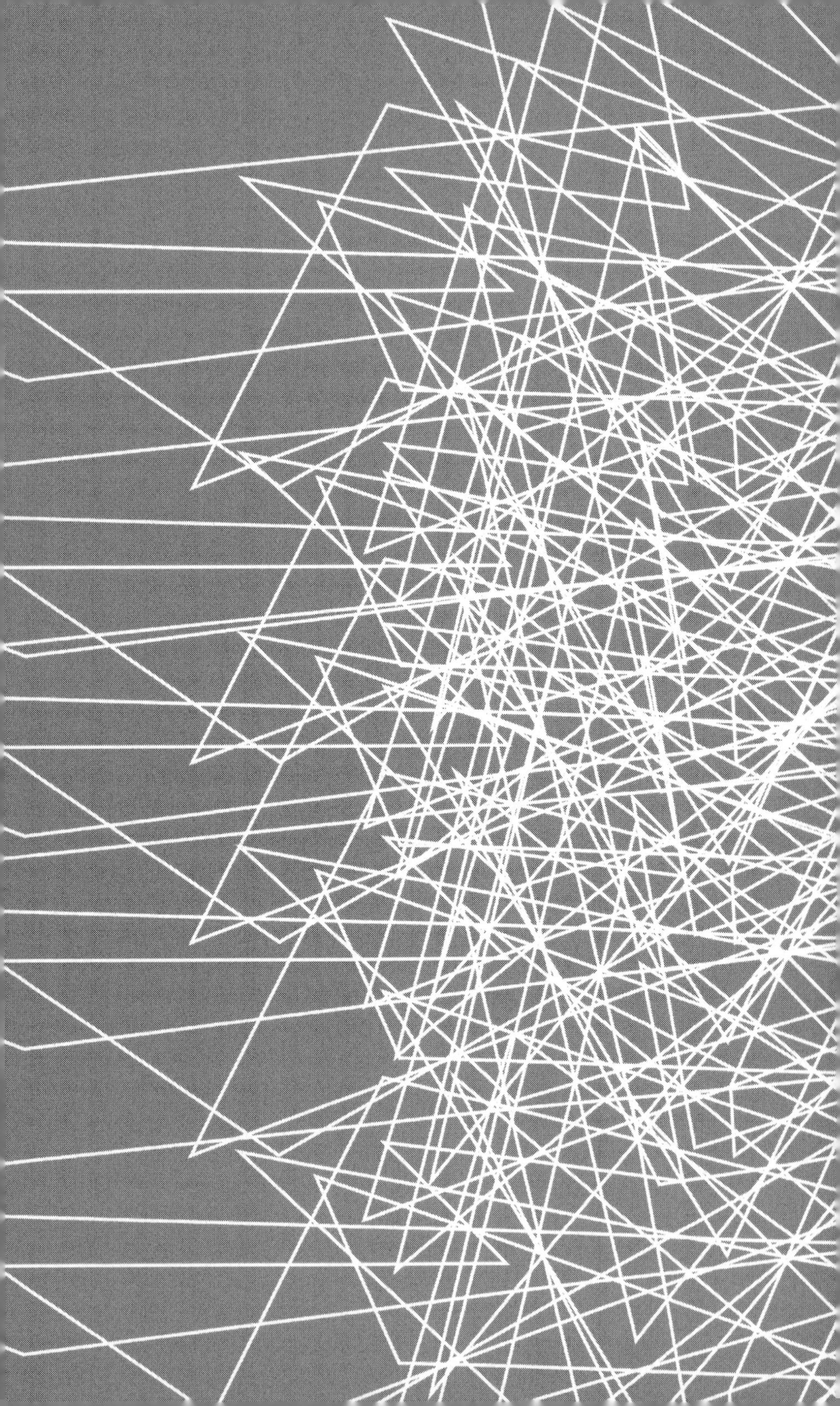

part 1

ARE PEOPLE LETTING YOU IN OR SHUTTING YOU OUT?

Just because something is legible doesn't mean that it communicates; it could be communicating the wrong thing.
David Carson

Many times, conventional wisdom about communications and marketing is wrong. It mass markets, force-feeds and assumes people are just waiting to hear what you have to say. Are you unknowingly falling victim to believing five myths about getting the word out?

chapter 1
THE MYTH: YOU ARE IN CONTROL

> **One of the ways we elicit wonder is by scrambling the self temporarily so the world can seep in.**
> Jason Silva

Every person has a unique framework of ideas and beliefs they use to interpret the world and interact with it—a worldview. A person's worldview encompasses his or her experiences, wishes, biases, values and assumptions. Good communication is not so much about sending the right message as it is about releasing the right response. The right message assumes you and the other person will respond in the same way. A person's worldview shows up before you do, and that is the reality of the message you send. It's not what you say; it's what people hear. And, while you might not be able to control what people see or hear, you can do a better job of trying to anticipate it.

IT'S A FRICKIN' ELEPHANT!

I heard a story about a grandpa helping his four-year-old grandson learn to read. The boy pointed to a picture in a zoo book and said, "Look, Grandpa! It's a frickin' elephant." The grandpa took a deep breath and asked, "What did you call it?"

His grandson repeated himself.

"It's a frickin' elephant, Grandpa! It says so on the picture!"

And, so it did. When the grandpa looked down at the picture, it read,

"A F R I C A N Elephant."

It's not what you say; it's what people hear.*

* Think you may have heard this before? It's the subtitle of a book by corporate and political consultant Frank Luntz: *Words that Work.*

ARE BIRDS TOO FEMININE?

Believe it or not, we processed this real question as a ministry team. The question arose when we were evaluating whether or not to use the image of a bird on our website. We also discussed whether our baptism graphic resembled a female body part. Both of these conversations were totally serious and appropriate.

It is important that you're willing to ask these types of questions before using graphics and images:

- Does this graphic support or compete with the intended experience for our audience?
- Does this visual help accomplish the desired objective or not?
- Does it have potential to attract or repel?
- Does it add to or take away credibility?

Several years ago, Pepsi ran a short-lived billboard campaign for their Pepsi ONE[1] product.

What does this mean?[2]

When I saw it, I wondered why Pepsi was using a drop of blood to advertise their cola. The billboard would have made more sense for a hemophilia center or blood bank, but it did not make me want to drink Pepsi One, that's for sure. After some research, I discovered the experience they intended for their audience. The little circle guy is supposed to represent one calorie. The little drop guy is supposed to represent taste. And, isn't that cute—they are coexisting happily together. See, you really can have it all.

Except, that is not the message I got driving down the road at 55 mph. They weren't in control of the message. **Sometimes, you need to evaluate a graphic's potential to take on a life of its own.**

In the end, we decided the particular bird image we were considering would send a more feminine message than we wanted. Although, we did all agree that a cardinal can put on a mean face.

IT TAKES TWO

Do we think about how what we say is going to affect others, or do we just think about what we have to say? I've heard David Armano, a user experience design guru, say it this way:

> **"What are we trying to communicate?" implies a one-way conversation. Maybe we should ask ourselves: "How can we facilitate?[3]"**

I was once forwarded a response to a form letter someone had received. It's a real-life demonstration of a message action and the reaction it triggered. I'm changing some names and details to protect the innocent, but here's the gist:

SUBSCRIPTION SUSPENDED

I'm disappointed.

You requested a subscription to our magazine, and I started that subscription for you in good faith. But so far, you haven't held up your end of the bargain.

I have no choice but to cancel your subscription unless we receive your payment in the next 10 days. Please mail it today.

This simple letter from the magazine seems harmless and normal enough, doesn't it? That is, until you see how it made the reader feel. The recipient tells the rest of the story in a candid response that gave voice to what many others feel but rarely communicate aloud:

DEAR EDITOR,

When I was six, I regularly bullied my sister.

When I was 10, I stole candy from the Dollar Store, even though I had the money to pay for it.

When I was 14, I broke my mother's heart by yelling at her to leave my baseball game because she was embarrassing me.

When I was 19, I regularly pilfered wads of toilet paper and Ziploc bags of hand soap from my place of employment.

I'm impatient with my kids. I'm selfish. I judge people harshly. I'm not as kind to strangers as I should be. I don't like animals. I take the miracle of my life for granted. I'm ungrateful. I'm obscene. I make absurd banalities into "issues" just so I don't feel boring. I once instigated a fight with my wife over green beans.

I am not as good as I could be. Of this, there can be no doubt.

Two months ago, I filled out a little card requesting a free copy of your magazine. After reading through it, I chose not to subscribe. Was I disappointed in the quality of the writing? Did I find it overpriced? Did I get busy with giving birth and raising an infant and forget all about it?

You didn't ask, and I am disappointed. Had I received a kinder message from you such as, "I'm sorry you chose not to subscribe to our magazine. Please keep us in mind in the future. Please have a nice day," I would have considered sending a check for $12.95.

Please take me off your mailing list. I have enough to feel ashamed of in my life without more guilt trips from you.

It makes me think of this new response I've been seeing lately when I unsubscribe to mailing lists or opt-out of subscription pop-ups. Retailers—or worse yet, content providers I'm following—ask too much as I manage my personal influx of information.

- ☐ Yes! Please sign me up for more insights with regular emails to my inbox.
- ☐ No! I don't want to be more effective in my work.

That cleverly-worded choice doesn't make me second-guess my decision, it reinforces it! Geez, magazine. Thanks for trying to take me on the biggest guilt trip of my life. But, honestly, our relationship status isn't even close to that level.

If we asked, I wonder what candid feedback we'd hear about emails we send? Or, the status updates we post? How often do I draft my correspondence, seemingly harmless enough, without concentrated consideration as to how it makes the recipient feel? Do I test my words against the objective I'm trying to accomplish?

I appreciate the insight I gained from this honest response to a thoughtless form letter. When I'm able to get insight such as this, it helps me anticipate responses. Only then am I able to communicate in a way that opens doors instead of closing them.

WAIT FOR IT!

I don't necessarily like surprises, but I do love the unexpected. I love it when someone breaks away from the norm to introduce a fresh approach. When I can't predict what's going to happen, I'm left going, "Huh. How about that?" I like it when that happens.

A close friend of mine once attended our weekend service and sat down behind a family whose teenage son was playing his handheld video game. As the service began, my friend was irritated that the boy continued to play. The longer the service went on and the longer the boy kept playing, the more agitated my friend became. The game was on mute, but it was still distracting and unnerving to see the teen playing in the middle of the service.

My friend was just about ready to ask the boy to put the game away when something caused him to stop. He waited a few minutes, then finally leaned forward, tapped the boy on the shoulder, and said,

> **"I've got the guide with all the moves to beat that game if you want it."**

Huh. How about that?

What my friend did not know was that the teenage boy in front of him was autistic. He also did not know the boy's family hadn't been able to attend church for years because of their son's inability to sit still. They had been asked to leave public places numerous times because of the boy's erratic behavior. When the boy's parents saw my friend lean forward and tap their son on the shoulder, they immediately assumed the worst: "Here we go again."

But, they experienced an unpredictable comment, wouldn't you agree? It even took my friend by surprise, and he's the one who said it! I am so glad he kept his heart open and was slow to speak.

It's easy to judge people who are not like me. It's easy to dismiss people who act in a way I just don't understand. It's also easy to slip into this complacent mode where I think, "I've got it all figured out." When that happens, my unsolicited sermons into those people's lives are destructive because I don't have all the information. I end up keeping score based on my own personal worldview—a worldview that lacks important context outside of my individual walk.

> **Your life bears a message, a message of hope and redemption. But, before people in your world encounter your message, they encounter you.**[4]

Ouch.

When Rob Wegner was the pastor of Life Mission at my church, he spoke about the two parts to the great commission. Part one is, "How do we get people into the church?" Part two is, "How do we get the church into the community?"

He said the only way to accomplish these objectives is to make some "missional moves." In other words, move on mission. Even if those moves are small, they have the potential to make a seismic impact (for better or worse).

Case in point? Rob is the friend I just wrote about who almost jumped all over that kid for playing his game during church. But, he didn't. And, that's what's so honorable. He didn't forget that Jesus gives us multiple spheres of community influence. Be it for the one, the few or the many, we're responsible for handling every interaction with care.

> “ **Everything that irritates us about others can lead us to an understanding of ourselves.**
> C. G. Jung

IS YOUR INFORMATION RELIABLE?

I was driving home from visiting my sister in Cincinnati, and as I passed an eighteen-wheeler, the driver honked. My first instinct was, "Hey, I'm in my lane...what are you honking at?"

I drove a little farther, and another truck honked as I passed. This time, I wondered if I had a flat tire or if something was sticking out of one of my doors. I checked my gauges. They all looked good. I continued driving.

Then another truck honked at me! This time, I confess, my mind went here: "Well, I am aging gracefully. I guess I shouldn't be surprised I can still get the attention of a trucker. I should be flattered."

As I drove for the next thirty miles, four out of five truckers honked as I went by. As deluded as I may have been in the previous paragraph, I am not an idiot. Something was wrong, and I knew it. I'm not all that, and even if I were, there aren't that many cavemen on the road at once.

It was only then that I caught a glimpse of my kids, Emmi and Easton, in my rearview mirror, pulling an imaginary chain in the air as we passed another truck. Oh.

Turns out, all of those cavemen on the road weren't honking at me; they were engaging in a childhood game* that has been passed through the generations. They were just playing along and honking their horns in response to my kids' hand motions.

* Children act out pulling an imaginary rope as every truck passes on the highway to make the big ol' semi honk. If the trucker honks, kids laugh and squeal. If the trucker drives on by with no honk or wave, then kids are sad until the next try.

Awwww. In an instant, they went from perverts to participants. From cavemen to child advocates.

See how easy it is to mistake personal perceptions with the greater reality? Or, am I the only one who does that?

YOU'RE NOT THE BOSS OF ME

Once upon a time, Google tried to "protect their brand" by posting alerts and sending letters about the proper and improper ways to use the word google in a sentence. Their *helpful tips* were an attempt to rebound from the word *google* slipping from trademarked status into common usage. It was frustrating to read.

The short story? Google was slapping our collective wrist for how we use their corporate name in our conversations. Apparently, their huge success and influence on pop culture was distressing to their trademark lawyers, and they wanted us to know what we could do about it.

Yougottabekiddingme.

To: GOOGLE
From: KEM

You've lost some street credibility and are facing some mocking and ridicule by making an issue out of this. Somebody in marketing or legal forgot about the attributes that got you to your place of influence in the first place. It was never all about your technology or legal name...it was about the value you gave away for free...it was about how you let people explore without prescribing a forced path...
it was about how you pushed the envelope of invention and didn't fit the mold.

You built a loyal fan base by making it feel like it was all about us...and we loved you for it. You changed the way we talk, research and see "the Cloud." But, then, when you got defensive for a minute and made it all about you, our radars went up. And, now, your fan loyalty is threatened a little. Because, now, you look like everyone else.

In some instances, **a message might be important to your INTERNAL corporate audience but completely absurd for your EXTERNAL audience.** Do you know the difference?

I'm still a fan of Google. And, I'm glad they're not still making a big deal out of how I google that meme or how I use *googlicious* in a sentence (although, they still haven't taken down the original post from 2006).[5]

NOBODY LIKES TO PLAY WITH A CONTROL FREAK

For the first decade of my son's life, nothing made him happier than LEGOs. It seemed he could assemble any pre-made kit in minutes and create masterfully thought-out showpieces with the extra bricks in the time he had left over. I don't even want to know how much money we spent on LEGOs during those "builder" years. (Thank God he grew out of it before the LEGO movie came out. I would have gone bankrupt buying all the merchandise.)

Anyway, it's safe to say I still spent too much on LEGOs to keep the little guy building. I couldn't stop myself. And, when I ran out of options at my local store, and then the regional LEGO store ninety minutes away, I went online to LEGO's corporate site to see what else I could buy.

Here's the actual screenshot from my computer. At first I thought it was a joke, but it was the real deal.

LEGO removed the notice from their home page shortly after they posted it. I was lucky to capture this moment of history in real time. But, they do still include it on their Fair Play guidelines and policies page.[6] And, fans are still mocking it today with blog posts, articles and comic parodies.

It's not so bad to bury some legal notice at the back of the interwebs to make sure somebody, somewhere got it right. I mean, at least the LEGO team employees should know how to use their name, right? But, who seriously approved this "IMPORTANT NOTICE" to their customers? What message were they trying to send?

Who were they trying to serve—the customer or themselves? I can just imagine the conversation in the boardroom:

"So, hey everybody! Our LEGO bricks are a household name. Everybody talks about them. Everybody plays with them. Everybody buys them for their kids and builds cities with them. But, you know what, people? We're failing at our job because nobody's saying it right! They call them 'LEGOs' instead of 'LEGO toys' or 'LEGO bricks.' The nerve.

"Our customers are getting it all wrong, and we've got to set them straight. We need an important notice on our website. Quick, before one more customer gets it wrong!"

Note to self: don't be a control freak with corporate communications.

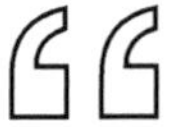

I'm sorry for my inability to let unimportant things go.
Jonathan Safran Foer, *Extremely Loud and Incredibly Close*

THINK IT OVER
BUSTING THE MYTH: YOU ARE IN CONTROL

- ☐ How can I stop myself from trying to push my audience to a decision or to my point of view? Are there incremental steps I could lay as groundwork to pull people into the content I have to offer?

- ☐ Where am I imposing my worldview on others? Am I inadvertently putting out a message to meet my needs rather than thinking through the worldview of my guests? How can I habitually give people the benefit of the doubt on a daily basis?

- ☐ In what ways could my message be misunderstood based on the worldview of my audience? What could help prevent that? Has there been an instance where I failed in communication by assuming the wrong thing?

- ☐ Where am I engaged in corporate self-talk? Are there formal or informal feedback mechanisms in place to help identify my communication misses? Something that reveals when I sound ridiculous or out-of-touch to outsiders?

- ☐ Where am I trying to force behavior in someone, versus nurture the potential that's already there?

- ☐ When do I think I have all the answers? Are there places I need to go, people I need to see or experiences I need to feel to keep my mind and heart open? Do I surround myself with "yes" people? Am I avoiding the hard work of differing perspectives, seeking only input and answers that support my thoughts and views?

chapter 2
THE MYTH: THE MORE CHOICES, THE BETTER

> **The ability to simplify means to eliminate the unnecessary so the necessary may speak.**
> Hans Hofmann

Information used to be as rare and precious as gold; now, it is so inexpensive and plentiful that most of it, when we have the choice, ends up being overlooked, deleted or tossed like garbage. A Sunday edition of the *New York Times* carries more information than the average nineteenth century citizen accessed his entire life.[1] A snapshot in 2013 counted more than 100 billion emails sent and received per day.[2] The total number of websites[3] is expected to stabilize at a count over 1 billion by 2017. By the last count I could find in 2014, Apple was growing by more than 1,000 apps a day.[4] Google processes more than 40,000 search terms per second.[5]

Regardless of the technology threshold or the generation, the barrage of data to which we are constantly exposed carries a cost—physically, mentally and financially.

More isn't what people are looking for; *relief from the pressure of more* is what they're looking for.

INFORMATION OBESITY

Information overload occurs when we receive more info than our brains can process. Even if it is good information, too much of a good thing is just not good—it's bad. (Think "more pain than gain.") Whether you're an info addict or a Zen advocate, information overload affects us all.

It's not new; information overload dates back to Gutenburg.[6] But, the 24/7 digitization of information has blown up data access/bombardment to infinity and beyond. In 2011, it even got its own diagnosis (IFS: Information Fatigue Syndrome).[7] Think Simple Now is just one of hundreds of sources that breaks down the cost of overfeeding the information appetite. (Ironic, isn't it?)

- **Productivity Loss.** In the face of too much information, we can easily get lost in the details. We waste time focusing on unimportant information and lose sight of our goal and purpose.
- **Mind Clutter.** The noise created by media and other sources of information clutters our minds and takes away from our inner peace.
- **Lack of Time.** Rich or poor, young or old, we all have the same limited amount of time in a day. And instead of spending a good chunk of my day filtering through incoming information, I'd rather spend the energy on bringing more enjoyment and fulfillment into my life.
- **Lack of Personal Reflection.** I find that if I am constantly consuming information, then I forget to connect with myself (and others). I realize that valuable personal reflection comes when we create a "space" for it in our lives. If there is always noise, then we won't have the mental capacity to reflect within.

- **Stress & Anxiety.** Information inflow creates the illusion that we have more tasks to fill our lives than we have time for. Often, we might suddenly feel nervous without understanding why. Every piece of information carries with it energy, which demands our time. Even if we consciously ignore it, a part of us saw that data and recorded it within our subconscious.[8]

Life is overwhelming enough as it is. Your church or organization shouldn't pile more on top of an already mounting problem, especially when people are looking for answers that will make a difference.

If you want to be a credible source for those answers, look for "opposite thinking" ways to help reduce that load:

- **Stick to the facts.** Don't over-sell, over-explain or over-control. Just provide the information someone needs to self-sort and self-decide. People don't need a page on the philosophy of each ministry, activity or event. They do need to know who it's for, when it happens and how to get there or sign up. Too often we justify added content with a lazy "it doesn't hurt; just in case" rationale. Before you let yourself off the hook so easy, ask this instead: "Does this content help?" If the answer is no, cut it.
- **Stick to the point.** Start with the end in mind before you're about to do something. If you can identify the one actionable purpose behind your mass mailing, status update, email, blog post, direct mail postcard, etc., it will be easier for you to stay focused and on track. If you lose sight of what you want to happen as a result of your communication, it's hard to recognize your own excess. Do you want people to show up or respond? What are you asking them to do? If you can't answer that question easily, they won't be able to either.

- **Consider the crowd.** Does your announcement (handout, online or verbal) apply to everyone or just a handful of people? If it's not affecting the masses, it's just going to land like dead weight. Don't punish the crowd to keep a few people happy (even if they are the most vocal). Find a way to deliver your news in appropriate venues. Ask yourself questions like, "Does this apply to the whole weekend service, or just fifth grade parents?" "Is this a question 5,000 people are asking, or is it more helpful to a targeted list of fifty?"
- **Don't intrude.** Unless they've asked for it, people welcome unsolicited emails as much as a door-to-door salesperson during family dinner. Respect personal space and put information in an easy place for people to find it when they want it.

In 2012, the American Psychological Association CEO spoke on a panel[9] about how stress undermines our health. He stated 75 percent of healthcare costs are associated with chronic illnesses. And, the key driver of chronic illnesses? Stress.[10]

Marketers have responded with superficial, tranquility promises: happiness in a perfume, peace in a lotion, focus in a drink, euphoria in a bubble bath, sex in a lip gloss, etc. **Our response should be less complex, more authentic and, ultimately, life-giving—it's as simple as dialing back the volume.**

POTATO CHIP DECISIONS

I heard author Gail MacDonald speak about a friend of hers who had moved overseas for mission work. One of the first questions Gail asked her friend when she returned home after being gone for four years was, "What's changed most in America since you've been away?"

The thing that changed the most in four years wasn't technology, health care or architecture. It was the potato chip aisle in the grocery store. When she left to go overseas, there were only a few types of chips to choose from, and when she returned, there were hundreds of choices in multiple aisles.

Although that wasn't the answer Gail was expecting, after reflection, this was her takeaway:

> **Are we spending all of our time on potato chip decisions and wondering why we don't have any energy left for the good stuff?**

And, here is my takeaway:

> **Are we wondering why people don't have any energy left for the good stuff when all we're giving them are potato chip decisions?**

(If you didn't just say, "Aha!" aloud to yourself, you need to go back and reread the question.)

Practically speaking:

- The more events you promote, the less important each event becomes.
- The more promises you make, the lower the chance you can deliver.
- The more announcements you have from a platform, the less people hear.
- The more handouts you add to the pile, the harder it is for people to find what they're looking for.
- The more logos you create, the less cohesive the overall church or organizational identity becomes.
- The more space-filler posts you publish to your Facebook or Instagram account, the more out-of-touch each update is perceived to be.

Now I like potato chips as much as the next person (especially barbeque), but I argue this is a principle of stewardship. Are you responsible with information you have to share?

IS CHOICE REALLY SUCH A GOOD THING?

In theory, more choices may lead people to find exactly what they want. But, research shows that when given too many choices, people actually feel worse. Too much choice leads to one of three results: regret, shutdown or paralysis. It looks different depending on the generational attributes, but "give them more choices" is often an ineffective communication strategy for people across all generations. For example:

- Boomers get overwhelmed and shut down.
- GenXers think they want the choices (and expect them), but labor over whether or not they're making the right decisions.
- Millennials just ignore you and move on to whatever interested them in the first place.*

That said, demographics don't tell the story like behavior does. Our brains are rewiring on the fly—adapting to new ways of life. I know that I, for one, don't fit perfectly into any one of these categories. And, my response to too many choices depends on the circumstance. I've experienced them all.

And, if I know what it feels like, I'm wondering if you do too.

At least once a year, my church has a weekend message series about volunteering. It's when we cast the net far and wide, educating and encouraging the people in our church to find their fit on a ministry team. Over the years, we tested various vehicles to help equip people with the information they needed to make a move. I fondly remember one of those vehicles several years ago—a bulletin insert for our Ministry Fair.

* "Boomers," born during the 1946-1964 baby boom, are the first group raised with televisions in the home. Generation X thinking, born 1965-1980, has significant overtones of cynicism against things held dear to previous generations (mainly the Boomers). Millennials, born roughly 1981-2001, are shaped by the rise of instant communication technologies and have a reputation of being peer-oriented, instant gratification seekers.

I helped pull together the content for this insert. By the time we were done, it was four pages, single-spaced, with every team and volunteer role that existed in our church. And, I was proud.

Logically, this made sense, right? People weren't volunteering because they just didn't know what was available. I thought that if we showed them everything that was available—the hundreds of opportunities to choose from—they'd be able to find what they were looking for. Sound familiar?

What we learned is that people aren't motivated to move in the face of hundreds of choices. In fact, they were feeling frazzled about where to start and left feeling overwhelmed. The next year, we condensed the copy from more than fifty teams into eight categories.

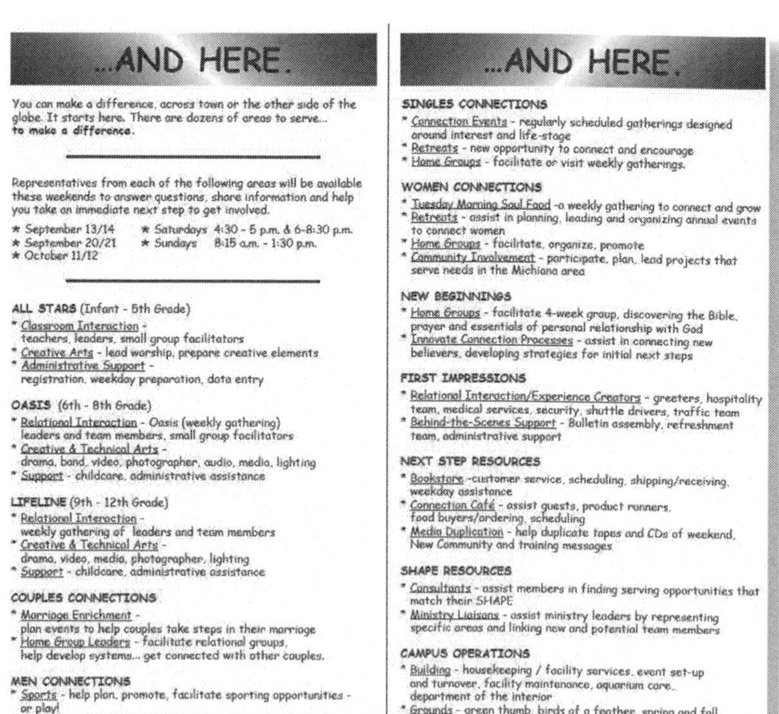

...AND HERE.

You can make a difference, across town or the other side of the globe. It starts here. There are dozens of areas to serve...
to make a difference.

Representatives from each of the following areas will be available these weekends to answer questions, share information and help you take an immediate next step to get involved.

★ September 13/14
★ September 20/21
★ October 11/12

★ Saturdays 4:30 - 5 p.m. & 6-8:30 p.m.
★ Sundays 8:15 a.m. - 1:30 p.m.

ALL STARS (Infant - 5th Grade)
* Classroom Interaction - teachers, leaders, small group facilitators
* Creative Arts - lead worship, prepare creative elements
* Administrative Support - registration, weekday preparation, data entry

OASIS (6th - 8th Grade)
* Relational Interaction - Oasis (weekly gathering) leaders and team members, small group facilitators
* Creative & Technical Arts - drama, band, video, photographer, audio, media, lighting
* Support - childcare, administrative assistance

LIFELINE (9th - 12th Grade)
* Relational Interaction - weekly gathering of leaders and team members
* Creative & Technical Arts - drama, video, media, photographer, lighting
* Support - childcare, administrative assistance

COUPLES CONNECTIONS
* Marriage Enrichment - plan events to help couples take steps in their marriage
* Home Group Leaders - facilitate relational groups, help develop systems... get connected with other couples.

MEN CONNECTIONS
* Sports - help plan, promote, facilitate sporting opportunities - or play!

...AND HERE.

SINGLES CONNECTIONS
* Connection Events - regularly scheduled gatherings designed around interest and life-stage
* Retreats - new opportunity to connect and encourage
* Home Groups - facilitate or visit weekly gatherings.

WOMEN CONNECTIONS
* Tuesday Morning Soul Food -a weekly gathering to connect and grow
* Retreats - assist in planning, leading and organizing annual events to connect women
* Home Groups - facilitate, organize, promote
* Community Involvement - participate, plan, lead projects that serve needs in the Michiana area

NEW BEGINNINGS
* Home Groups - facilitate 4-week group, discovering the Bible, prayer and essentials of personal relationship with God
* Innovate Connection Processes - assist in connecting new believers, developing strategies for initial next steps

FIRST IMPRESSIONS
* Relational Interaction/Experience Creators - greeters, hospitality team, medical services, security, shuttle drivers, traffic team
* Behind-the-Scenes Support - Bulletin assembly, refreshment team, administrative support

NEXT STEP RESOURCES
* Bookstore -customer service, scheduling, shipping/receiving, weekday assistance
* Connection Café - assist guests, product runners, food buyers/ordering, scheduling
* Media Duplication - help duplicate tapes and CDs of weekend, New Community and training messages

SHAPE RESOURCES
* Consultants - assist members in finding serving opportunities that match their SHAPE
* Ministry Liaisons - assist ministry leaders by representing specific areas and linking new and potential team members

CAMPUS OPERATIONS
* Building - housekeeping / facility services, event set-up and turnover, facility maintenance, aquarium care, department of the interior
* Grounds - green thumb, birds of a feather, spring and fall

Before: two of four total pages.

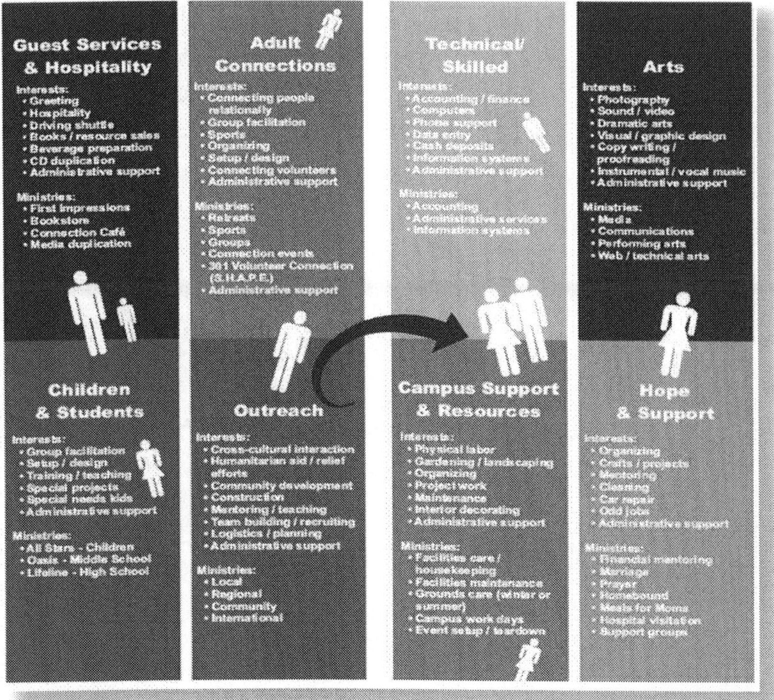

After: one page.

Here is how we explained the minimalistic approach.

> People are busy and life is hard. They have too much information bombarding them from everywhere (not just one hour on Sunday) and never enough time. But, they're still looking for answers that make a real difference in their lives. Being part of something bigger than you makes a difference. And, people experience that life change one step at a time. **The value we provide grows in direct proportion to how easily people can find and say yes to their next step.**

And, the opposite is true: the value we provide decreases in direct proportion to how hard we make it for people to do what they're trying to do.

The minimalistic approach here is all about breaking a big leap into smaller, incremental steps. A person's journey away from God does not happen in one step, but rather in a series of steps and decisions that seemed otherwise perfectly rational at the time. One day, he wakes up and realizes just how far he's traveled as a result of the sum total of his steps in the wrong direction. And, what about when he's ready to start taking steps back to God? How hard are we making it?

YOUR NEW IS NOT NEWS

I commonly get questions about how to "launch" new websites, apps or logo re-designs. My answer is always the same—don't talk about it; just do it. If it's good, people will notice. More to the point, your new website, app or logo is not newsworthy in itself. It just helps deliver the newsworthy items. Talking about it is just goofy.

Katya Andresen, veteran marketer and nonprofit professional, puts it this way:

> "You should not communicate what is new in your universe. You should communicate what matters to your constituents. If you have a new logo or brand* look-and-feel, that's nice, but it doesn't mean a thing to the outside world. What matters to the outside world is how they experience you.
>
> "If you're launching a new blog, app or website, figure out what's incredibly interesting INSIDE of that new blog, app or website. Show your audience what they have access to or can do now they couldn't before."[11]

I recently got an email from my bank announcing, "You'll notice our e-news has a new look!" And, that was it. That was the news. That was the full objective of the communication: to let me know they had updated the e-news look. I'm no hater. I'm sure some hard-working digital designer spent a lot of time on the makeover. I'm glad they did. The old one looked like something my cat designed right after he got declawed. (Just kidding; my cat isn't declawed.) But, the fact they sent me an email about it left me feeling annoyed.

* Contrary to popular belief, a brand is more than a logo. In this context, "brand" is referring to the collection of descriptive verbal attributes and symbols (e.g., name, logo, slogan, design) used to convey the essence of your organization, product or service.

You know how lame it would look to hog the spotlight when you give someone a gift? You would never say, "Look at me and the gift I picked out! Isn't that just the greatest news ever?" (At least I hope you wouldn't.) It's kind of like that when you update your logo, blog design, website, etc. **Just give someone the gift without trying to bring attention to yourself.**

LESS PROMOTIONS = MORE PUBLICITY

Instead of asking what else you can do or create to get the word out about your awesome event or service, what if you look to where people place their trust before making a decision about trying, or buying, something new? After all, it's about the quality of an experience, not the quantity of promotions, that spreads the word and influences decision-making the most.

Nielsen's 2015 Global Survey of Trust in Advertising still ranks recommendations from friends as the most credible form of advertising at 83 percent (compared to trust in online videos at 48 percent or social network ads at 46 percent).

So, if the secret is to get satisfied customers talking (our most powerful and trustworthy source of advertising), why aren't we giving it the attention it deserves? We're still banking on Facebook broadcasts, mass mailings or giant email blasts to get the word out. Of course, there will be occasions where it makes sense to invest in these efforts for special promotions, but none of these "campaigns" are the heavyweights we make them out to be. They are more support cast, not the lead.

Randall Beard, President, Nielsen Expanded Verticals says, "While advertisers have started to follow consumers online, about a third of online advertising campaigns don't work—they don't generate awareness or drive any lift in purchase intent."[12]

If you want the biggest ROI in everyday promotions, it's best to focus time, energy and money on two primary things to get the word out:

1. **Satisfied customers.** Give people an experience to talk about. They'll tell their friends so you don't have to.
2. **Invite tools for the satisfied customers.** While your website and social media accounts can add a level of "legitimacy" to your brand, they're not what gets people talking. Give satisfied customers a variety of tools to help make it easier for them to tell their friends.

So, counter to the impulse to blast another message to the masses—naively expecting that to do the work of our persuasion—what if we turn things upside down? Philip Kotler and Joanne Scheff write about five major things that influence audience behavior in their sourcebook of marketing strategies, *Standing Room Only*:[13]

- **Macro-environmental trends.** Social, political, economic and technological forces.
- **Cultural Factors.** Nationality, subcultures and social class.
- **Social Factors.** Reference groups, opinion leaders and innovation.
- **Psychological Factors.** Personality, beliefs, attitudes and motivation.
- **Personal Factors.** Occupation, economic circumstances, family and life-cycle stage.

Ironically, if we are looking to impact the factors at the top of this list, we must begin by making a connection with the practical realities at the bottom. That small personal connection is what

makes people want to respond to the big issues.
Denise Lee Yohn, author of *What Great Brands Do,*[14] asserts that the smallest details make the biggest difference when connecting with your audience. She says:

> "Great brands may think big, but they sweat the small stuff. They know that all the little things they do or fail to do in person shape brand perceptions far more than the big things they claim through mass media. So they design their customer experiences down to last detail, and usually appeal to as many of the five human senses as possible, since they know those experiences are so much more impactful, distinctive, and memorable than any advertising or marketing program they could run."

Sweating the small stuff means caring about details like flooring, as well as lighting, wayfinding signs, display materials, uniforms, smells in the bathroom, door handles, carry-out bags, receipts… Everything communicates. Every touchpoint matters.

So. Start small. Pay attention to every detail people are connecting with and develop your approach from there.

THINK IT OVER
BUSTING THE MYTH: THE MORE CHOICES, THE BETTER

- ☐ How can I get in touch with things people are already connecting with to develop my approach, instead of creating a separate track they ignore?
- ☐ What can I do to make it easy for people to say yes to the next small step—not everything at once?
- ☐ Am I responsibly managing the information I have by giving people only the best, or am I contributing to information overload by burdening people with potato chip decisions?
- ☐ Where am I bombarding people with information and draining their ability to be inspired?
- ☐ Which communication vehicles in my church or organization are most effective, and why? Which tools would not be missed if they were gone? Can I identify communication pieces that exist purely to serve the internal politics of the organization?
- ☐ If I evaluate the last three communication pieces I created, how much was simple and succinct? How much was detail overkill?
- ☐ Where am I promoting big, but delivering small? How can I improve the experience without increasing promotions?

chapter 3
THE MYTH: ADVERTISING CREATES INTEREST

> **Conventional wisdom can be the comfortable thing to do. Many times, the comfortable thing is not the right thing.**
> Tony Blair

Advertising doesn't create interest; at best, it creates awareness. And, that is not always a good thing. Cancer has awareness, and nobody wants that.

I once heard about a national research survey asking the American public what top five things need more government regulation. Get this: advertising was ranked #4—after air pollution and before nuclear safety! And, that survey went down before spam was such an evil force in our society. What people want is a promise they can trust, consistency, something worth telling their friends about—an experience. Instead of investing efforts in promotions to get attention, we should be getting attention with what happens when people show up.

TRANSPARENCY

One way to help keep a team aligned is to broaden perspective as a team; get in touch with your audience and culture. And, to be successful in the process, it's important to foster an environment that allows honesty about what people discover—inside and outside of themselves.

Are you and the people on your team willing to share what you see or hear transparently with each other? Do you foster a safe environment for candid, constructive observations, even if they are unpleasant or uncomfortable?

Here's an excerpt from an email I received from a key leader in our church. He sent it in response to the question, "What do you think contributes to the decline in local church attendance?" He is strong in his faith; committed to the mission, vision and values of our church; dependable; and high-capacity. And, he is transparent in his risky observations about the church:

NEW EMAIL

Sometimes I feel the church over-promises and under-delivers. I guess that's part of feeling as if you've been sold a bill of goods. It promises love, joy, peace and purpose. It says give and you'll receive. It says be a good person and good things will happen to you. Become a Christian and your life will change. Yeah, sorta...

It reminds me of a network marketing organization (many of which, by the way, are launched within church setting). You have a bunch of people who aren't good at sales out trying to sell with a little bit of information about their product. They over-hype and make promises they can't possibly keep. It's a second-class, circus-like sales organization that people don't take seriously. "Oh. It's a network marketing company? Great. You're one of those people." "Oh. You're telling me I need church and God? Great. You're one of those people."

After all, liberals have a valid argument about the "Christian Right," don't they? Divorce rates are similar. My own daughter is in spiritual limbo after growing up in the church. My in-laws are on the brink of divorce. My wife and I still have fights and have hard times "on the brink." I'm estranged from my best friend and haven't spoken with him in years. I've had business failures. I've felt crushed under the burden of debt. Hmmm. Yeah. I'm much better off than people who don't go to church and those who don't tithe!

Why do so many Christians sell Jesus "pain-relievers"? Man, I must have missed that pill. He does rescue. He does save. But, I still feel pain. And, so did He.

So what is it? What is it that truly adds that value to life? For one, I have to remind myself it's not about here. Our life on earth is temporary and our purpose is not an unwavering pursuit of happiness, wealth and health here...NO! We struggle, we work it out and we deal with it. We're not immune to it...but our hope, prize and purpose is and will be with Christ. Shame on us for over-selling life here on earth.

Can the church offer happiness? Healing? Financial relief? Longer life? Christian kids? Can it promise the fruits of the Spirit without being the Spirit? Many do.

What is it that we can truly promise a seeker or a believer? I could go on, but I'll stop there for now. I believe we can do better. We just need a better plan.

Being transparent is not only being honest about who you are, it is also about being honest about how you are perceived by others. It's risky, but worth it. **It could make the difference between high-impact and no impact at all.**

LAWS OF ATTRACTION

Only when you're attractive will you have the ability to attract. To *attract* is to "cause to approach or adhere." If you have a message you're sending out, isn't it worth the extra effort to make the message attractive? Let's take the ever-popular "no soliciting" sign as a case study for attraction.

I will most likely walk right by this without noticing, even if it's 4′x4′ and bright red. It's boring and invisible—which is fine, if that's what you're going for.

I will probably try to go in and sell them a candy bar for my kid's fundraiser anyway.

Attractive! No bright color or expensive surgery.[1]

I noticed it right away and it made me laugh. Because I appreciate the extra time somebody took to have some fun with a standard message, I'm going to respect their wishes and go sell my candy bars next door.

When we're on our game, we'll pay attention to how we present ourselves, even if it's a temporary sign we tape on the door.

The offices of Granger Community Church will be closed Christmas Day, Sunday December 25, 2011 until our Saturday December 31st's service. One service will be held at 5:00 on the 31st. at this campus or at our Elkhart campus. Doors will open at 2:00 pm

Normal office hours will resume on Monday, January 2nd, 2012

Should you need assistance, contact your ministry leader or leave a message at the general mailbox of Granger Community Church. A staff member or ministry leader will respond the week of January 2nd.

Have a very blessed Christmas and a Happy New Year!

Granger Community Church
574-243-3500

BEFORE: Technically, all the information on this sign is correct. But, ewww.

We're busy at home with family, making things merry and bright.
Our offices are closed from Christmas Day, Sunday, December 25 until the New Year's Eve service on Saturday, December 31 (service is at 5 p.m.).
574.243.3500
GCCwired.com
25

AFTER: Merry and bright! correct.

A tale of two signs—but one is arguably more attractive (and effective). **Which one will you be?**

WHO DO YOU LOVE MORE - THE WHAT OR THE WHO?

We should be asking ourselves this question in all communication efforts: am I more attached to what I have to say than how I say it? Everywhere in our life—whether it's at work or play, internal or external—people tune out if the content is abrupt, lofty, bossy or boring. If they're in a bad place, they might even rebel against the pettiest things.

Even if it's just a sign you hang in your corporate kitchen, people are more inclined to read and respond if there's something in it for them—a laugh, a reward, a compassionate tone delivered from their point of view.

I remember a few years ago when we needed to roll out a new employee handbook at our staff meeting. You know the drill—hundreds of pages full of boring policies and procedures. But, there was also important new information everyone needed to observe, whether they knew it or not, whether they cared or not.

The easiest thing to do would have been to simply hand out the manual and tell everyone they had to read it. Instead, my boss at the time, Tim Stevens, took the extra time to consider his audience. He dedicated time to prepare a careful presentation that valued the message recipients.

This is just part of the pop quiz he created to roll out the new staff handbook to the team. We had a blast at that staff meeting. Everybody laughed and interacted; it was amazing to observe people having a merry ol' time around the employee handbook.

If you don't know how to add inspiration and motivation to your information, find somebody around you to help. Everybody needs an image consultant. Even for kitchen signs and employee handbooks. (And solicitors!)

Employee Handbook – POP QUIZ

Students, be sure to use a #2 pencil or Sharpie Magnum. Carefully listen to each question and then circle the letter of the correct answer, which, by the way, is "C." Yes, that's right, the correct answer for every question is letter "C". Cheating is encouraged.

Do not work ahead of the class. Your teacher (the bald, good-looking guy at the front of the class) will lead the class in reading each question.

---

1. I need to sign an acknowledgement stating I've read the new handbook because...
   a. I'm not trusted.
   b. Some lawyer says its' a good idea.
   c. There's some new stuff I need to know.

2. There is a section called the "Statement of Ethics" in the handbook that outlines...
   a. How to ethically cheat on your taxes.
   b. When I need to wear my seatbelt.
   c. The rules of the game for staff members of GCC—they will keep you from being sidelined due to perception of wrong doing. (Pages 11-12)

3. When it says that we maintain an "at will" employment policy, it means...
   a. You must do anything your supervisor asks (i.e. like wash their car or polish their shoes).
   b. You work for free.
   c. It is legalese that complies with Indiana hiring law and means you don't need a reason to quit and GCC doesn't need a reason to terminate your employment. (Page 13)

Page 1

A page from the Granger Community Church Employee Handbook Pop Quiz.

ADMIT IT. YOU LIKE PEOPLE WHO ARE LIKE YOU.

Stephen Denny is a marketing expert with proven performance connecting brands to the wants and needs of technology users. He's helped manage the people, strategy and budgets at brand name companies such as Sony, OnStar and Iomega. Years ago, I read a simple post on his website about how one business was finding things in common with their audience.[2]

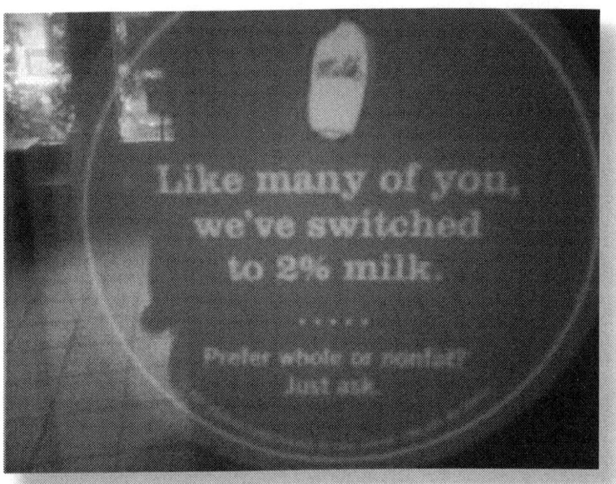

Snapped outside Starbucks. Poor quality, but caught in the real-life moment on Stephen's vintage flip phone.

"Did you know that Starbucks is just like you? They use 2% milk, too. You guys apparently have something in common! And that's great. Consider the alternatives. They could have said, "We only serve 2% milk. Whole or skim on request (or extra). They could have just switched and not told anyone." It's not rocket science—got milk? But, seriously. It is a legitimate brain science that can work for or against you.

Just think about how your opinion of a store softens a bit when they close shop on Thanksgiving. Admit it. In your mind, they leave the dark side to join the Jedi Order in a blink. (You've GOT to get that reference. But, if you don't, it's OK. Move on.)

What about REI's unprecedented move in 2015 to close 143 stores on Black Friday? Not only did they step back from short-term profits on the biggest shopping day of the year, they won the hearts and minds of the globe by demonstrating a policy of generosity and consideration.

Businesses are going the extra mile, past the transactional relationship, to think like their customers and make a meaningful connection. Don't you think we should work harder at this virtue, too?

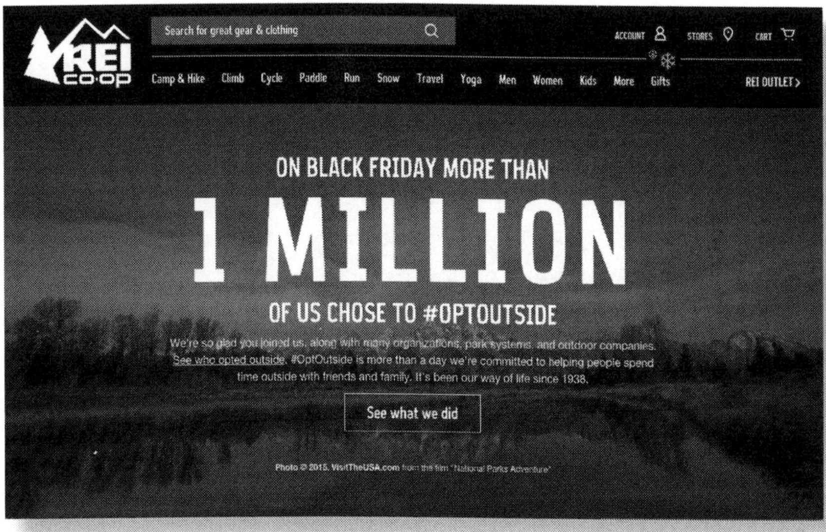

REI's #OptOutside hashtag measured a pop-up movement of over 1,000,000 people who skipped shopping to spend time outside with friends and family.

Businesses are going the extra mile, past the transactional relationship, to think like their customers and make a meaningful connection. Don't you think we should work harder at this virtue, too?

IT'S NOT WHAT YOU SAY; IT'S WHAT PEOPLE HEAR.

If you advertise a product (or platform or message) without taking into consideration all the things that happen when someone comes in contact with that product (or any part of your organization), it can actually work against you. What we say to address one group of people can actually alienate another. Sometimes, it's worth it. The objective is not to try to please the world. However, it is helpful to evaluate whether it needs to be said in a different setting, or if it needs to be said at all.

I got to thinking about this a few years ago when Rusty Weston, a writer for *Fast Company* magazine, devoted an entire article[3] to his perception of "Christian staffing."

Here are just a few excerpts from that article:

> Christian staffing. Do you work in a predominantly Christian workplace? Increasingly, Christian job boards are making this mission, as some put it, a reality.
>
> My take on the job boards that match "followers" with "Christian employers" is that a Christian workplace is at least partially about excluding non-believers who may undermine their value system.
>
> This statement on *Christian Staffing*'s website summarizes the mindset: "Have you dealt with staff problems including stealing, fraud, sexual harassment, lack of work ethic, tardiness, etc.? We did, and so we have decided to try to hire people we knew had a good reputation … and more specifically followers of Jesus Christ."

***

> What is unclear to me is how a Christian employee differs from, say, a Hindu, Islamic or Jewish employee. Of course, it's no secret that religious cultures and subcultures often hire amongst themselves; what's different here is these job boards are explicit about it.
>
> Biases are part of the American fabric, right? The federal government, including the U.S. Justice Department, recruits from Christian law schools and colleges. (That hasn't gone so well.)

***

> For many cultures and subcultures, a homogeneous, immersive environment is the most appealing way to live and work. But where are the winners here? People who seek faith-based work environments lose the value of collaborating with people from different cultures, who offer different ideas and perspectives; and people who are excluded from faith-based workplaces may be victims of discrimination.

The justification for a Christian staffing source is not what caught this writer's attention. It's how it's talked about. Now, take a step back to think about how you talk about your own "products." Think about how the language you use for your events, your weekend service, your fundraising, your email subject lines, your social media posts, etc., sound to someone who doesn't run in your circle. Do you sound controlling? Superior? Judgmental? Out of touch?

Sometimes, we can't see it ourselves—that message we unintentionally send. It helps to hear an outsider's perspective. Playwright Anton Chekhov said, "Man will become better when you show him what he's like." I know it's true. **Who you are is important, but don't underestimate the value of how you are perceived.**

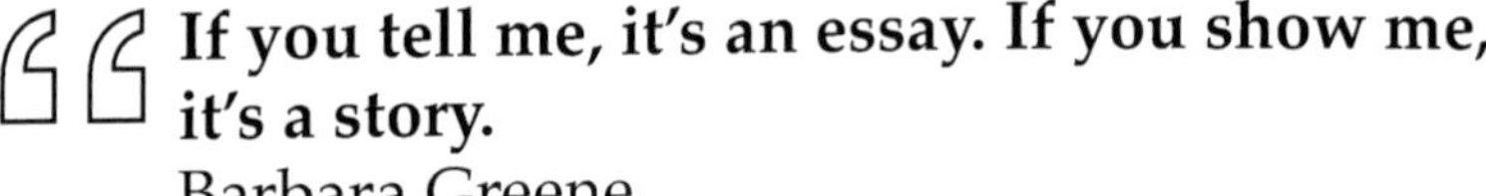

> **If you tell me, it's an essay. If you show me, it's a story.**
> Barbara Greene

LESS PROMOTIONS = MORE PUBLICITY

How do you get through in this low-trust, high-volume world? Simple. You cut out all the extras, so the real message can be heard.

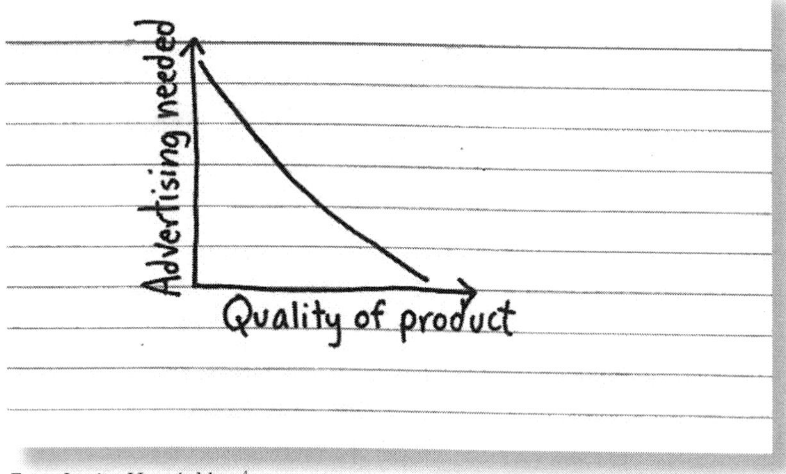

From Jessica Hagy's blog.[4]

People don't need as much background information as you think they do. Providing background details might seem essential to you, but it actually seems like hot air to your audience. They'd rather you get to the point and share the essential information they're looking for to make a decision.

People don't want to read more corporate copy from paid professionals about what makes this or that a "don't miss" event. They want to experience it for themselves, or ask their friends for the real scoop. Your job? Eliminate the weight of bullhorn self-promotion, and make your offering easy to find. And, if what they find is worthwhile, it will speak for itself.

Can your content and design pass these filters?

1. **Useful.** Emphasize the usefulness of a product, disregarding everything else.
2. **Understandable.** Self-explanatory.
3. **Unobtrusive.** Leave room for the user's self-expression.
4. **Honest.** Don't manipulate the consumer with promises you can't keep.
5. **As little design as possible.** Don't burden users with non-essentials.*

Here's a great example of a design from McDonald's that clears all five of the above filters:

McDonald's free Wi-Fi advertisement.

* This list was inspired by a good design list by Dieter Rams. I excerpted and edited but got original content from vitsoe.com/gb/about/good-design.

McDonald's didn't drone on and on about their multiple locations, new buns, white-meat chicken, $1 menu or hours. They stuck with one main theme that appealed to a mass need: free Wi-Fi. That one thing pulls us into the rest of what they have to offer.

Stick to the facts, and dispense with the fluff. **Clarity is creativity.**

THINK IT OVER
BUSTING THE MYTH: ADVERTISING CREATESINTEREST

- ☐ Do I foster an environment that allows honesty about what people discover—inside and outside of themselves? Am I, or the people around me, willing to be transparent and share what we see, even when it's uncomfortable and hard to understand?
- ☐ Am I more attached to what I have to say, rather than how I say it? Do I have someone around me who can help identify if my content is abrupt, lofty, bossy, boring or out-of-touch before I finalize it?
- ☐ Am I actively learning about new trends and how these trends are changing the way people are doing life? Who can help me in my discovery?
- ☐ Is there a simpler or more compelling way to communicate our message?
- ☐ What am I overselling? Where do we, as a church or an organization, under-deliver?

chapter 4

THE MYTH: IT WORKED BEFORE, SO IT WILL WORK AGAIN

> **Stubbornness is an unintelligent barrier, refusing enlightenment and blocking its flow.**
> Oswald Chambers, *My Utmost for His Highest*

History books talk about a time when you could mass market to a captive audience. You may even remember a time when the family sat together around the radio, or when there were only three network TV channels. Everyone experienced the same thing at the same time.

That's not the world we live in anymore. With the internet, email, satellite TV, Netflix, Hulu, Amazon Prime, smartphones, app stores and more communication channels you can count, the masses are spread out; tuning in or out as they choose. People are ignoring sterilized marketing copy and looking for recommendations from their friends. They're supplementing face-to-face interpersonal relationships with their online networks, looking for comrades and firing back at foes.

You can ignore the world around you and use old techniques you're comfortable with. Or, you can learn how people are really connecting to content in today's culture and join the conversation.

ARE YOU TOO FAMILIAR?

You wouldn't expect to find parallels between video game developers and ministry discipline, but that's exactly what I found when I read an article about *Halo*'s development team. I was inspired by three particular strategies they "played" by:

1. They watched people play *Halo* and noted problem areas they, as the game creators, were too close to see. They watched facial expressions, body language and player results, tracking everything from favored weapons to how and where players most frequently got killed.

   As a result, they discovered flaws between what the game creators thought people should do and what they actually did. They went back and corrected bugs and graphics that were ineffective.

2. They analyzed the change in their team dynamic and processes in the face of growth. When they started developing *Halo,* they could all sit in a single room and communicate by yelling over their shoulders, or peer at each other's cool creations on screen.

   As a result, they discovered that the pressure to deliver the previous version nearly destroyed them. Separate teams formed to design each level of the game, but they didn't coordinate their efforts. When they assembled all of their pieces for the first time, they discovered that the story was incomprehensible. They actually had the guts to throw out 80 percent of their work and start over.

3. They watched the stats and looked for positive and negative trends. These trends were one of the probes they used to find trouble.

As a result, one report revealed an unusual number of "suicides" among the players piloting the alien Wraith tank in an upper level. They discovered that the firing line of the guns was misaligned, inadvertently killing (and frustrating) the players. They went back and fixed the guns, and the suicides stopped.

What do church and organization leaders have to learn from game developers?

- **Every stakeholder aims for the same goal: keep players in a "flow" state—constantly surfing the edges of their abilities without bogging them down.**

  Are we intentional about watching the flow experience for our guests? I'm reminded to create space to watch people experience our creations—watch facial expressions, body language and traffic patterns the first time they encounter a touchpoint at our church. One weekend, I sat on the far right of our auditorium and watched people as they read (or didn't read) the bulletin and listened (or didn't listen) to the video announcements. I observed them at different points in the service for positive (or negative) responses. I watched where people went, and listened to what they said as they left the auditorium after service. I was a covert spy, and I learned many of my assumptions were wrong.

- **Game makers give people the tools, clear the way and allow people to find their own way of achieving their goals.**

  Do we provide the tools and create the environments for people to find their own way to connect with resources and each other? Or, do we force our prescribed paths and make it hard for people to do what they're trying to do? I've worked with a couple of churches who wouldn't stream their services or post their messages online because they wanted to force people to come in person.

Even forward-thinking churches who think they're making things accessible can make them difficult. More than once, I've gone looking for podcasts from a church. But, I can't make sense of the message list because they haven't labeled the episodes by series subject or topic. Labeling your message archive with the week number, date or out-of-context sermon title doesn't help your audience connect with your content.

- **Game makers eliminate battlefield areas where players are bored, stuck, killed or simply baffled about where to go.**

Do we take notice when people are doing things we never thought, or taking a different path than we planned for? Do we alter our flow when people are stuck and not responding the way we want them to, or do we stay the same and expect them to change?

Our Student Ministry Director, John Keim, noticed declining youth group attendance between middle and high schoolers. Instead of dismissing it as something he couldn't control and chalking the decline up to kids "not getting it," "aging out" or being "too busy," he dug in and talked directly to the high schoolers who had stopped attending. In the process, he found out that some had stopped attending because of busy schedules, but others had stopped attending because they didn't like the small groups.

He learned that they valued being part of a community, but didn't want to be "assigned" friends like in middle school. They also said the small groups around a table made it hard to invite friends. John took that information back and restructured the way high school did community. He created mid-size tribes for high schoolers to connect with organically, and attendance started growing again.

- **Game makers watch the stats to find what's working and what's broken.**

  Do we plow ahead, making assumptions and support needs that don't exist? At one time, my church looked at the data to find four out of 5,000 people from the weekend service downloaded our online discussion guides. You read that right: four out of 5,000. Before looking at the numbers, we assumed "everyone" was using those guides. After a brief consult with the real story, we were able to redirect the writing team to places where they could make a bigger impact.

Ed Catmull is co-founder of Pixar Studios and President of Pixar and Disney Animation. A quick glance at his long list of accomplishments (former VP at Lucasfilm, multiple Academy Awards and lifetime achievement recognitions in multiple fields, etc.) demonstrates that Ed knows a few things about how ideas are implemented.

In his book *Creativity, Inc.: Overcoming the Unseen Forces That Stand in the Way of True Inspiration*, Ed says, "When dynamics are working, you will solve your problem every time and do remarkable things. **Every once in a while, the system collapses. That's when you need to sit up and start paying attention to the people. Know that you're more wrong than you think you are."**

Who said computer games and cartoons are a waste of time? Game developers and animators are modeling ways to make connections and change lives. We can learn something from them.

CREATE CONVERSATIONS, NOT CONTENT

David Armano has been talking about the "conversation economy" for quite a few years. Consider these thoughts from one of his early articles[1] in *Business Week* magazine:

> Once upon a time, we were consumers. We took in the messages that were communicated to us. We didn't really get to talk back.
>
> Marketing has traditionally been about messages. Now consider this: the medium is the message.[2]
>
> Great experiences are a start, but they aren't enough. Communities are forming around popular social platforms such as YouTube, Facebook, Twitter [SnapChat, Instagram]—the list goes on and on. These platforms facilitate conversation. Conversation leads to relationships and relationships lead to affinity.
>
> [Technology] is changing how we interact with each other and with brands. Does this sound like marketing? Well, it is. It's how we market to each other. Yes, that's right—we market to each other. We always have, in fact, but now, we're doing it in a more digitally connected way. We swap stories about products and services we like or dislike. We share knowledge and expertise. **We define a new kind of currency fueled by conversation and founded in meaningful relationships.**

I can imagine what some of you might be thinking as you read this:

"What does this have to do with anything? I'm not in marketing—I'm in ministry. I don't even use SnapChat. You might as well be speaking Greek to me."

In fourth grade, we had a week of indoor recess. The teachers let us bring games and music from home to keep ourselves entertained.* I couldn't wait to bring my favorite album to share with everyone. It was *The Very Best of Herman's Hermits* from my parents' music shelf, and I knew every word of every song by heart. I was positive the class would love it as much as me. I imagined smiles and laughter as we sang along to "Henry the Eighth" and "I'm Into Something Good." But, when the day came, it was nothing like I dreamed.

No one appreciated or enjoyed the music I shared—at all. Instead, they mocked me for being such an out-of-touch loser. Nobody wanted to hang out with me after the Herman's Hermits incident. I was a laughingstock and it took years to recover.

It didn't matter; my intentions were good and my heart was pure. I was speaking a language nobody understood by playing music nobody around me was listening to.

So what is the church or your organization to do in this new generation that speaks a different language—with mobile phones as an extra appendage, and technology shortcuts you couldn't have dreamed up, even on a high dose of hallucinogens? (Notice I said "in" this new generation, not "with"... because like it or not, you're in it.)

* Now would be a good time to grab a tissue.

Haydn Shaw recently published one the most important books in the history of the planet.* *Generational IQ*[3] is about our how lack of generational intelligence causes us to overreact to the small things, ignore the big things, and do the wrong things, making our relationships worse.

Shaw says, "The older generation saw my generation's behavior as moral failure and essentially told us, 'The way we've always done church should be good enough for you, too, so get with the program.' The younger people came across as attacking the leadership, as demanding and disrespectful. I didn't know any of the sociological words for what was happening, but I could tell that much of it was over styles and preferences, not right and wrong. It started with people from different generations and ended up with a fight."

For those of us who think we're always right: perspective.[4]

Do you react to the new behaviors and philosophies of technology-native generations around you because they don't fall in line with "the way we do things"? Do you tune out or, worse, admonish them?

* Seriously, though. For the first time in the history of the planet, we have five generations in the church. Haydn's book walks you through these generational differences and paints a vision of hope for the future. I think the book is so good, you might want to put this book down and go buy his to read first. If not, promise me you'll read his book next.

If you have ever said, "I just don't get social media," or, "I'm not into all that technology stuff," or, "Why do people have their phones on them all the time," then you have announced to the world that you are out-of-touch. Worse yet, y**ou're perceived as someone who doesn't care to connect with any generation that acts differently than you (even if they face different challenges, and a different world, than you).**

I'm not saying that's who you are or what you believe, but like it or not, it is how you're perceived. Shaw brings an alternative approach into perspective: "When we start to understand another generation—rather than attempting to maneuver others into seeing things our way—we open ourselves to new possibilities are relating, helping, reaching, encouraging, and loving them."

Even if you're not ready to start interacting online, you have a responsibility to at least get online to watch others interact. Or, start a conversation with someone about their favorite apps. You'll be surprised at what you discover about them, and yourself.

Life change happens in relationships, and today's human behavior around technology is still centered around relational collateral. And, if we stop finding a way to meet people in their mobile and social spaces (the medium is the message), we won't have a clue what people are talking about, wrestling with and connecting to.

And, fourth graders will call you a loser. (I'm still not over it.)

WHAT HAPPENED TO OUR ATTENTION SPANS?

According to a recent study by Microsoft,[5] the average human attention span has fallen from twelve seconds in 2000 to eight seconds in 2015. Goldfish, meanwhile, are believed to have an attention span of nine seconds.[6]

I believe it. Our brains are rewiring themselves based on how we use technology. Generations of people are losing the ability to concentrate.

Have smartphones killed our attention spans?[7]

Besides missing that whale that just swam by, people don't read all that lovely content you've written; they skim and scan it. They're looking for a keyword that catches their attention or hits a nerve with something they're dealing with. And, they're impatient sitting still, unable to absorb long lectures.

Noah Zandan, CEO of Quantified Impressions, shared a Prezi (presentation software for cool kids) with the five metrics you need to know to give a great presentation.[8]

Obviously, Noah knows about the goldfish:

- **1.5 seconds**: the amount of time you have to make a positive first impression.
- **2.5 minutes**: the average audience attention span (down from twelve, then five in past ten years).
- **150**: average number of times the average American checks his/her phone in a twenty-four-hour period.
- **12**: maximum number of words that should be projected on your screen at a time
- **100:** percent of your audience will appreciate your speech ending on time

Some cognition experts have praised[9] the effects of tech on the brain, lauding its ability to organize our lives and free our minds for deeper thinking. Others fear tech has crippled[10] our attention spans and made us uncreative and impatient when it comes to anything analog.

Technology isn't making us stupid, it's making us different. And, different isn't always bad. In 2014, the third highest reason people gave for their increased Bible reading was, "Downloaded the Bible onto my smartphone or tablets."[11]

Do people need to get a life, turn off the computer and put down their phones? Yes, sometimes. But, the answer isn't to unplug to stay smart. We may just need to flip-flop how we supplement our knowledge. That is, in the past, we had to create the space to go online to enhance our learning and social networks. Now, we need to create the space to go offline to do the same.

We need to acknowledge that our brains process information differently today than they did even five years ago. Look at the regular communication channels you're using (e.g., weekly bulletin, email blasts, website, etc.) on a quarterly basis. Are you presenting too much information for people to absorb? Chances are you'll find paragraphs (and maybe pages) of content that's been added over time.

Bloated content doesn't make a powerful impact, it diminishes or eliminates it. So, the responsible choice here isn't whether or not you make the cut, it's what you're going to cut.

THE PROBLEM IS NOT THE PROBLEM

Kare Anderson wrote about the dilemma Walt Disney World executives faced when they discovered what really held the attention of the theme park's youngest guests:

> A few years ago, Disney World executives were wondering what most captured the attention of toddlers and infants at their theme park and hotels in Orlando, Florida. So they hired a few consultants to observe them as they passed by all the costumed cast members, animated creatures, twirling rides, sweet-smelling snacks, and colorful toys. But after a couple of hours of close observation, they learned that what most captured the young children's attention wasn't Disney-conjured magic. Instead it was their parents' cell phones, especially when the parents were using them.
>
> Those kids clearly understood what held their parents' attention—and they wanted it too. Cell phones were enticing action centers of their world as they observed it. When parents were using their phones, they were not paying complete attention to their children.
>
> Giving undivided attention is the first and most basic ingredient in any relationship. It is impossible to communicate, much less bond, with someone who can't or won't focus on you.[12]

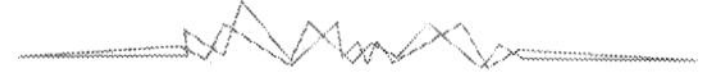

So what's a theme park to do? Contrary to what you might first think, mobile phones aren't the problem in this story—they're the opportunity.

Last summer, I went to Disney World's theme park in Orlando. And, while all the traditional Disney magic attributes that we'd come to know and love were still in practice, we encountered a new layer that took our experience to a deeper level. The catalyst to that experience might surprise you: it was a mobile phone.

Instead of banning phones at the park entrance, or training characters to perform wilder, attention-grabbing tactics, they actually incorporated phones into the experience. We were part of a secret mission that had us using a smartphone to weave in and around the park on a scavenger hunt adventure. Instead of drawing our attention away from each other, or the park magic around us, we actually found more hidden gems we never knew existed, and connected with each other like no other trip to any amusement park—anywhere, anytime.

It wasn't the new multi-million dollar ride, elaborate show or giveaways that brought us together (and increased our fandom to epic levels), it was a funny, fast-paced, interactive, memory-building bonding experience using a phone. We still talk about it to this day.

Whatever you pay attention to—or don't—has a huge effect on how you see the world, and how you feel about it. Disney saw phones taking parents' attention away from their kids and, consequently, pulling kids' attention away from the park. They saw those same phones not as a problem, but as a tool they could use to solve the problem.

You don't have to be Disney to conquer this challenge. My kids are in high school now. And, I'm amazed by the teachers who don't ban phones because of the distraction the classroom, but use them to enhance learning. They'll ask kids to pull out their phones for timed quizzes and surveys, leveraging the competitive gene of the students in the classroom. More students are engaged and learning because teachers have found a way to turn a problem into an opportunity.

Before you dismiss that [insert pet peeve of choice], look for ways to use it to enhance the overall experience you're trying to deliver.

THAT'S NOT HOW I REMEMBER IT

When my son, Easton, was seven years old, I came home from work and found a note on my desk with this picture:

Apparently, he was designing new logos for Google, and he wanted me to send his concepts to them for consideration.

It was one of the first times I paused to really reflect about some of the parts of normal, daily life for my kids that didn't exist when I was growing up. Besides Google, there are:

- **User names**. My kids were in first and third grade when I first heard them in the backseat talking about various user names for their classmates. This is not what my friends and I talked about on the bus growing up.
- **GPS**. I was wrong when I thought God created Dora the Explorer* so kids can learn what maps are actually used for, because her cousin Diego came along and threw the map out for gadgets.
- **Channel 31**. My kids have hundreds of television channels to choose from. I had five.
- **Code blue drills**. When I was growing up, we had fire drills. My kids have drills to protect themselves from terrorist attacks.
- **In-flight Wi-Fi.** When I was a kid, I took coloring books on road trips. Now my kids can watch movies, TV, email and text 30,000 feet in the air between Iowa and Alaska.
- **FOMO**. While I may have been anxious as a child about an occasional slumber party invite, constant social media access and warped online identities have teens and adults alike experiencing new levels of anxiety and compulsion with a "fear of missing out" syndrome.

* A few short years ago, *Dora the Explorer* was a popular cartoon for preschoolers on Nickelodeon. The Map was a supporting character on every episode, providing travel guidance and advice.

Even though I'm familiar with most of what my kids are talking about today, I'm not as tuned in as I was a year ago—and I imagine the gap will continue to grow as they do. When I find myself clueless about words they're using, I actively research to learn what they're all about. I can't afford to write it off to "kids these days," or I'll lose touch with their culture. Occasionally, I'll hand them my phone and tell them to surprise me with a new background. It's amazing what I learn about them when I do.

These days, there's no excuse to live in a cave. It's easier than ever to learn anything about everything with a Google search. I land on these sites the most during my pop-culture "research":

- **Wikipedia.com**: a searchable online encyclopedia.
- **UrbanDictionary.com**: a searchable archive of contemporary American slang*, listed in alphabetical order.
- **azLyrics.com**: a searchable song lyrics database.
- **Homeword.com**: I subscribe to their culture update newsletter, which arrives in my inbox every Friday. It includes the top trending items from the Internet, music, TV and movies for that week, as well as topical articles with psychological and sociological insights.

When I'm engaged in my kids' culture, I can stay in relationship with them. This is true of your audience and the emerging culture around you, as well. What are you actively doing to learn more about your staff, your church or your neighbor?

* This site should be rated R for mature audiences. As with any slang, some definitions get racy. There is no obscenity filter included.

MOBILE CULTURE

When I pulled into the parking lot and saw a car parked sideways with a woman slumped over in her seat, I didn't stop to offer assistance. I didn't even slow down. I didn't assume she was in medical distress or dead. You and I both know already: she was texting.

Just a few years ago I had to turn my phone off during flights. How inconvenient. Now I can use "airplane mode" and in-flight WiFi at 30,000 feet to stay connected to my little handheld device and all my life's assets.

Do you think people are addicted to technology? Do you think social media and texting are "replacing" real relationships? Are you afraid people don't know how to have a conversation anymore? Does it annoy you that people can't turn off their cell phones for an hour?

Kelley Hartnett, a colleague of mine, posted[13] about leveraging technology to enhance relationships, not replace them:

> I'm connecting with people—more frequently and more consistently than I ever have. In the last few days, I've gotten real-time updates from friends about a death in the family, a sudden hospitalization, a first-ever homecoming date and reactions to the presidential debate. I learned that a quiet church guy has an incredible wit, and I discovered that another church guy and I share the same wacky taste in music. All of my in-person interactions with these folks have an undercurrent of community that I'd not experienced before.

I have to agree. In the past few years, my on-the-go access to technology has allowed me to learn from people more effectively and more efficiently than ever before. I don't have to be at my desk to learn from other professionals in my field, my life stage or hobby of interest. I'm learning what events I need to attend, what books I need to read and what resources to access for help. When I run into roadside technical trouble, I can instantly post an SOS to a guru friend of choice who can offer immediate, sage advice. And because all of those people know other people, I have a virtually unlimited, instantly accessible network of really smart people at my disposal.

If used appropriately, mobile access gives us opportunity to love more authentically and more freely than before. It may seem idealistic, but it's true. Yes, plan A is to have backyard BBQs with our buddies every evening. But, when that's not possible, at least we can share the best BBQ experience together on Yelp.

Yes, it's nice to pick up the phone and call someone to offer a kind word and some encouragement. And, I do that too. Just in new ways. More than once, I have had the chance to visit someone in the hospital as a direct result of a Facebook post asking for prayer. I wouldn't have had the chance to be there in person if I hadn't heard about it online.

THE ART OF LETTER-WRITING IS FAST DYING OUT. WHEN A LETTER COST NINE PENCE, IT SEEMED BUT FAIR TO TRY TO MAKE IT WORTH NINE PENCE ... NOW, HOWEVER, WE THINK WE ARE TOO BUSY FOR SUCH OLD-FASHIONED CORRESPONDENCE. **WE FIRE OFF A MULTITUDE OF RAPID AND SHORT NOTES, INSTEAD OF SITTING DOWN TO HAVE A GOOD TALK OVER A REAL SHEET OF PAPER.**

THE SUNDAY MAGAZINE

1871

IT IS, UNFORTUNATELY, ONE OF THE CHIEF CHARACTERISTICS OF MODERN BUSINESS TO BE ALWAYS IN A HURRY. **IN OLDEN TIMES IT WAS DIFFERENT.**

THE MEDICAL RECORD

1884

WITH THE ADVENT OF CHEAP NEWSPAPERS AND SUPERIOR MEANS OF LOCOMOTION ... THE DREAMY QUIET OLD DAYS ARE OVER ... FOR **MEN NOW LIVE THINK AND WORK AT EXPRESS SPEED.** THEY HAVE THEIR *MERCURY* OR *POST* LAID ON THEIR BREAKFAST TABLE IN THE EARLY MORNING, AND IF THEY ARE TOO HURRIED TO SNATCH FROM IT THE NEWS DURING THAT MEAL, THEY CARRY IT OFF, TO BE **SULKILY READ AS THEY TRAVEL ... LEAVING THEM NO TIME TO TALK WITH THE FRIEND WHO MAY SHARE THE COMPARTMENT WITH THEM** ... THE HURRY AND BUSTLE OF MODERN LIFE ... LACKS THE QUIET AND REPOSE OF THE PERIOD WHEN OUR FOREFATHERS, THE DAY'S WORK DONE, TOOK THEIR EASE ...

WILLIAM SMITH, *MORLEY: ANCIENT AND MODERN*

1886

We've been complaining about relational inattention[14] since long before mobile phones arrived.

Constant connection can appear threatening if you don't hear all sides of the story. And, the more you learn, the more you will discover that culture hasn't shut down, it has just shifted and the space in which we interact looks different.

THINK IT OVER
BUSTING THE MYTH: IT WORKED BEFORE, SO IT WILL WORK AGAIN

- ☐ Are we providing tools, creating the environment, and allowing people to find their own ways to connect with next steps and each other? Or, do we prescribe rules, force paths and do their thinking for them?

- ☐ Do I dismiss people who are baffled about where to go, don't do things the way I think they should, or respond in ways I didn't anticipate? Or, do I look for new ways to open the flow and eliminate frustrations?

- ☐ Are we confident enough in our mission to discard "battlefield areas" where people are bored and stuck?

- ☐ Am I resistant to watching the new environments where people are interacting (online and mobile) before I jump to conclusions? Am I so egocentric that I believe my perspective is the only one that matters?

- ☐ What are we doing to learn about new methods and trends to understand how and why people are drawn to them?

- ☐ Can I identify *The Very Best of Herman's Hermits* in my organization? What out-of-date tool are we blindly holding on to because of habit or nostalgia?

- ☐ Is there a problem I could turn into an opportunity?

chapter 5

THE MYTH: PEOPLE CARE ABOUT WHAT YOU SAY

> **Educating the mind without educating the heart is no education at all.**
> Aristotle

You think people care about what you have to say? The truth is that the average person doesn't notice you. And, if they happen to have a different point of view than you do, they'll flat-out dismiss you as a non-option. It's not that you're not likeable or smart; it's just a matter of survival for people in today's world. There is simply too much out there and not enough time to take it all in.

Spotty memories and decreased benevolence are on the rise, and people are shutting down in an effort to make it through another day. The last thing they're looking for is unsolicited information, or someone to tell them to change their ways. They will, however, take time to read or hear something that reinforces an opinion they already have, or speaks to a real need in their life. If they're not looking for it, they won't hear it. But, if you take the time to learn what they're looking for, you can get in on a conversation already in progress.

EMOTIONAL IGNORANCE

Dr. Mark Goulston, author of *Get Out of Your Own Way: Overcoming Self-Defeating Behavior*, shares a list of misconceptions about how others view you and ten more about how you view others. It's a perfect illustration of the idea that "what you don't know can hurt you." Don't you want to know?

MISCONCEPTIONS OF HOW OTHERS VIEW YOU

Believing you are:	While perceived by others as:
Influential	Sly
Confident	Arrogant
Humorous	Inappropriate
Energetic	Hyper
Having Strong Opinions	Opinionated
Passionate	Impulsive
Strong	Rigid
Detail-oriented	Nit-picking
Quiet	Passive or Indecisive

MISCONCEPTIONS YOU HAVE ABOUT OTHERS

Assuming they are:	When they are actually:
Moved by passion	Moved by facts
Moved by facts	Moved by passion
Fun-loving	Serious
Serious	Fun-loving
Looking for a reason to buy in	Looking for a reason to buy out
Looking for a reason to buy out	Looking for a reason to buy in
Wanting to be told	Wanting to be asked
Needing to be convinced	Ready to buy
Ready to buy	Needing to be convinced
Excited about your organization	Thinking your organization is a dog

Absorb these insights to significantly influence self-awareness* and increase favorable interactions with others. Ignore them at your own peril.

* I'm pretty sure I'm perceived as arrogant and inappropriate. Little do people know how confidently humorous I really am.

I HAVE ACRONYMPHOBIA

What is it with the need to turn everything into an acronym? I saved this ad from a magazine about, of all things, customer service:

TFWM PARTICIPATING IN THE FOLLOWING SHOWS FOR 2008:

ISE
Jan. 29-31, Amsterdam, the Netherlands

ENTECH
Feb. 11-13, Sydney, Australia

NSCA
Feb. 21-23, Dallas, TX

NAB
Apr. 14-17, Las Vegas, NV

INFOCOMM
Jun. 18-20, Las Vegas, NV

PAL/MIAC
Aug. 27-28, Toronto, ON, Canada

PLASA,
Sep. 7-10, London, UK

LDI
Oct. 17-19, Las Vegas, NV

And, in case you're wondering, there was no key or legend anywhere in the article to decode what these acronyms stood for. I was left wondering what the purpose for the advertisement was. If people don't have the superpower to break the code, acronyms add no value.

Acronyms happen in the technology and political sectors at an annoying rate. But, it's even more disturbing to see churches frequently use acronyms as an everyday communication practice. Too often, people throw out inscrutable acronyms that few people outside their bubbles can understand or relate to.

How do you make sure you're not one of them?

- Do a health check. How freely are you using acronym shortcuts in your communication materials? For starters, look at your pre-service slides, your bulletin, Facebook posts and website.
- Who are you talking to? Are you using a language that only you understand?
- Are you taking shortcuts that make it easier for you, but harder for your community at large to connect the way you intended?

Best case with most acronyms is that people just won't get them, or they end up taking on a different meaning because the abbreviation is already owned by text lingo you don't know about. Sure, everyone's familiar with the benign starter list that includes BRB (be right back), TTYL (talk to you later) and OMG (oh my God*).

But, the list of text and hashtag shortcuts is longer than you can imagine, and your FYI (for your information) may end up being TMI (too much information) or NSFW (not safe for work) if you're not careful. One of my husband's favorite abbreviations is BM. (He's not talking about a bowel movement, but it's all I associate that acronym with and I throw a flag every time. I think he uses it more often because it bugs me so much. He's funny like that.)

Minimizing the use of acronyms in your communication will have a powerful effect on how you relate to your audience. Making this seemingly small change could be a game-changer—for the better—in how you relate with your community.

* I'm sure it's the praise version.

NOBODY'S LISTENING

> **Everything that needs to be said has already been said. But, since no one was listening, everything must be said again.**
> André Gide, *Steal Like An Artist*

Making announcements? Whether it's at your service, meeting, or event, there are eight great things you should know about people if you want them to hear what you're saying.

This list may not make your job easier, but I guarantee it can help make you more effective:

1. **People aren't open to your change prescription.** Of course, we want to inspire people to be part of something bigger than themselves, to break unhealthy patterns, and live a life of purpose. But, when we dictate, "You need to step it up," or, "It's time to go deeper," we imply that we have all the answers, and we think people aren't OK where they're starting. They already know they're not as good as they want to be, and we just make it worse. Instead, open their minds and get them thinking. Try: "This might be your next step," "Here is an opportunity for you to consider," or ask the question, "What is your next step?" Remember, everyone's next step looks very different. One person's next step might be to invest or volunteer more but, for another, it may be to finish out the evening without leaving early. And, each of these next steps is equally important.

2. **People aren't motivated by your need.** When people hear, "We really need small group leaders," or, "We really need your help," they perceive desperation and self-centeredness. And, since they've got needs of their own, your ask feels like one more obligation to add to the pile. Your message should be about the great things that change life for the guest, not about what you (or your church or organization) need. When you communicate, "Here's a cool opportunity not everyone knows about," or, "You might want to be part of this one-of-a-kind experience," it makes it about them, not us, and it motivates people to move.

3. **People don't know who you are.** Even if you keep it short, always take the time to introduce who you are and why you're there, even if it's just for the benefit of one new person in the room. When you just get up and start talking without introducing yourself, you communicate two things to new people: exclusivity ("Everyone's already in the club except for you.") and pretentiousness ("Everyone already knows who I am.").

4. **People multi-task and can't remember squat.** It's human nature to tune out the talking head in the front of the room as you look through your purse, replay the drive to church in your mind, or mentally run through your to-do list for what's next. And, if a speaker is lucky enough to have a room full of people with full attention spans who are actually listening, there is no guarantee they will remember what you said when they walk out of the room and back into their lives. Visually support your verbal announcement to grab and hold your audience's attention, clarify information and raise their interest level. It doesn't have to be fancy or elaborate. A printed pro-

gram, slide, table tent, or sign all work fine. Just remember, don't read directly from your visual aids. They're not your script, but a separate component that reinforces your words.

5. **People are turned off by lack of preparation.** Prepare your announcement so your audience "catches it" within thirty seconds. If it's important enough to announce, then it's important enough to prepare for. Try to cast vision by answering these questions: What is so special about this opportunity? Why should I spend my time on it? How is it going to make my life and me better? Remember, you've got no more than thirty seconds.

6. **People can relate when you talk about them or people like them.** Tailor your announcement to your audience. Whenever possible, customize a broad message to a specific audience to make a bigger impact. Even if the announcement doesn't change, it makes all the difference when you find a way to highlight a unique attribute for your specific audience. For example, if you're talking to a group of moms about volunteer opportunities at the food pantry, tell them to bring their kids. If you're talking about the same volunteer opportunity to a group of students, tell them about the free donuts you'll have. Help them see how they can specifically use the information you're sharing.

7. **People feel left out and frustrated when you use insider language.** Don't assume everyone is in the know; most people aren't. Avoid the use of acronyms or nicknames, or you run the risk of alienating guests. Does everyone know what "The FUSE," "TRL," or "Lifeline" is? Be specific and clear,

not clever. If a program or event is for middle schoolers, say so. Once people are on the inside, feel free to use insider language. But, it's never cool to use it in announcements for large groups, connection events, first-serve opportunities, etc.

8. **People are not impressed with your technical vocabulary or holy dialect.** Use normal, everyday language. Skip the phrases that are weird and scary to normal people. Don't know what I'm talking about? Picture yourself walking into a professional office setting and trying to have a normal conversation using words such as *saved, sanctified* and *washed in the blood of the lamb.* If we use religious words, guests either won't understand, or they'll run from us so they don't "catch it." Keep it simple and keep it real. Avoid over-spiritualizing and over-complicating your conversation. Your announcements aren't any more credible with an entire list of "blessed" or technical phrases.

BIAS AWARENESS

My neighbor "Jim" is one of the nicest people I've ever met. He's outgoing, funny, kind, hardworking, family-focused, generous and just an all-around great guy. He makes a difference in his neighborhood and community. Anyone who knows him loves him.

One weekend my husband, Mark, and I stopped by Jim's house to return some things we had borrowed. We happened to walk up on a candid, honest and unguarded conversation he was having with his friends.

Jim was sharing the real-life stories about his interactions with church people—from my church—and at one point, he summed it up this way: "I can't stand them." It was clear that Christians were the reason he didn't go to church.

Jim had always been friendly to us, but guarded. After hearing him say, "I can't stand Christians," it became clear why he had kept a safe distance from us after we moved in. All he knew about us was that I was on staff at Granger Community Church and that Mark was "heavily involved." I'm sure he had been sitting across the street waiting for us to "pounce" on him like church people. This guy wasn't looking for someone to change his mind.

I get it, my friend. I feel the same way.

Mark and I had some beverages, ate some snacks and stayed a while with Jim and his friends. We talked about NASCAR, biking, kids and lack of sleep. We weren't there to sell anything; we just hung out.

And, to be perfectly honest, I respected Jim more for being honest, rather than being safe and politically correct. I sincerely considered his opinion constructive for all of us.

No one is immune to an outsider's perspective. It doesn't matter if your ministry is progressive and contemporary, traditional and conservative, or relevant and real—**we all know insiders who get in the way of outsiders experiencing Jesus.**

> “ **One of the most compelling sounds for the human ear is the sound of another human voice talking about something they care about.**
> David Candow, National Public Radio

What are you doing to help educate your church body about how others see them?

I CAN'T SEE YOU. OH, WAIT! NOW I CAN.

Chris Forbes is a marketing coach and consultant for faith-based nonprofits, organizations and films. He has one simple secret for reaching more people: **reach fewer people more times.** Brilliant. Go back. Read it again. Wow.

The secret is for churches and other organizations to narrow their focus and reach fewer people more times. There is more to the secret, of course, than just narrowing your focus onto a smaller group of people. You have to understand the people you want to reach. But when your focus is smaller, this is possible.

This one simple secret is so simple, it even works with kittens:

> People only pay attention to what their brains tell them they need. For example, when my children were younger, they decided they wanted a pet kitten. We all agreed it would be okay for the children to have a kitten. The next day, I began to notice all the kitten communication in my community. I saw "Kittens for Adoption" and "Free Kittens" signs everywhere it seemed. I overheard people talking about kittens. I even saw stray cats! What made the difference from the day before? On that day, I "needed" a kitten for my daughters.

> The fact is people's needs drive what people pay attention to. People usually only notice what will benefit them in some way. As a marketer, you need to understand people's specific needs. When you know who you are trying to reach and begin to understand their needs, your communication can be presented in a way that speaks directly to their needs. That means they will pay attention to your communication and not block it out.[1]

For years, we had record numbers attending our informational meetings for our quarterly mission trips. When numbers started declining, we started ramping up the promotions exposure. We'd send more emails, create more bulletin inserts and post more social media reminders. Attendance still didn't grow to the levels it was at before. As a matter of fact, it seemed to be declining, and our ministry leaders thought it was from lack of communications. So, with outreach being one of our core purposes, we elevated promotion of this quarterly information meeting to the weekend service with a dedicated message, video, bulletin ad, platform announcement and home page banner on the website. And, when the meeting rolled around, only a handful of people showed up.

Frantic attempts to generate more interest with more promotions wasn't yielding anything but wasted energy and loss of promotion equity.

So, why was attendance so high in previous years? Upon reflection, we recalled the small, repetitive and focused arena where this event was shared in the first place. For a season, we had a series of core class members cycled through six to eight times a year. The fourth and final class was all about "finding your mission."

At the conclusion of that class (thirty to sixty people at a time), we'd share the quarterly mission meeting as a next step. When we stopped hosting core class 401, it affected the outcome event (the next step quarterly mission meeting). Do you see? **We had higher attendance promoting this event six to eight times per year to a group of thirty to sixty people who were highly interested in the topic than we did when we pulled out all the stops for the entire weekend crowd of 5,000.**

That's the definition of a felt need—anything people consciously lack, desire or need help with (time and money management, relationships, stress, pain, etc.). Connect with a felt need, and you will connect with an audience. On the other hand, if you share information without wrapping it around a felt need, it is almost impossible to make a connection. **Remember, it's easy for people to miss what they're not already looking for.**

THINK IT OVER
BUSTING THE MYTH: PEOPLE CARE ABOUT WHAT YOU HAVE TO SAY

- ☐ Runners strip themselves of any unnecessary weights so they can run unencumbered.* What weight is holding me back? Is it a weight of culture? Tradition? Extended family expectations? Or, are there unresolved issues in my heart that I need to deal with such as anger, fear, insecurity or jealousy?

- ☐ How many ways can I connect with my audience—naturally, uniquely and on a one-to-one level? What do I have in common with a parent, a student, a retired person, a neighbor or someone who avoids "church people"? How can I learn to "love the one I'm with"?

- ☐ How would I change a recent presentation I've given or conversation I've had—same room, same slides—if my audience was totally comprised of recent immigrants? From Russia? Who were blind? But loved country music? And were afraid of horses? But loved square dancing? In each case, how would my presentation subtly change?

- ☐ Is our church or organizational communication aligned with our DNA? Are we using the same filter as an overview for everything we create? Is this what we really mean to say? Does it sound like us?

- ☐ What can I do to help educate my church or organization about how others see them? Who can educate me?

- ☐ Where am I speaking to the needs of a focused audience? Am I blasting promotions to the masses for an event that applies to a few?

* 1 Corinthians 9:24–26; Hebrews 12:1–2.

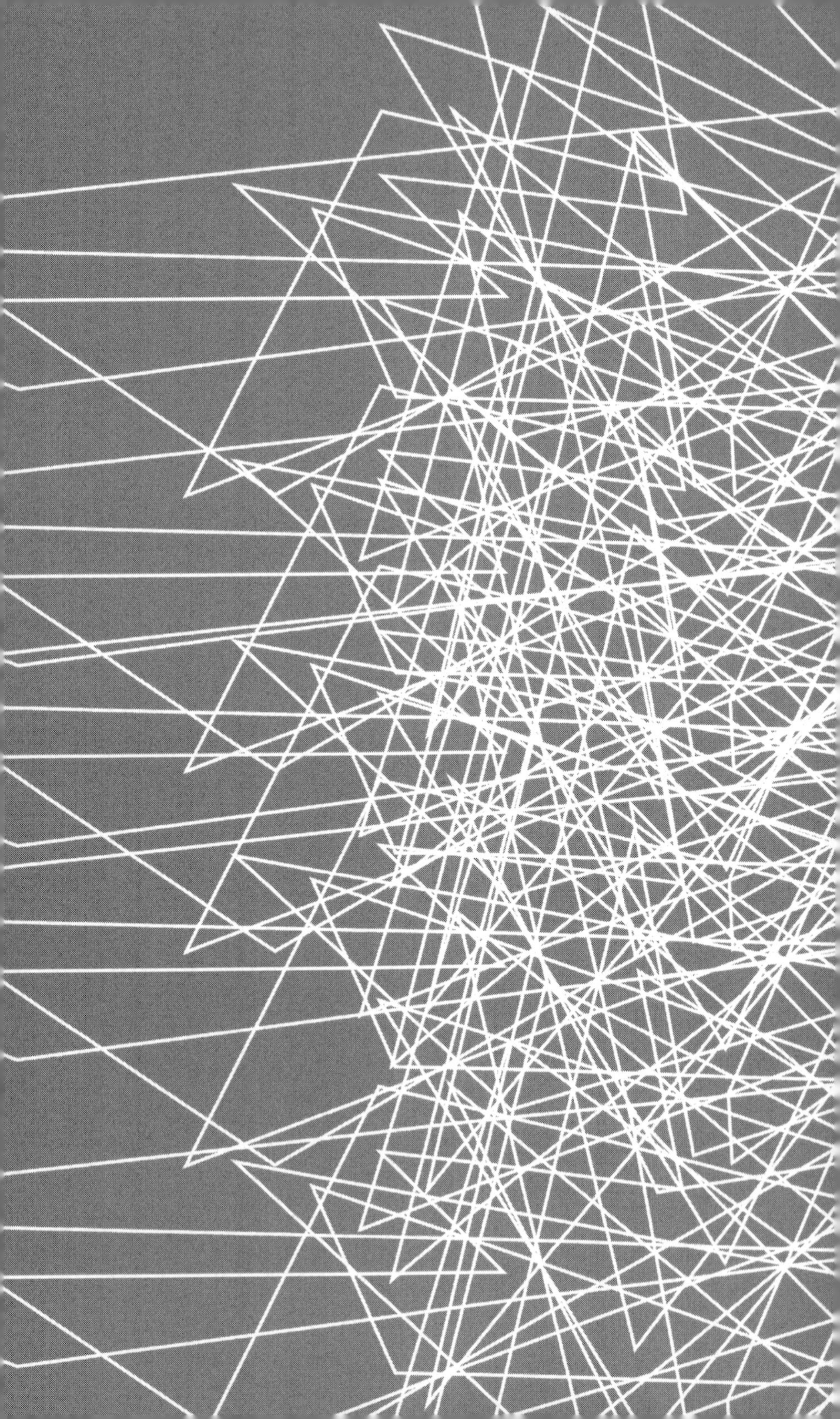

part 2

BEST PRACTICES MAKE A DIFFERENCE

If we're growing, we're always going to be out of our comfort zone.
John Maxwell

I heard it said somewhere that information is giving out, but communication is getting through. You should have just had an "aha" moment reading that. If you didn't, go back and read it again. This is why we need to consider our approach when it comes to communicating. We can't be lazy and speak from our selfish, one-sided point of view if we intend to positively influence perceptions and persuade decisions. A few "best practices"* can help change our vantage point from "what I think needs to be said" to "what my audience thinks they need." Yes, this might be counterintuitive, given that most of us typically think we have all the answers, and people don't always know what they need. But, as you'll see, it really works.

* What's a best practice? A reliable technique with proven results.

chapter 6
KNOW YOUR AUDIENCE

“ **Everybody experiences far more than he understands. Yet it is experience, rather than understanding, that influences behavior.**
Marshall McLuhan

If people are struggling to figure out what will make a difference in their daily grind, why would they spend their time and attention on you? In his book *Get Out of Your Own Way,*[1] Robert Cooper says, “The more you engage with things that inspire you emotionally, the more powerful is your motivation to achieve them.” The same is true for your audience. So who are you talking to? Do you even know these people? And, for the record, the answer doesn’t lie in demographic insights alone. To communicate effectively with someone, you have to get at the *psychographics*—the attitudes, interests, lifestyles—to connect with the emotion in his or her real world. Only then will you be able to begin to learn what might make you worth his or her time.

CULTURE DEFINED

Years ago when I was working for a consulting firm, I attended a cross-cultural communication workshop.[2] Although the workshop was geared toward software developers and technical writers, my takeaways applied in a variety of contexts.

Here's what I uncovered when I recently pulled out my old notes for a fresh opportunity to look at what we do in ministry and why:

> **"The term *culture* has been defined in a variety of ways. Even among anthropologists, there is no agreement on a single definition of the term. In fact, researchers Kroeber and Kluckhohn identified over 167 definitions of *culture*.**[3]

Wow. That's not 167 cultures, but 167 *definitions* of the word. Interesting.

You know me by now. I'm all about less chaos, less noise. So I'll share six of the 167 definitions. That's more than enough to get us going.

Culture is:

- How people think, feel and act;
- A system for creating, sending, storing and processing information developed by human beings;
- A program for behavior;
- The collective programming of the mind, which consists of patterns of thinking, feeling and acting;
- Software of the mind;
- The way in which a group of people solves problems.

Too often, I think we're all guilty of defining culture as "the way we do things around here." The good news is, we don't have to stay that way.

Historically, the word *culture* derives from the Latin word *colere*, which could be translated "to build," "to care for," "to plant," or "to cultivate."

This is where it gets good. And, this is our opportunity within the church: to use this definition to drive ministry decisions about our programming and communication priorities. **Not "this is how we do things around here," but instead, to build, to care for, to plant or to cultivate the communities we are surrounded by.**

THE PSYCHOGRAPHICS INSIDE THE DEMOGRAPHICS

Sociologists, national advertising agencies, consumer-marketing companies and political strategists all use ethnography, the study of living cultures, to explore the social relations that structure everyday lives of society. By observing behaviors "in the field," they learn what it is people want and think they need. They work hard to figure out how they can answer the questions people are asking. They are discovering the space in which people rally, and they go there. They continually learn how to get outside their own bubble to attract and move people to buy products and get votes. Richard Reising[4] tells a simple story that brilliantly demonstrates a practical application of ethnography:

> A woman is driving down a pitch-dark road late at night and sees that she is almost out of gas. Her fear is somewhat relieved as she sees two gas stations up ahead.
>
> If these two gas stations are equally accessible, and the gas is equally priced, which will she choose?
>
> Simple. She will choose the one with better lighting. Why? At that moment, her primary need is safety.
>
> Better lighting makes her feel safer. Her response is natural—just as natural as the first conclusions that people commonly draw about churches.
>
> Imagine the owner of the less-frequented store. He tries to solve the problem by dropping prices, hiring a new graphic designer, making a new sign and increasing inventory...but his sales do not increase. He is missing the connection. He doesn't understand what drives people.

I have a question for you. How strong is your connection? Is your church providing the right light or are people headed to the other station?* If you don't take the time to learn about your audience, you'll never know.

This may or may not be surprising to you, but many of the primary ethnology research techniques sociologists employ are "soft" and "emotive," not scientific and absolute. They include:

- First-hand observation of daily behavior;
- Casual conversations and in-depth interviews;
- Discovery of local beliefs and perceptions.

What are you waiting for? Find the answers to these questions, and learn about people that you are trying to reach:

- Why would people want to spend their time and attention in your church instead of on the couch, at the mall or at the club? Consider what they're looking for and rallying around.
- What unique value do you provide that makes changing their schedules worth the hassle? Consider what they find or experience at your church that isn't available anywhere else.
- How does your programming fit into the grind of their lives? Consider the reality of their career demands, sports schedules, financial strain, relationship and family dynamics, etc.
- Consider their comfort zone; where they spend free time and money. Do you know what they love and hate? Are you aware of the emotional triggers that could attract or repel?*

* Are you wondering what the result of all this questioning looks like? I thought you would be. And, that's why I put a sample "mindset profile" in a place I affectionately refer to as "the back of the book."

If you really care about connecting with the audience you say you care about, part of your daily discipline should include amateur sociology. Much like intramural sports provide us the opportunity to play collegiate basketball without a scholarship, ministry provides us the opportunity to become ethnographers without a degree. Make it part of your job description—**become a student of people.**

And, you know what? It's just not as hard as we make it out to be. Most of the time, it can be as simple as a change of scenery. **How can we change our perspective if we don't change our view?** We can't judge our station without getting out from behind our desks and actually seeing what it looks like to people driving by.

THE WORLD AS YOU SEE IT

As a spiritual discipline in my life, I consistently pray and work on renewing my perspective. Let's just say I never run out of real-life situations that challenge me to look at things from somebody else's point of view. Sometimes, I'm intentionally seeking it out. And, other times, it's a hard life lesson I run into face-first (like a brick wall).

> **It is the function of art to renew our perception. What we are familiar with we cease to see.**
> Anaïs Nin

I still flip through magazines whenever I can just to browse the print ads: the best inspiration for how to tell a story on one page. When I saw this ad, I immediately thought about how it applies to the church. What a profound illustration to the point.

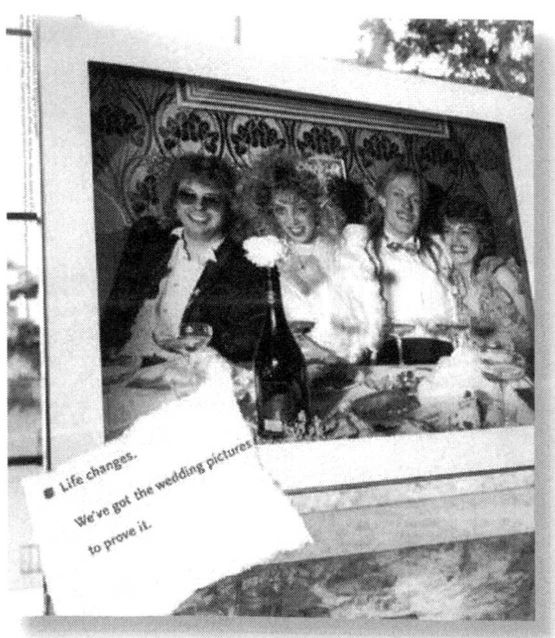

"Life changes. We've got the wedding pictures to prove it."

What does an old wedding picture with big hair and bad clothes have to do with ministry? Well, to be honest, sometimes, we're still trying to relate to people in a world that no longer exists. Our frame of reference and perspective are as out-of-date as my prom dress from 1986.

So, how do you see the world—as it is, or the way you are? What are you doing to learn about people today who don't see things the way you do? As a church leader, would you be willing to:

- Go on vacation with an atheist?
- Eat dinner at a smoky, local bar with people who swear like truckers?
- Listen to secular music (with the explicit label) and learn what the lyrics mean?
- Read a racy, nonfiction or non-Christian advice book from the *New York Times* Bestseller list?
- Make friends with pornographers or strippers?

Any of these could, and should be, uncomfortable. Maybe even controversial. But, too often, we get so worried about what other church people will say that we forget how Jesus tells us to live. And, he never told us to live in a bubble.

I'm just asking: what are you willing to do to learn about people who don't see things the way you do?

DON'T ASSUME THEY'RE BAD APPLES

We're all prone to "filling in the blanks" and making assumptions based on a snapshot. I've done it to others, and it's been done to me. It's particularly easy to do when someone's actions don't match up to what you're used to in your own life. I'm thankful for the hard lessons I've learned in this area, because I jump to conclusions a lot less often.

I'm learning that the actions don't tell the whole story, and I get the opportunity to dig deeper to learn about the story behind the person—behind the behavior. I'm better because of it and would miss out on SO MUCH that's great in this world if I spent my days running away from, or fighting against, everything new and unknown.

The real boot camp experience for me came when my daughter hit turbulent times in the teen years. I'm convinced those times would have been a lot less turbulent if I hadn't feared some of the new things she was connecting with (i.e., social media, friends who dressed weird, scary music, alternative thinking, etc.). I reacted without first taking the time to learn.

Shepard Fairey is a street artist and designer (and founder of OBEY clothing) who emerged from the skateboarding scene. I once read an interview where he talked about the assumptions people made about his alternative journey. His insights were helpful:

> "My attitude was never, 'I want to be an isolated person and do my own thing in direct opposition to the mainstream;' it was more like, 'I need to be doing what I'm doing, and I need to figure out how to keep doing it by any

means necessary.' A lot of people think if you are into some sort of subculture or alternative culture that means you are anti-mainstream. My idea was always, 'Well, mainstream is kinda sucky a lot of times, but does it have to be?' It would be cool to educate people about the stuff that I'm into. Sort of, enlighten the mainstream—raise the bar all across the board rather than having to feel like an outsider forever."[5]

Geez, Louise. He's right. Too often, I have assumed the wrong motives. **I defaulted to, "If they don't think like us, they must be anti-us."**

A word to myself? Chill. To other people? Chill. To churches? Chill. Let people color outside the lines. You just might learn something.

I'll bet some of you might be struggling with this principle, believing it's your holy responsibility to live "separate from the world" and fix the sin of anybody you come in contact with. Allow me to rattle your cage.

In his book *Lasting Impressions,* Mark Waltz talks about the difference between being responsible to people versus being responsible for them:

> We can easily make our approach—our programs, services, classes and groups—more important than the people we want to help. When we do, people feel disrespected, insulted and parented. We are not responsible for people but to them. Being responsible TO our people is quite different. And incredibly freeing.

- When I'm responsible to people, I understand they have a choice. When I'm responsible for people, I think I should decide for them.
- When I'm responsible to people, I know they must figure out their next step. When I'm responsible for people, I try to tell them what their next step is.
- When I'm responsible to people, I allow them to bear the brunt of the consequences for their own chosen actions. When I'm responsible for people, I assume the guilt—or worse, the shame—for them.
- When I'm responsible to people, I engage in their journey, offering encouragement and teaching. When I'm responsible for people, I try to direct their journey, never allowing them to wrestle, mess up or make a wrong turn.
- When I'm responsible to people, I talk to God on their behalf. When I'm responsible for people, I talk to people a lot on God's behalf.[6]

You don't have all the answers, so you can quit operating as if you do. Someone might find the courage to take his or her next step toward Christ because you get out of the way.

HOW FAR WOULD YOU GO TO SEE THROUGH THE EYES OF YOUR GUEST?

> **You have to be interested in culture to design for it.**
> Lorraine Wild

You get it by now. We're talking about spending lots of time getting to know the people you're trying to reach. But, here's the kicker. Your job is never done because you can never learn enough about them. Your audience keeps changing.

If you flip through my journal, you'll find this handwritten prayer:

Jesus, please don't let the fire in my mission die.
Keep me close to the flames and keep me bothered.
Don't let me lose touch with real life and real people.
Show me people's hearts and pain, so I remember
the stakes are high.

Even though I wrote that original prayer over a decade ago, it hasn't waned. It's a classic song I still have on replay as I continue to discover new ways to adjust my perspective to see through the eyes of other people. Without even leaving my office, I'm challenged daily about how far I would go to understand the reality of my co-workers', extended family's and enemies' worldviews.

It really is an exercise in dying to yourself. And, for the record, I in no way, shape, or form have it mastered. (But, I am in a constant state of pursuit, just in case you were wondering.)

I'm inspired by the lengths the Walt Disney Corporation takes to accomplish this:

- Disney Imagineers have gone as far as wearing kneepads and crawling around their parks to experience them from a child's perspective.
- Every Disney employee is trained in the art of "guestology"—learning who the guests are and what they expect when they come to visit. It's a standard part of every employee's job.
- Disney guest services teams set up incognito "listening posts" all around the parks to capture candid feedback about guest impressions.[7]

Why aren't these standard practices for the church? They should be!

We should care about what guests say about us—not just the positives, but the negatives as well (denial is not a good strategy). But, you know the funny thing about negativity? We get the chance to turn it into a positive.*

It's probably not practical for me to ask you to go crawl around your lobby wearing kneepads tomorrow, but there are some practical places you can get started to get to know your audience. The more you know about your guests, the better you can communicate with them.**

- **Watch online chatter.** Set up a Google alert, use the advanced search features on Twitter and Facebook or use a social media monitoring tool like Mention or Hootsuite to watch your brand. Start with a simple search for your church and pastor names to see what results you find. It's really helpful to discover what people say about you when you're not around.

* Funny, isn't that what God does for us every day? Ironic.
** A big part of this list was originally inspired by posts I read on ChurchMarketingSucks.com.

- **Enlist secret shoppers.** Invite people who don't attend church to visit a service, your website or browse your social media activity and offer their candid reactions. People love to give their opinions, especially when there are no strings attached. I heard of one church that invited an atheist to review their service on his blog. I love that.
- **Take surveys.** Use short-formal and informal polls to see what people are thinking and get feedback about what they believe works and what doesn't. Use different channels—online and off—for a variety of responses. For the best results, make sure your questions force a choice between two options. If you give people a chance to sit on the fence, they will.
- **Join in.** Watch the shows people are talking about. Eat where they eat. Read what they read. Sit in a different seat. Take a different route. Try different times. The more you understand life outside your own routine, the more you know how other people outside your slice of the world are connecting. A friend of mine got on Twitter and followed everyone within a ten-mile radius of the church to see what they were talking about.
- **Watch.** Instead of doing what they do, observe how they interact with what they do. Tag along with someone for a day. Grab a friend—or better yet, an acquaintance—and plan a field trip. Off the record and outside your usual environment, watch what makes them laugh, what makes them cry. What scares them? What moves them to action?
- **Round it out with the demographics.** It's the rest of the story. It doesn't show the whole picture, but including the demographic information in your audience profile is important. The best part is, someone else has most likely already done the research for you and you can get it free.*

* Looking for places you can get free market research? Go to the "back of the book."

And, when you're done with all your learnings, then what? Document them and keep them in front of you. Share the summary with your writers, designers, communicators and key leaders to keep in mind as they do their daily jobs.

Without that constant reminder of the bigger picture, it's too easy to fall back to creating your task list and materials for whoever is in front of you—not necessarily the audience you're trying to reach. Many times, they're not the same.

THINK IT OVER
ADOPTING THE BEST PRACTICE: KNOW YOUR AUDIENCE

- ☐ How am I defining culture? Do my priorities, actions and decisions help the church "to build," "to care for," "to plant," or "to cultivate"? Or, am I living out the definition as "the way we do things around here"?

- ☐ Am I finding ways to become an amateur ethnographer? What are people rallying around and connecting with? Am I there? Am I finding ways to speak to the need?

- ☐ What new things am I willing to do to step outside my comfort zone to learn about people who don't see things the way I do?

- ☐ If relationships are built on trust, then no one sells better than a peer does. Who are my audience members most like? Who would they rather hear this from than me? How many other people, similar to them, have already gone down this path? What role could they play?

- ☐ How can I promote and perfect the art of "guestology" in my ministry? How will it impact my role, department and task list?

- ☐ Is the audience we're currently reaching the same audience we want to reach? Do we know the difference?

chapter 7
REMOVE BARRIERS TO ENTRY

> **The problems we can fix, we should.**
> Bono

Distractions are roadblocks, and they can blind an audience before they ever get the chance to hear, see or click through your message. Potential distractions exist all around you—from sights, sounds and smells to facilities, signage, preconceived notions, language, graphics and information flow. Your best defense? Identify the distraction and eliminate it. And, you're going to need help with that because most distractions for others are invisible to you. Much like the elephant in the room, sometimes the best way to remove a barrier is to acknowledge it.

THAT'S JUST GROSS

Have you heard about the toilet bowl restaurant in Taiwan?[1] (Yes, I used the words "toilet bowl" and "restaurant" in the same sentence.) When I first read about it, I was baffled. A restaurant that decorates, seats people at, and serves food in toilets?[2]

Ewww. Seriously, what's the appeal? I've lost my appetite. I don't get it.

This restaurant seems like a good fit for Survivor contestant training, but wide appeal? I just don't know that many people who want to eat with their friends in the bathroom, out of the toilet.*

Think about your ministry programs. Do you have any toilet bowl opportunities you're promoting? In other words, does your audience "get" you (or do only you get you)? **Are you freaking people out, or helping them lower their defenses?**

The ministry promotions I'm going to share with you now may not be as gross as eating out of a toilet bowl, but they are gross examples of real communications misses:

* Believe it or not, they're so successful, they've expanded to multiple locations. However, consider this restaurant an exception to the rule, and don't use it as a model for your ministry.

- Promoting a men's retreat as a place to "go deeper and develop relationships with other men." *Try selling that one to your neighbor. Uh…it's not what it sounds like.*
- Providing postcard invitations to your congregation that have, "Share this with your unchurched friend," printed on them. *Talk about feeling targeted. What an awkward feeling for the "unchurched friend" when they read that. Are they a person or a project?*
- Asking a newcomer to stand up to be recognized during the service. *This embarrassing moment commonly brought to you by many well-meaning local churches.*
- Using words such as "commitment" and "challenge" in the content of your welcome packet or first-contact invite tools. *I'm already over-challenged, overcommitted and overwhelmed. More commitment? My first impression: I don't think I can take* it.
- Jumping in someone's path to shake his or her hand and make them feel welcome at church. *There is such a thing as personal space. I'm glad you noticed I'm here, but not glad to feel assaulted.*
- Use a picture of people holding hands in a circle with their eyes closed to promote small groups. *I'm not sure that's what attracts me to go to someone's house to meet with total strangers. You want me to join a small group and hold hands with total strangers? Try a more inviting first impression.*

The examples here just might create some barriers for people. Wouldn't you agree?

GET OUT OF YOUR OWN WAY

A friend of mine was asked to tour a church that needed help growing their dwindling attendance numbers. Here's an excerpt from the email he sent me about his experience:

Their Goals

1. They want to attract younger people to the church.
2. They want to create a newer, fresher image and use it to cultivate awareness of their church.

Their Barriers to Entry

1. The median age of the members is seventy years old.
2. Commemorative plaques were located throughout the building dedicating every upgrade to the church (e.g., parking lot paving, welcome center, foyer decor, etc.) to the memory of someone who had died.
3. About forty really big boxes of Kleenex were located under every pew just inside the aisle. As you walked in they really stood out.
4. A wall of photos in the baby room dated back to the 1930s. The faces of the people were circled with a number next to their face. No explanation about the circles and numbering system existed.
5. The fellowship hall smelled like the inside of a moldy hope chest.

6. A large, framed artist's rendering of what the building would look like after a major stewardship program dated 2001. The campaign was abandoned, but the picture remained in a prominent location.
7. An old-fashioned church attendance reporting sign hung by the "Welcome Center" boasting fifty-five members in attendance, thirty-three in Sunday School and an offering of $500.
8. The building was made of cinder blocks painted white with a brown roof and surrounded by a weedy lawn. The only color on the entire property was a tombstone-like plaque in a garden dated 1998.

When new ideas were introduced to make their environment inviting to others, they faced resistance from existing members. Somewhere—somehow—these things became sacred and changing them was as unthinkable as desecrating someone's grave.

The late William Perry, a well-known educational psychologist, used to say "Whenever someone comes to me for help, I listen very hard and ask myself 'what does this person want and what will they do to keep from getting it."[3] In other words, **if we want a deeper understanding of the prospect of change, we must pay closer attention to our own powerful inclinations not to change.**

How sad is it that this reality plays out repeatedly as the things we are used to become more important than the goal of reaching our original objectives? God called you for a worthy reason, and that reason is not included in any of the eight things listed here.

FLETCHER
"We're hoping you'll lead us on a journey of transformation without requiring any real changes."

Comic softens hard truth.[4] But, it doesn't completely take away the 'ouch,' does it?

The right thing to do is simple, although it is rarely easy. Whether you are a pastor, church leader, or volunteer, do not fear the wrath of existing members. Instead, fear the thought of people who never get the chance to experience the love of Christ. When you make the right changes for the right reasons, you'll sometimes experience loss for a short while. It is worth it.*

* But, don't bull ahead until you finish part three of the book: the responsibility of buy-in.

HOW DARE THOU?

Have you ever been around someone from a specialized industry who speaks fluently in technical jargon as you sit there with a big question mark in the thought bubble above your head? I don't know why groups default to these little lexicons of unique jargon only understood and appreciated by their members. It's hard to sift through a steady stream of information without interpretation.

- Do we have an SME who works on this?
- I'm taking a VFR Approach to MHTG.
- Look at your P2P traffic.*

Let's shift gears. What about you? Have you been swimming in the church subculture for a while? It's possible your conversation has been infected with "Christianese"—a language that feels normal to you, but leaves others confused.

You might need an intervention if you converse like this:

- Thanks! *"I'm just humbled God can use me as a blessing to others."*
- How is everything going with your new job? *"I'm just trying to let go and let God."*
- Why do you like your church? *"They just preach the gospel, you know?"*
- I'm worried about my family. *"Just pray a hedge of protection around them."*
- Thanks for inviting me today. *"The Lord placed it on my heart to witness."*

* For those of you who are going crazy and about to put this book down to look up what these cryptic acronyms mean…let me save you the trouble:

SME = Subject Matter Expert (corporate-speak).
VFR Approach to MHTG = Visual Flight Rules to Tegucigalpa-Toncontin International Airport (aviation-speak).
P2P = Peer to Peer (geek-speak).

- Why do you volunteer? *"I feel a burden for the lost."*
- Are you coming to Jim's party? *"I'm looking forward to the fellowship."*

I have good news. It is possible for you to talk like a normal person again. But, only if you're willing to give up clichés. You may think it makes you sound like a wise, sage Yoda. But, trust me: it doesn't. It just makes you look full of yourself.

Say it with me now: **"The first step is to admit I have a problem. I confess I might be speaking a language that creates an exclusive and intimidating environment. Sometimes, I use words just to feel a sense of belonging, identity and maybe even superiority over others."**

I'm proud of you!

Make it a normal practice to regularly evaluate your language in the context of guests. Set aside the insider speak and avoid using words that people have to look up. Recognizing that regular people are consumed with the pressures of life (i.e., pressure to keep up, loneliness, sadness, fear, skepticism, pride, guilt and anger), their filter is set to cope or comprehend based on their "everyday." So, you should just use "everyday" talk, too.

I walked through this exercise when I first joined the team at Granger to identify a few words we regularly used "inside our walls" that needed to change to help improve the way things translated "outside our walls."

Say this:	Instead of this:
Connection	Intimacy
Group	Small Group
Volunteer	Fellowship
Team	Committee
Community	Ministry
Guest	Target Audience, Unchurched and Visitor
Volunteer Expo	Ministry Fair
Next Steps	Go Deeper
Invite	Recruit
Opportunity	Need to Help
Experience	Attend
Explore	Commit
Growth	Maturity

This list isn't static; it needs occasional revision, as words take on new meanings in culture. But it is a helpful frame of reference to revisit to keep our voices in tune with "everyday" vocabulary.

Mark Twain said,

> **The difference between the right word and the almost right word is the difference between lightning and the lightning bug.**

What are a few small changes you can make to communicate more effectively, in a way that resonates with guests?

MARKETING MAD-LIBS

George Bernard Shaw said, "The problem with communication is the illusion that it has been accomplished." Why, then, do people use important words and complex sentence structures to sound more impressive?

Matt Linderman, co-author of *Rework* and *Getting Real*, has been a long-time champion of saying "goodbye to bloat." He shared an opening line from an email he received that was full of bloat:

> "[Redacted] creates the conditions for experimentation and quantitative understanding of the impact of novel management practices in large companies."
>
> The sentence is structured like this: "We create _____ for _____ and _____ of _____ of _____ in _____." It's tough to have anything make sense within that structure.[5]

Here's another example from the world of local government:[6]

> "The sustainability group has convened a task force to study the cause of energy inefficiency and to develop a plan to encourage local businesses to apply renewable energy and energy-efficient technologies which will go a long way toward encouraging community buy-in to potential behavioral changes."

Or, this example from a well-known place of happy:[7]

> "The mission of _________________ is to be one of the world's leading producers and providers of entertainment

and information. Using our portfolio of brands to differentiate our content, services and consumer products, we seek to develop the most creative, innovative and profitable entertainment experiences and related products in the world."

What the heck?

Would you have guessed that mumbo-jumbo is on Disney's corporate site? What about the verbiage you use on your "about us" page? What does your mission statement or vision look like? It doesn't sound like this, does it? If it does—priority one—change it!

Trying to say too much is a constant job hazard. I worked for a finance company where this type of writing was an operational value. I remember asking about it once, and an executive told me, "We're dealing with quants* here. They won't take us seriously if we don't sound as smart as them. This is what they're looking for."** And now, I work with pastors and ministry leaders who argue the same point.

It has taken me years to unlearn this phantom logic.

Why do we believe the more important or intelligent something is, the more deep and complex we need to make it to legitimize it? It's seems to be a constant pattern for humans. Way back in the day, the Pharisees constantly over-complicated things. They begged Jesus for the "higher level" answers, but he gave them less chaos, less noise EVERY TIME. "Love God. Love others." He made it simple.

You want to stand out from the crowd? Stop writing nonsense and clear the hurdles from the track.

* In the investment industry, people who perform quantitative analysis are called quants.

** No liberties were taken with this example for dramatic effect. It was a verbatim quote from a very smart man I used to work with. While he was very successful, I'm not convinced this was a very smart statement.

THEMING A CAPITAL CAMPAIGN

Every one of us has the tendency to turn inward unless we're reminded to turn outward. It's human nature to default to, "It's all about me." So, instead of fighting it, we just went with it and themed one of our capital campaigns "My Life."

BELONGING. CHANGING. SHARING.

At first, this might seem like a contradiction to the desired spiritual growth we're teaching about (i.e., "It's not about me"). But, see if this rationale doesn't help connect the dots:

1. **Until somebody owns it, he or she is not likely to go the extra mile.** Regardless of age, environment, or spiritual health, there's an immediate connection and sense of ownership when "it's all about me." You can get a lot of mileage out of it; it's my story, it's my decision, it's my chance to make a difference, it's my place, my space, my life. I own it.
2. **It's a multi-dimensional message.** Belonging. Changing. Sharing. The tagline projects movement and addresses all parts of the journey—personal, church, and community. It progressively moves from felt need to action.
3. **It's believable.** It's personal and doesn't sound like a national sales convention or fundraiser. It creates possibilities.
4. **It's simple.** Short and to the point, it's easy to remember and easy to use in creative storytelling.

Ah, there it is. The stories—in print, video, online and live from the platform. It's in those stories of changed lives where people get inspired and shift their thinking from self to others.

I heard Erwin McManus describe "first space" as the space where we engage with people who like me because they are like me, and the "second space" as the place you earn the right to be heard and interact with others. **If we don't create a first space in the church, people will never experience the church in the second-space moments of their world.**

MICKEY'S TEN COMMANDMENTS

In the book, *Be Our Guest*, Walt Disney's Vice Chairman Marty Sklar shared the list of design principles he created for how Disney delivers its service themes and standards. He said he created the list from what he learned from his principal mentors, Walt Disney and John Hench.

Think about your church as you read his list. Think about the individual ministries and departments. Think about your postcards, your website, your lobby, your social media content, your email blasts—every touchpoint a guest experiences. Ready?

1. **Know your audience.** Before creating a setting, obtain a firm understanding of who will be using it.
2. **Wear your guest's shoes.** That is, never forget the human factor. Evaluate your setting from the customer's perspective by experiencing it as a customer.
3. **Organize the flow of people and ideas.** Think of a setting as a story and tell that story in a sequenced, organized way. Build the same order and logic into the design of customer movement.
4. **Create a visual magnet.** It's a visual landmark used to orient and attract people.
5. **Communicate with visual literacy.** Language is not always composed of words. Use common languages of color, shape and form to communicate through a setting.
6. **Avoid overload—create turn-ons.** Do not bombard customers with data. Let them choose the information they want when they want it.
7. **Tell one story at a time.** Mixing multiple stories in a single setting is confusing. Create one setting for each big idea.

8. **Avoid contradictions; maintain identity.** Every detail and every setting should support and further your organizational identity and mission.
9. **For every ounce of treatment, provide a ton of treat.** Give your customers the highest value by building an interactive setting that gives them the opportunity to exercise all of their senses.
10. **Keep it up.** Never get complacent, and always maintain your setting.[8]

And, there you have it. The keys to the Magic Kingdom. Ten ways Walt Disney harnessed the talents and hearts of his "cast members" with one vision to create unparalleled entertainment experiences. If it works for a mouse, why aren't more churches following these commandments?

THINK IT OVER
ADOPTING THE BEST PRACTICE: REMOVE BARRIERS TO ENTRY

- ☐ What are a few small changes we can make to our organizational language to communicate more effectively in a way that resonates with more people? Are we consistent with the language we use in all of our media (e.g., messages, bulletins, newsletters, signage, events, social media posts, etc.)?

- ☐ Am I focusing on my content over communication? What information is not being presented for interpretation?

- ☐ How can I uncover the barriers to entry that are invisible to me in our environment? Once identified, am I prepared to make a change?

- ☐ Where am I fearful to change because of the resistance I'll experience from the regulars or staffers stuck in a rut? How can I avoid a classic case of misplaced priorities?

- ☐ At the end of the day, am I taking down roadblocks between our guests and God? Am I the roadblock? What do I need to unlearn?

- ☐ What do my guests see, hear, smell and feel in our environment? Does it attract or repel?

chapter 8
REDUCE THE NOISE

> **Noise and activity are the refuges of the bereaved and guilty.**
> Tris Prior, *Insurgent*

People are stressed out, fed up, overcommitted (in time and money), and overstimulated. Under any kind of stress (i.e., traffic, deadline, crying kids, finances), the loudest signals your brain sends out are about what's happening right at this moment and how to survive it. Anything that's not critical to this moment is physiologically drowned out. It's how God designed the human brain to prioritize. People need inspiration first, so the information will sink in. Many times that inspiration will come from how you make them feel, not by what you have to say. People argue, "It doesn't matter how we make people feel; our job isn't to make them feel good. Our job is to tell the truth in love." Does it matter how people feel? If your goal is effective communication, then yes, it matters immensely. A person needs to be reachable before they're teachable.

YOU GOT FAMILIES IN YOUR CHURCH?

If you have families in your church, I wonder if you know what they're dealing with outside the church walls.

I'll use my friend Michelle as just one example. She has two girls in school—one in third grade and one in fourth grade. Just five days into the school year, the girls had brought home over 100 pieces of paper. One hundred pieces of paper in five days. For two children. Just two.

From Michelle Wegner's blog.[1]

There is something terribly wrong here. How many weeks of school are there? After one month, her two girls had brought home over 200 pieces of paper between them. Michelle asked, "Can you help me figure out what is important and what I should keep? I went to college, and I can't figure it out."

Before my kids reached high school, it used to take me twenty minutes to sort through the handouts, flyers and forms they brought home with them every day. (I don't know if the school stopped sending them home, or if the kids just stopped bringing them home.) That may not sound like a lot. But, with a young family and two working parents, our time was stretched and we were tired. There wasn't a big emotional margin to solve the daily paper puzzle from the kids' school. It was frustrating trying to figure out what to keep and what to throw away, what to pay attention to and what to ignore, and what was due when; everything was treated the same. How could I figure out what was important when they communicated that *everything* was important? It stressed me out, and it felt like someone else was taking control of my life and my kitchen counter by overwhelming me with clutter.

You might be asking yourself, "Why is she telling me this?" You might catch yourself thinking, "Look, missy, your issue is not my issue."

Well, maybe. And, maybe not. Before you drop another postcard to your entire database or send that mass email,* ask yourself,

> **Will this information I intend to be helpful just add to the clutter?**

If you can't be sure, go farther.

> **Is there any way to simplify what my audience sees to make their experience with the church easier and more rewarding?**

Because, Lord knows, the public school officials aren't asking themselves these questions. It's the least we can do as the Church. Our job isn't to add stress—we want to reduce it.

Don't you think?

* As I type this chapter, Barracuda network has blocked more than 256,847,725 spam emails so far today (it's barely noon and that's the stats for just one saecurity network). Can you tell me why your email is different?

IS THE CHURCH BULLETIN DEAD?

I remember the first time I heard about a church killing its bulletin. My friend Tim worked at Park Community Church and, at the time, their decision to kill the weekly bulletin was a bold move. But, they didn't enter into the decision flippantly. The alternative solution they came up with—the monthly bulletin—was a strategic win in their setting.

Here's why it makes sense for us.

1. **We are a young church.** Not young in the sense of how long we've been around (twenty years), but in the sense of our average age. It's twenty-nine.
2. **We are a "mobile" church.** Our people work in the Loop, live by their smart phones, are single, on Facebook, texting and Twitter.
3. **Our content was stagnant.** On any given week we were just shuffling around the same information in our programs, maybe adding only one or two new things.
4. **Uh, hello.** Every week we threw away scores of bulletins people left behind. It was crazy.

The pros of our choice.

1. **Budget savings.** We cut our monthly printing budget by 75 percent.
2. **Environmental savings.** It's a "green" choice the people in our church rally behind.
3. **Smart resourcing.** It forced our organization to plan out events in advance instead of waiting to the last minute. This was our old mode of operation.

4. **Focus.** We went from thoughtlessly publishing everything, to choosing only to publish the things that would further the mission and vision of our church. And, what we do decide to communicate has to be done in a few sentences, not an entire paragraph.[2]

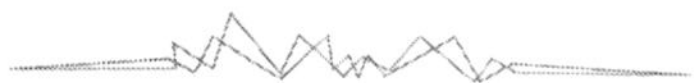

Even if it makes sense for you to let your weekly bulletin live, Tim makes some interesting points about Park's decision we should all at least consider. The first question, incidentally, isn't whether or not we keep our bulletin, but how are our people using (or not using) it? Remember, it's important to determine the purpose of your bulletin before you evaluate what changes need to be made.

- Is it a wayfinding tool for new guests, or a newsletter that highlights family news for the folks who are already part of your church?
- Do you want people to sit down with a cup of coffee and read it like a magazine, or be able to easily scan it for the most important, highest-value next steps for the season?
- Do you want people to use it during the service, or find enough lasting value in it that they feel compelled to take it home and share it with someone or hang it on their refrigerator?

Once you determine the primary purpose and audience for your bulletin (guide, program, etc.), then you'll be able to determine what changes need to be made: what's included, how it's organized and how often it's updated. The bulletin isn't dead, but the world around it has changed. Consequently, the emphasis and purpose of the bulletin should change too.

WHO MAKES THE CALL?

"Who decides how, what and where things gets promoted?" This question is probably the one I hear the most. And, I never answer it. Because it's the wrong question. You can't build an effective communication strategy by asking someone to play referee.

Instead of, "Who decides it?" ask, "What drives it?" By answering that question, you can start to work toward not only making it easy to get the word out, but more importantly, easy to find once it's out there.

If you want to maximize promotional impact, start by drafting two documents:

1. **Communication values.** How you communicate (and how you don't).
2. **Communication priorities.** What has the highest emphasis and where it gets promoted.*

If I were you, I'd be asking, "What are two documents going to do for me? I'm not trying to create more tasks on my to-do list. Just answer the question!" Stay with me. I promise these tools will actually reduce workload.

As you face growing demands and changes in an organization, "on the fly" doesn't fly. You're left in a constant state of frenzy, having to figure it out repeatedly with each individual request. But, when you decide in advance how and what you communicate as an organization, you can help reduce noise for both internal and external audiences.

* You can find a sample of both documents in "the back of the book."

Donald Sull is management guru and former professor at Harvard and the London Business School. Kathleen M. Eisenhardt is a professor of strategy at Stanford's school. They got together and wrote a book called *Simple Rules*. It's one of my favorites.

In it, they state, "Simple Rules are clear guidelines for well-defined activities or situations. Their purpose? **To help you make good choices when things start to get convoluted.** Simple Rules reduce the factors you have to consider in a situation by highlighting the crucial, thus preventing you from ruminating over trivial details."

As you're creating the framework for your own communication values and priorities, keep these guidelines in mind:

- **Prioritize based on scope.** While everything may be important, not everything is EQUALLY important and appropriate for "all church" consumption. When you treat everything the same, it gets noisy. Depending on the amount of people it affects, items could fall into one of the following categories:

Heavy	Medium	Light
The 20 percent of what's happening that affects 80 percent of the audience—this week in the main auditorium, next steps out of the weekend and all-church events.	Mid-sized events that affect a larger group, but not 80 percent of the audience—student ministry, financial class during a marriage series and men/women retreats.	Niche news, team meetings or small volume events.

- **Invest minimal resources into print materials.** Don't attempt to go for the "sell" with ministry or event brochures or long-winded online content. Instead, invest that energy into personal invites and the event experience. Why? Print materials have a limited shelf life (especially with the pace of ministry and volunteers), create a lot of production activity and cost with little return and add to the clutter. Long-winded online content gets skipped or deleted. Skip the elaborate design and marketing copy to focus on the basic questions people have: who, what, where and when.
- **Identify one place to keep all information up-to-date.** Your website is an easy-access hub to update all news in one place for everyone. It doesn't matter what your role is (e.g., staff, volunteer or attendee) or what question you have—everybody will know the one place to go for the answer. In other words, you don't need to answer to everything all at once, but you do need to know where to go when you need the answer. You don't have to create special materials for the info counter; they can use the website too. If a guest needs a handout, they can print it right on the spot. Resist the temptation to duplicate all information in all channels (e.g., e-newsletter, bulletin, etc.). It might help to think of spreading out your content like a progressive dinner, not potluck. But, you should use all channels (appetizers) to drive people online (or to the guest services desk) for the rest of the details. Stick with that one hub and drive everyone back to it for the main course.

Make use of the Pareto Principle: what's your 80/20? With a few simple rules in place for the routine activity (80 percent of the time), you leave more room for options and creativity when the unexpected and out-of-the-ordinary happens (20 percent of the time).

GET REAL

In *Getting Real,* the best-selling book from 37signals (makers of Basecamp), the authors set a new bar for corporate self-control. The book is a few years old, but has fast become a modern classic. It's a quick scan packed full of stories about keeping it simple to achieve successful projects in a complicated industry. It starts with their *modus operandi:*

> "We believe software is too complex. Too many features, too many buttons, too much to learn. Our products do less than the competition—intentionally. We build products that work smarter, feel better, allow you to do things your way and are easier to use."[3]

That is beautiful. Somebody hand me a tissue. No, I'm serious. Their book is not a rant about technology and project management. It has broad principles that apply to all of mankind.* If you're a designer, teacher, marketer, developer, executive or entrepreneur, you can find contrarian value and empowerment in this book.

Look at the transferable principles I found in their introduction alone!

What Is Getting Real?

- Getting Real is about skipping all the stuff that represents real and actually building the real thing.

* Am I being too dramatic? I think not.

- Getting Real is less. Less mass, less software, less features, less paperwork, less of everything that's not essential (and most of what you think is essential actually isn't).
- Getting Real is staying small and being agile.
- Getting Real starts with what the customer actually experiences and builds backwards from there. This lets you get it right before you get it wrong.
- Getting Real delivers just what customers need and eliminates anything they don't.

More than once, I've used these bullets as talking points to brainstorm our print project list and our website and app navigation. Just because you can do something, doesn't mean you should.

Good idea.[4] Noble intentions. Ironic execution. We've all done it.

What could it look like to get real in your environment?

- **Admit it might be time for a little nip/tuck.** Identify how bloated your website, e-newsletters or print materials have become. After adding so many pages and graphics and paragraphs over the years, people may have stopped reading them. If it's not helping, it might be time for some liposuction.
- **Design for action.** Change your online navigation from fat menus with lots of pages to browse and read like a library of articles to action-oriented links. In other words, instead of trying to figure out what needs to be said (i.e., a menu option for every ministry department), figure out what tasks people are trying to get done (i.e., what volunteer job openings are available, where do I get help when I need it, how do I register for the next event, etc.).
- **Show some personality.** Take the suit off your content and dress it in khakis or jeans (whatever fits your corporate personality). Give people access to real-time human content and conversations on a few staff blogs, links to your leader's Twitter or Instagram stream or church Facebook feed. The imperfect, human interaction is more inviting and share-worthy than sterilized corporate content.
- **Give search prime real estate.** How can you give people access to stuff they want, instead of creating more pages for the stuff you think they need? Make sure your site has a search feature and make sure it's right up front. You may not know what everyone wants, when, but you can make it easy to get to with search.

It's worth setting aside the time to ask yourself how to get real instead of trying so hard to appear real.

PLEASE DON'T MAKE ME WORK SO HARD

We've all been there, in the middle of the hustle—busting tail to cross another thing off the growing to-do list, jumping the next hurdle, returning phone calls, racing the clock and trying to tame the monster that is our inbox. Then, it happens: that long-winded email arrives, exhausting you the minute you open it. Immediately, you're bombarded with tiny fonts, run-on sentences and single-spaced lines, or you're faced with volumes of seemingly senseless content with no consideration for the task list or brain space you're already trying to manage.

Many times, there actually may be an important action item or value-add buried in there. But, you're going to have to go on a search and rescue mission to find it. You're forced to take the time to sort through the overgrown mass because the author didn't take the time to do it for you. It can be frustrating when someone carelessly dumps more work on top of your already towering plate load.*

I don't have the time to do someone's work for them. Who does? Well, OK, just this one time. Let's use this email from a randomly-selected insurance company as a case study.

Before:

Dear UnumProvident Customer:
A lot has changed over the last several years, and in many respects we are a new company today—one that is better positioned to capitalize on the tremendous opportunities that lie ahead. One of our goals for 2007, in addition to continuing to build on the momentum we've established, is to enhance the marketing of our products and services.

* There's only one circumstance where I want my plate load to tower as high as possible. That's when I'm at my favorite "build your own stir fry" bar. One plate, one price. In that case, and that case only, pile it on, baby!

> With this in mind, we have been undertaking a complete brand review with the intention of developing a new brand identity that better leverages our unique strengths in the marketplace.
>
> As a first step in what will be some exciting changes to our brand, I'm pleased to announce today that we are changing our name to Unum. The name is intended to simplify the brand, without losing sight of the valuable brand equity we've built in the marketplace over many years. In addition to having strong awareness among customers and brokers, the name Unum also provides a better fit as we focus more of our efforts on being a leader in benefits sold to and through the workplace. In many respects, this action is simply formalizing what many of you have already been doing—abbreviating our name to Unum.
>
> The names attached to the legal insurance entities we use to market our products, such as Unum Life Insurance Company of America, Provident Life & Accident Insurance Company, The Paul Revere Life Insurance Company, and Colonial Life & Accident Insurance Company, will remain the same. We plan to share more with you on our branding initiatives, including a new corporate logo, later this spring. In the meantime, the correspondence you receive from us many still carry the UnumProvident name, as we phase in our new name.
>
> Thank you for your continued support of our company. We value the opportunity to serve your employee benefits needs, and we look forward to a continued partnership between your organization and the new Unum.
>
> Sincerely,
> Tom Watjen
> President and CEO

Unum is a good company with plenty of completely satisfied customers. But, this email leaves you asking, "Huh? Why did you send this to me, and what am I supposed to do about it?"

Do you have any idea what they're saying and why we should care? Me either, but I can guess. And, here's how I would rewrite the letter for them. Free of charge.

After:

Dear UnumProvident Customer:
We wanted you to know, we're changing our name to Unum. It's simple—which is probably why many of you are already abbreviating it anyway. We're just following your lead. The transition will take just a little while to phase into, so you might receive some correspondence from us that still carries the old UnumProvident name. Thank you for your business. We value the opportunity to serve your employee benefits needs.

I'm not picking on Tom (or his staff). We've all been known to talk too much about ourselves and forget to filter our message through the eyes of our audience. How about that last family Christmas letter you sent out?

Every year I receive family Christmas letters from people I know, love and who add value to my life. But, their Christmas letters sure don't. I don't even read them. They're too much work! I even received a corporate Christmas letter this year from a company I trust and choose to do business with. I would recommend them to friends. But, I did not read their letter. It went straight to the recycle bin.

This image is a re-creation of an actual Christmas letter I received this year:

Dear Mark & Kam,

Thank you for your business. Merry Christmas.

Aliquam Suspendisse

The format and word count are identical to the original. But, the content and author have been changed to protect the guilty.

In contrast, here is a copy of a Christmas letter that took a different approach and delivered the holiday cheer, big time.* Not only did I read it immediately, I read it multiple times and shared it with anyone who visited. It wasn't a self-indulgent, run-on dissertation. It was personal. It was handmade and imperfect. It was delightful:

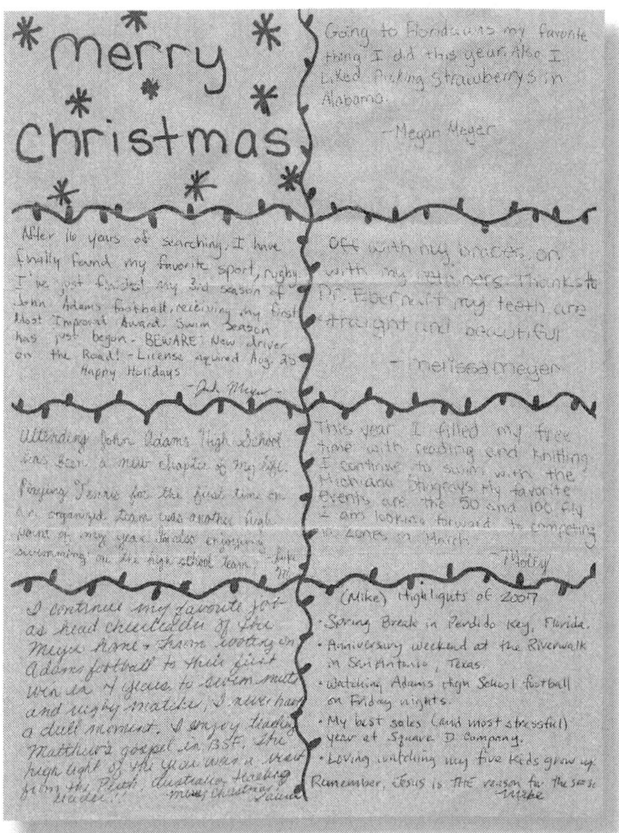

Merry Christmas

Going to Honduras was my favorite thing I did this year. Also I liked picking strawberrys in Alabama.
—Megan Meyer

After 16 years of searching, I have finally found my favorite sport, rugby. I've just finished my 3rd season of John Adams football, receiving my first Most Improved Award. Swim season has just begun. BEWARE New driver on the Road! —License aquired Aug. 25
Happy Holidays
—Josh Meyer—

Off with my braces on with my retainers. Thanks to Dr. Ebernardt my teeth are straight and beautiful
—Melissa Meyer

Attending John Adams High School has been a new chapter of my life. Playing Tennis for the first time on an organized team was another high point of my year besides enjoying swimming on the high school team.
—[illegible]

This year I filled my free time with reading and knitting. I continue to swim with the Michiana Stingrays. My favorite events are the 50 and 100 fly. I am looking forward to competing in zones in March.
—Molly

I continue my favorite job as head cheerleader of the Meyer home + team rooting on Adams football to their first win in 4 years, to seven meets and rugby matches, I never had a dull moment. I enjoy teaching Matthew's gospel in BSF. The high light of the year was a visit from the Perth, Australia teaching leader!!
Merry Christmas!
[illegible]

(Mike) Highlights of 2007
- Spring Break in Perdido Key, Florida.
- Anniversary weekend at the Riverwalk in San Antonio, Texas.
- Watching Adams High School football on Friday nights.
- My best sales (and most stressful) year at Square D Company.
- Loving watching my five kids grow up.

Remember, Jesus is THE reason for the season
—Mike

My sister-in-law let each family member do their own talking and gave them one box to do it in. One page. One-sided. One family. Top seven highlights.**

Churches can be the worst about playing the "too much" card. But, it's not too late to break the cycle. Say less. Value people's time.

* It's true. Big things do come in small packages.

** (This is a little sneak-peek illustration of the "Freedom within a Framework" principle we'll get to in Chapter 13.)

FREQUENCY CAN ADD TO THE CLUTTER

A common pillar of social media advice is that post frequency is the secret to success. People say the more you publish, the higher your readership will be. I've been successfully using and happily consuming social media for over a decade and have never agreed with this advice. Not every social media account needs to deliver a daily dose of wisdom or multiple updates a day.

I can't find many people who agree with me at the onset of my contrarian declaration; they're amped up and heavily armed with research that argues for the standard advice. But, if you dig a little deeper into that research, you'll find there's always more to the story. By the time we finish this story, you just might be nodding your head in agreement as a post frequency contrarian, too.

Social media is an enduring reality of online communication. I agree that everyone needs to find a way to engage, but be wary of one-size-fits-all advice. Big social media numbers don't mean big activity.

- Just because you have followers, doesn't mean you have an audience.
- Just because you have likes, doesn't mean people are doing anything about it.
- Just because you have a lot of site traffic, doesn't mean anyone is engaging.

With billions of people hanging out on social media, post frequency doesn't guarantee the bullseye—you still have to aim.

Did you know there are over sixty virtual communities that have over 1 million active users?[5] Not only is it difficult for people to cut through the clutter with hyper-frequent posts; the pressure to post frequently can lead you compromise content quality. But, enough about what's wrong. Let's talk about what to do about it.

Neil Patel, Chief Evangelist of KISSmetrics, recommends you answer four questions to slice through the confusion:[6]

1. **Where is my audience?** The primary question to ask about social media is where your audience is actually spending time. What social media outlets are they on?
2. **Where is my audience active?** A social media user needs to be using the site for them to be of use to you. For example, in early 2015, Facebook reported around 170 million fake users,[7] and possibly many more that they aren't quite aware of yet.
3. **Where is my audience searching?** People use social media for searching, not just socializing.
4. **What niche social media sites are right for me?** Some businesses are missing out on a deluge of warm leads, because they are absent from niche social media sites.*

Make sure you can identify what you want to happen before you hit "publish." If you can answer these four questions, it will be easier to figure out what networks to join, your optimal messaging and, yes, your post frequency.

If you've ever felt the pressure to post daily (or multiple times a day), I'm here to tell you to breathe easy. As an individual, I give you permission to post when you're inspired, and don't when you're not. As an organization, post only when you have something worthy to add to your audience.

* With the massive platforms like Facebook, Twitter and Instagram, it's easy to get lost in the shuffle. Like it sounds, niche social media sites are popping up to serve specialized community subsets. Think CaringBridge, CafeMom and Goodreads.

My kids' youth group has a Facebook account that may average one post a week, at most, during the majority of the year. But, a few times a year (during major events and key seasons) it's the go-to, active source for travel logistics, registration information, emergency alerts, fan photos, fun facts, behind the scenes info and FAQs. The team has built a dependable, one-stop hub for parents and students alike—with a very inconsistent post frequency—because they know who they're posting for.

I don't need news from them daily, but when I have a question about back to school or the travel logistics for my student's mission trip, I'm counting on more frequent posts. And, when they're away at camp? I'm living on that page, constantly hitting refresh for new photos and video posts, to catch just a slice of the experience.

Alternatively, I stopped following my own church's Instagram account for a season because the posts were too frequent. My feed was clogged with volumes of quality photos that, ironically, didn't add value or hold my interest. Too much traffic from one account can overshadow feed real-estate like a ball hog. It's worth it if I'm getting something out of it (e.g., inspiration, inside scoop, entertainment, etc.), but if it's neutral, I'm going to unfollow.

I'm not a hater. I'm not making a relationship status statement. I'm just trying to curate my social media feed traffic. And, so is your audience.

The point? We all have trusted accounts we follow faithfully and engage with sporadically. Whether it's business or pleasure, social or marketing, don't let frequency become your goal. Instead, aim for the most helpful, rewarding content you can provide your specific audience, and the frequency will follow.

THINK IT OVER
ADOPTING THE BEST PRACTICE: REDUCE THE NOISE

- ☐ Do I look for ways to alleviate the barrage of information my audience receives from me? Do I proactively look for ways to make it easier to sort and digest, or do I just throw it all up at once, leaving my audience to pick up the pieces?

- ☐ It has been said that the brain can only absorb what the seat can endure. Am I still talking when my audience's seat is beat?

- ☐ If I go back and look at what we're putting out there for people to read with new eyes, how much can I cut to value people's time?

- ☐ What corporate communication are we sending that's babble? What opportunities do we have to get real instead of trying so hard to appear real?

- ☐ What content do we include because "it doesn't hurt to have it in there" that is out-of-date, redundant, self-serving or irrelevant? Can I answer the question, "How does this content help me get to my desired outcome?" as my new content filter?

chapter 9
TELL ONE STORY AT A TIME

> **Think long. Write short.**
> George Lois

One thing is more important than all the rest in what you're doing. Do you know what it is? Can you communicate it in one sentence? Theologian Joseph Priestley says, "The more elaborate our means of communication, the less we communicate."[1] If you don't know what that one sentence is, how do you expect other people to figure it out? Each communication piece is a valuable tool with the opportunity to unify all communications or dilute them. How many stories are you telling? Sometimes the secret to finding the right thing to say is in knowing what *not* to say.

LIVING OUT YOUR STORY ONLINE

Everything you do is an extension of your story. Does your communication strategy consider that story at every touchpoint? For example, have you thought about how your story plays out on your website?

A lot of churches are giving their online spaces more attention—bringing their websites up-to-date with new graphics and features. This is a good thing. They're not stuck. But, more often than not, these makeovers and technology upgrades aren't getting them, or their audience, to a better place. Just a different place. They miss out on the power their website has to offer by skipping the foundational question at the start: who are we, and how does that play out online?

I mentioned before that I was first hired at Granger Community Church to lead and launch a new website. It didn't take me long to see that everyone had a different definition of the win—their own wish list, audience flavor and ministry needs. We had to take the conversation higher, to a place where everyone found value; a common ground (and common win) as a church family to build the project scope around.

Here's how we did it in 2002:

> In this era of information overload—and life at light-speed—we strive to provide escape hatches. And, our website is one of them. We've designed it to answer the two most important questions:
>
> 1. Is this a fit for me?
> 2. If so, what is my next step?

In 2011, our site was once again due for an overhaul. And, once again, we revisited our story before we started scoping out the website punch list. We used our vision and brand personality* as a filter. Here's what the starting point of our guiding principles looked like:

WHY

We will distribute high-quality content wherever and whenever it is possible. At any time we will be able to teach, train and inspire thousands of people as they gather from their home, church, business, or wherever they are located.

BY

- **Accessibility.** Any time. Anywhere. Bring the mission within reach for more people. Make it searchable. Scanable. Simple. Equip the church 7 days a week with access regardless of the timeline "we" are on. It's a kinder, gentler website. Not so self-centered.
- **Advocacy.** Not by creating more, but by making it easier to find, contribute to and share what already exists (video, articles, events and photos). Centralize the win, but decentralize the ownership. We will put people first by understanding context and minimizing distractions—starting with the unconvinced guy.
- **Analytics.** Watch and report on our activity to find trend indicators, watch organizational health checks and reveal data treasure finds to help us make better decisions within limitations. Our website is a vehicle, not a destination. We'll watch what's working and what's not. There will be no dead ends.

HOW

The same brand personality profile* that shaped our facility reconstruction will shape this online reconstruction. The essence of what people experience online is an expression of who we are:

- Creative
- Encouraging
- Unpredictable
- Relatable
- Empowering

* There's a sample for you in the back of the book.

These working documents helped us focus our work, words and priorities and prevented us from a chaotic, reactive, unfocused implementation. The talking points were used not only as quality control filters as we made content, technology and design decisions, but also in how we talked about them. It's amazing how one simple, unsophisticated outline can serve as the glue that holds the whole story together.

THE IMPORTANCE OF FLOW

One definition of flow is "to move or run smoothly with unbroken continuity." In other words, people shouldn't notice the process. If they do, it's broken.

I was staying in a hotel earlier this year. When the "0" on my room phone didn't call the operator (incidentally, the universal number to call an operator), I spent ten minutes trying to find the front desk button.

Flow? No go.

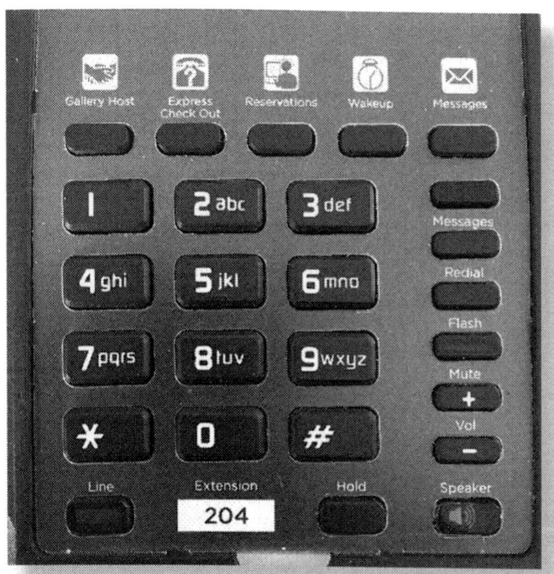

Spoiler: it's "Gallery Host."

What roadblocks get in the way of what people are trying to do in your church? There are plenty of areas to evaluate flow, and here are some places to start:

- **Eliminate the extra steps**. Don't make people "call for more information." Anticipate the basic questions they will ask, and give them a direct channel to show up, register or RSVP. If you're using this as your "connection point," I recommend you revisit that strategy. I love it when my doctor calls to remind me of an upcoming appointment. But, I hate it when they leave multiple messages asking me to call to confirm. Instead of "call [so & so] for more information," how about just providing the information people need up front? The basic who, what, when, where and how works almost every time. If I want to talk to someone, I can. But, don't make me.

- **Eliminate confusing treasure hunts.** Think of how people experience and navigate in a department store. The inventory is constantly changing, but the departments are constant. I know what direction to head, no matter what I'm looking for, and there are multiple ways to get there. Think about how you're asking people to navigate your site. Figure out the big categories that apply to everyone (e.g., events, volunteer or group) or just make your search feature front and center. By doing this, you'll have more time to focus on creating experiences and relationships on your teams and events, not by creating more content. And, the best part is people won't get lost on your site.

- **Eliminate assumptions.** Don't assume your audience will train themselves. They won't. Don't assume people wake up in the morning and check the church website or Facebook page. They don't. Don't assume people will tell you when a process or link is broken. They probably won't. Don't assume people outside your church won't read the stuff you're posting for the people inside your church. They do, whether you're talking to them or not. Don't assume people want or have the time to read the unabridged version of everything you think is important. They don't read; they skim and scan, looking for something (a keyword or header) that captures their attention or matches why they've come to you in the first place.

- **Eliminate extra work for others.** Instead of organizing your staff directory by department and name, how about arranging it alphabetically by frequently asked questions or by subject? Make it easy to find the right person by topic versus title. Instead of organizing your message archive by series name, how about making it searchable by keyword, emotion or topic? Think about how people search by need, not how you program your weekend calendar.

- **Eliminate the hold time.** Whenever I call my doctor's office, I'm never on hold for less than five minutes. Sometimes the wait is as long as fifteen minutes. That's fine. It is what it is. I'll put the call on speaker and keep working while I wait my turn. But, what bugs me is the story they tell when I'm on hold. In thirty second intervals, a voice breaks into the hold music to say, "Your call is very important to us. Please hold while we assist other callers." No matter how many times they tell me my call is important, the long and dated hold message says something different. Alternatively, I called Southwest the other day to make some travel changes. At the onset of the call, they told me my hold time could be as long as ten minutes. Then, they gave me a choice whether to stay on hold or leave my number for a call back when my place in line came up. It was a beautiful thing. You may not have a telephone hold time, but where else are you asking people to wait in line unnecessarily? Is there any way to streamline the traffic flow, children's check-in or event registration process?

The benefit of paying close attention to flow is a great experience. When everything flows naturally, your guests have a lasting impression of a place where the actions match the words, and the result is a trustworthy environment across departments and media.

When you break flow, you risk surprising people with conflicting personalities in the same experience. That's frustrating to people, and it's not the story you want them to leave with and tell their friends.

YOU CAN'T SAY EVERYTHING AT ONCE

How many verbal announcements are appropriate from the platform? Research shows that after two announcements, people generally stop listening. But, even when we know the answer, churches still struggle when service time comes around. We believe there are so many important things that "have to be said" during the service, we just can't control ourselves. We think if we don't say it, people won't hear it. Well, they're not hearing it anyway.

Allow me to share a story that comes at it from a different angle. No matter how many times I was told, nobody could convince me it was worth the extra time to cut the plastic ring from the milk jug before I threw it away. I wasn't convinced it would make a difference for "the benefit of the environment." The constant reminders were annoying, and I tuned out every time. That is, until my kids showed me the picture of a poor deformed turtle. You know the one I'm talking about—the turtle that swam through a milk jug ring?

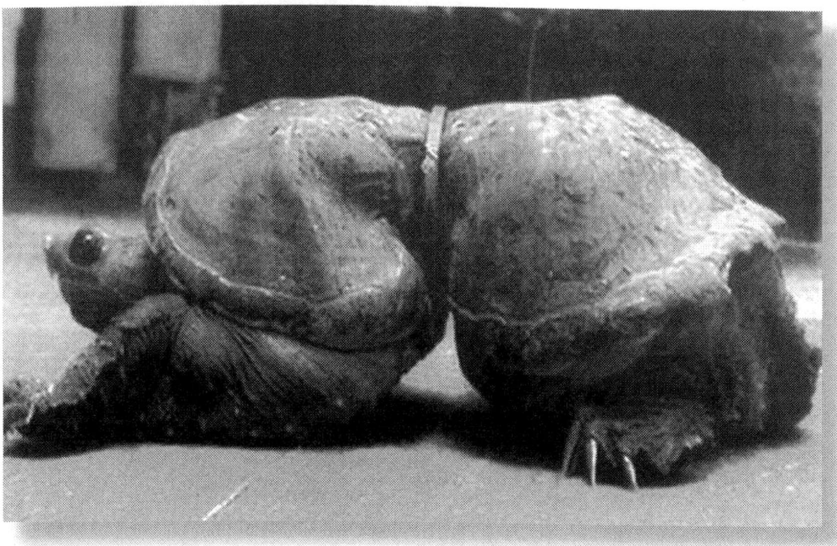

Poor little turtle.[2]

And, that's all it took. I will not be responsible for disfiguring a poor, little, defenseless turtle who was swimming along, minding his own business when—in an instant—his life's potential was cut short. Now I never throw away those little plastic rings without cutting them in half first.

Sometimes it takes just the right image for us to "get it." Well, we can thank my mom for emailing me this next photo. When I saw it, I immediately thought of what happens when we try to say everything at once.

Force feeding. It doesn't end well.

May this image be forever burned in your head as the little turtle image is burned in mine. Call it to mind to remind yourself to tell one story at a time. When you mix multiple stories in a single setting (e.g., meeting, service, website, brochure, letter), it blocks the message. Create one setting for each big idea.*

* If you must tell more than one story at a time, may I suggest you carpool? Try to tie multiple messages together into one cohesive thought. Group them. Theme them. One vehicle, many passengers. Make sense?

LESSONS FROM LUCKY

Here's a little blast from my past I'm going to share with you. I pulled it off my blog archives (the closest thing I've had to a journal since 2005):

- Today, January 12, 2006, I was almost killed by a vicious animal. I have the giant paw prints and witnesses to prove it.
- I was able to run for my flippin' life and make it into the house in time. Miracles do still happen.
- In the face of death, somehow I didn't pee my pants. This is truly amazing.
- I met my new neighbor for the first time when I called the police on her dog. Awkward.
- She tells me "Lucky" just needs to get to know me and that I need to come over to meet him. Uh, excuse me, are you high?
- The president of the homeowner's association stopped by to welcome me to the neighborhood. And, to find out why I had the street lined with emergency vehicles.
- I didn't feel very lucky when "Lucky," the 110-pound Rottweiler, was running directly at me, full speed, eyes locked, teeth bared, drool flowing, growl gurgling.

Days later, when I was over the trauma, I started reflecting on the "disconnect" Lucky created for the story his owner was telling me. She went on and on and on about how "Lucky isn't usually like this." Her mouth was moving, but the picture of the maniacal, ferocious killer in my head that I had experienced just moments before was speaking louder.

She continued, "He's so gentle and protective over the kids. He's usually so sweet. This is highly unusual."

This is what I hear: "Blah. Blah. Blah. Blah. Blah." Nothing she can do or say will erase the story I have in my mind.

"I'll have you over to share a bottle of wine." Nope. Your dog is still psychotic and dangerous, and I'm afraid to let my kids go in the backyard until he is gone or put on Prozac. Believe what you want, dog owner blinded by love. My reality is defined by my experience with Lucky, and it doesn't match yours.

The same is true in our environments. People leave with the "actual" experience, not our intended one, and that's what they talk about.

Rust-Oleum stops rust? How ironic.[3]

If we make one person feel unwelcome, forget to reply to an email, mess up registration because of disorganization—that's all they remember.

Sweat the details. Stay "on" at all times, and go out of your way to make positive first impressions—in your communications, your personal interactions and your organization. **Think about the individual guest over the institution at all times.** It's their perspective that matters first. It's hard to recover from a negative impression because, many times, people are gone before you even know you've messed up.

Things are going to happen. What's your plan when they do? If you find out about it, own it. It's a great opportunity to turn that negative into a positive. Apologize. Undo the perceived injustice. Don't make excuses for Lucky.

COHERENCE BEATS CONSISTENCY—ALL DAY, EVERY DAY

Coming from the marketplace with a background in technology, I was a zealot for consistency. I used to walk around wearing the badge of logo compliance officer with honor. Then, I invited my friend, Rick, to join my team as a volunteer advisor. Rick just happens to be a not-for-profit marketing guru, consultant and author of *Coherence.* I thought I had asked him to join the team to help us brainstorm creative campaign ideas, but he gave me more than I bargained for and challenged me about our brand coherence.

Up to that point, my corporate marketing experience weighed too heavy on ad campaigns and the graphics standards manual, and not heavy enough on brand wholeness. Brand integrity wasn't even on my radar. (And, just because you're in "church" work, don't assume you've nailed the whole integrity thing, either. People, we're the worst.)

You can read Rick's book yourself; it was a game changer for me. But, until you do, I'll share a few of the questions Rick asked us, along with the answers we discovered as a result of this honest audit.

Rick's starter coherence questions:

- What incoherence exists in our environment that kills connection?
- Where is our communication selling us short?
- Where are the contradictions in our story?

The answers we discovered as a result:

- Sometimes we communicate as if all of our needs are going to be met at church. "If I just show up to (something happening every day of the week), I will be in a better place."
- Time spent at "church events" is not the same thing as faith. "Church" is an expression of my faith. If I did everything we advertise, I wouldn't be a whole person. I would be very fragmented.
- Just because "church business" is our life, we can't assume it should be everyone else's life. Even staff members feel guilty when they don't do everything that's advertised. Sometimes we work so hard to provide next steps, it comes across like we're telling people what to do instead of encouraging them on their journey of faith (inside and outside of our walls).
- Church doesn't satisfy all needs, and it wasn't designed to. But, our communication fills in so many blanks that it appears as if it was. Our communication should dial back the volume of prescribed answers. Church INFLUENCES everything but doesn't ANSWER everything.
- People are looking for meaning, purpose, encouragement, discovering new ways to look at things, a challenge. When all we give them is an ad for the next service, they leave disappointed.

An honest inventory of how our communication was being perceived revealed some hard truths and some enlightening opportunities. And, none of them had to do with the quality of our video, logo measurements or pantone colors.

THREE EASY WAYS TO LOSE YOUR IDENTITY

Your identity is your brand. Not your logo. Not your design. Not your programs. However, you live out your identity through your logo, your design, your programs, etc. A common thread needs to string through everything you do to avoid committing brand suicide. One thread.

Jeremy Scheller is the "head honcho of a department of one" at the Sanctuary Church in Minneapolis. On the side, he's part of a three-person creative agency designed to help people enjoy a positive brand experience. I like to hear his thoughts from time to time because he calls it as he sees it.

In his typical style, he shares three easy ways to lose your identity:[4]

1. **Have too many of them.** Not everything in your organization needs a name, logo and stylesheet all to itself. When you over-brand, you dilute your core message. When everything has its own identity, you end up competing with yourself. It's like Fight Club all over again.
2. **Borrow it from someone else.** It's easy to get inspired by design. Some things are just drop-dead beautiful. But, it's hard to be yourself if you're trying to be somebody else. Be inspired, but don't imitate.
3. **Sparkle without substance.** If you oversell yourself, people will eventually figure you out. You can only fool people for so long. A candy-coated Brussels sprout isn't going to hide the bitter taste when you bite into the core.

Andy Sernovitz, author of the book *Word of Mouth Marketing: How Smart Companies Get People Talking*, makes it clear:

> **There is no 'and' in brand. A great brand can only be one thing. You can't sell yourself as fastest and smartest—people don't know how to process those conflicting ideas. Here's the test: Say what you do out loud. Is there an 'and' in there? If yes, you lose.**[5]

But, you're good at so many things! You're going to change the world! I know. I know. But, what's that one, specific, unique thread weaving through everything I experience at your church? Is it your compassion? Is it your arts? Is it your warmth? Is it your excellence? Is it your international impact? Is it your family focus? One thing, over everything else: *that's* your identity.

Granger Community Church is thirty years old this year. It has been through a lot of seasons and styles, but through it all, one constant mission has permeated the identity and influenced the brand:

> **Helping people take their next step toward Christ... together.**

One step at a time. The next right thing. No lone rangers. No isolation. This is the common thread, the one thing that permeates everything we do.

LET'S GO TO BRAND SCHOOL

Communication is tricky—especially organizational communication. So many people are involved, inside and out. With all of the objectives for effective communication, how do you cover all of them at once?

- **INSPIRATION:** information that motivates people to action.
- **OWNERSHIP:** mission, vision and values across teams and locations.
- **INCLUSION:** a common vocabulary for diversified audiences.
- **BALANCE:** just enough, but not too much.
- **LONGEVITY:** not just the here and now, but for the ongoing future.

These are loaded objectives, and I usually see two common responses to the challenges of meeting all five: control everything, or just give in to the free-for-all. Both approaches are counterproductive.

At this point, things could get complex if we let them. But we won't. Simple approaches do exist. The best way to get there is to start right, with a few basic essentials that apply to everyone.

A group of people with a clear understanding of the defined win can effectively create great work—easily. When everyone on the team collaborates to give it form, decisions are made and materials come together readily. And it starts with the same understanding of a key ingredient to our communication: the brand.

WHAT

A brand is not a veneer you apply to make something pretty. A brand begins to exist when you have something to offer the world; it's a promise of what to expect. Great brands are trustworthy. They keep their promises. Great brands like Starbucks, Nike, Apple and *Star Wars* are trusted because of the great experiences they deliver; not their logos.

Think *experience.*

WHO

Brands are made by people with a shared philosophy. They shepherd the brand's development as the brand's heart, head, eyes, hands, ears and voice. Everyone (and by that, I mean *everyone*) who affects any brand touchpoint is responsible for making sure its values remain intact.

Think *brand "handlers."*

HOW

Brands handlers need help. Again, it comes back to people. A communications hub team (or person) organizes the brand essentials so the "handlers" have what they need. Given the right tools and systems, a brand is like a person with good communication and adaptation skills.

Think *brand "advocates"*

Let's review. **Handle the brand with care. Don't manhandle the brand.**

Got it? Good. It's as if you just graduated from the fastest brand school in the universe. Move your tassel and go party!

VOW OF A BRAND HANDLER

As a brand handler, your job is simple. It all boils down to three basic mantras: **Love them. Own them. Live them.** And, everything else will fall into place.

1. Your job is much more about releasing the right response than it is about sending the right message.
2. You vow to reduce information obesity and simplify complexity.
3. Your commitment to effective communication comes from a level of self-awareness that is more of an attitude than a skill. It comes not from technique, but from being genuinely interested in what really matters to the other person.

I can just imagine what some of you are thinking right now: "Uh, technically it IS our job to send the right message." Before we get too far down that line of thought, just remember all the different ways Jesus framed the message to release the right response. Everything depended on who he was talking to at the time. He was never one-size-fits-all with His communication. This is proven not just by Jesus' example, but by scientific market research. Words not only explain but motivate. They cause you to think as well as act. They trigger emotion as well as understanding.

> **As a nation we have fallen in love with the concept of 'communication.' We don't always appreciate the damage being done by our over-communicated society.**
> Al Ries and Jack Trout, *Positioning*

People are so overwhelmed with information, their brains filter out most brands they encounter. A brand handler protects and simplifies the story so the brand personality doesn't get snuffed out.

YOU'VE BEEN FRAMED

Have you heard of the art of *framing*? It's the use of words, images and interactions to speak to, or avoid provoking, a bias someone is already feeling. It's how you piece all the parts together—language, images, environment—to tell a story. Framing is learning to communicate by seeing the world through someone else's eyes.

What story does this picture tell you?

It's not what you think.[6]

Without the proper framing, you probably wouldn't know that Mommy works at Lowe's and is selling a snow shovel. How you frame your story matters. What images you use matters. What language you use matters. The context in which you share it matters.

I heard that it's difficult to see the picture when you're inside the frame. How true. How true.

Framing is not the same thing as "spin." As a recovering corporate spin doctor, I'm opinionated about the difference between the two. It's clear to me: spin is selfish manipulation for personal gain. Framing is selfless, requiring you to step out of the frame to look at the whole picture for the benefit of others.

Mark Batterson, lead pastor of National Community Church in Washington, DC, talks about framing and leadership:

- A good coach knows how to reframe a game at halftime.
- A good psychologist knows how to reframe a problem.
- A good parent knows how to reframe spinach—the vegetable that will give you bulging biceps like Popeye.
- Good leaders are good at putting the right frame around a vision.
- Good preachers frame their messages with an organizing metaphor around biblical truths that make people say, "I've never thought about it that way before."[7]

He brings wise context to the subject. How we frame our message—challenges and opportunities—directly affects how people respond.

THINK IT OVER
ADOPTING THE BEST PRACTICE: TELL ONE STORY AT A TIME

- ☐ If I evaluate everything that happens at our church as a "story," is it cohesive and comprehensible? Do the environments feel as if they're from the same family, or like a hodgepodge of competing values?

- ☐ Are competing personalities on our team hurting the story? Am I afraid to deal with staff baggage proactively? How can I diffuse emotion to get people on the same page by encouraging cohesiveness, not cloning?

- ☐ People hate to be sold, but they love to buy. And, my audience is full of people who don't want to hear about how wonderful we think our product or service is. How can we breathe life into our flat "information" to help people imagine their owning and loving it for themselves? Is it something people will want to attach themselves to?

- ☐ How many stories are we telling with the amount of information we produce, the quality of each piece, and how we organize the information?

- ☐ What is the one thread of our identity? Is every ministry telling the same story?

- ☐ How can I better live out the mantra of a brand handler? How can I equip others to do the same thing?

- ☐ Are there areas where I can improve flow, make a process easier for our guests or shorten a turnaround time?

chapter 10
DECLUTTER YOUR DIGITAL SPACES

> **Innovation and creativity are processes. You can learn them and you can improve them.**
> Thomas M. Koulopoulos, *The Innovation Zone*

Bad websites happen to good people. If you code yourself or pay someone to do it for you, carry a selfie stick or a walking stick, are an online social media master or disaster, read your books on Kindle or turn the pages, spend your time downloading apps or downing appetizers—I'm talking to you. And, I'm going to tell you what you probably won't hear anywhere else. If you want a site that works, make paper first. [screeching brakes] That's right. I said "make paper." You see, the secret to making sites that work is to make the paper that holds the plan for your online strategy. That plan replaces the wrong questions with the right ones. The right questions prevent you from falling victim to one-size-fits-none solutions and flimsy technobabble. Do you want to unleash the power of the your online and on-the-go spaces? Start by asking, "What is the desired response we want?" instead of, "What do we want this to look like?" and work backwards from there.*

* The following pages don't hold answers to the "what" and "how-to" questions you can find yourself with a one minute Google search. They do, however, hold simplified and critical frameworks that can decrease your anxiety about online audiences and technology. Digest the thinking behind the following stories and you'll know what to do with the questions that don't have just one right answer, but many. Enjoy this alternative look at things and you'll be ready for anything.

WHAT IT IS AND WHAT IT ISN'T

We've come a long way since the early days of the Internet in the '90s. Websites are easier to afford, build and use today more than ever. Why, then, are we still experiencing so many bad sites and unsatisfied stakeholders?

My grandson is two years old. Recently, he wandered away from the crowd, quietly undetected, for just a few industrious minutes. You know how stealth those toddlers can be. By the time he was found, he had already attempted to make an official escape.

Just because you have the keys, doesn't mean you know how to use them.*

* Like you, I had a pseudo-heart attack looking at this picture. But, not to worry. No electricity connected with the keys and the little curious tot made it out of his experiment unharmed.

Bad sites begin with a bad definition. If you don't know what it is, then you're not going to know how to best use it. Am I right? Here's a list that might help reset some filters about what can make, or break, a website.

Websites are not...	Websites are...
a standalone deliverable	an extension of what you do
about technology	about communication
about adding more functionality	about adding more flow
about what you want people to do	about what people are looking for
about what you think people need to know	about what people are trying to do
where people go to read	where people go to solve problems
a destination	a vehicle
a place for content	a place to participate
sterilized	conversational
censored	social
long	links

When you are able to operate within this new paradigm, you will be more equipped not only to better control the flow of *information,* but also the flow of *attention.*

And, here is the best news of all. You don't need a big budget or a big brain to make your site work for you (instead of the other way around). All you need to do is ask the right questions about who is going to use it and how. Then, you can figure out what it should look like and what inventory makes the top shelf. The content you include and the design you use are decisions to make after you determine what your site does (and doesn't do).

Someone once told me we all have about seven trusted online agents; our go-to sites or apps for areas of our life (e.g., shopping, travel, weather, etc.). Think about the sites you use on a daily basis, on your phone and computer. Why are they part of your daily routine? Now, think about your church website. What unique problems does it solve? As an online spiritual agent, what can I get there that I can't get anywhere else?

So, if you haven't already, stop talking about your website as a piece of technology (or worse yet, an online brochure) and start treating it as another space you're hosting for people to gather and interact. That changes the rules of the game.

FINISH YOUR BLUEPRINT BEFORE YOU BREAK GROUND

You don't build a house one room at a time. You get the plans for the entire house before you make your shopping list and start hiring contractors. Nobody would look at a skyscraper after it was built and say, "I wonder how we're going to add a garage to that?" A website is no different; you need a master plan before you build. Here's a simple framework you can use, with sample questions along the way, to help you start the process of writing your web blueprint.

Phase 1: Discover

Fragmented identity equates to lost identity. That is why the process begins with questions about your organization—not your website. Use phase 1 to *discover* competing values and address them. Everything that touches your audience sends a message. Make sure you know what that message is, so you can positively reinforce the message you want to send—online and off.

- What is our ministry compass, our statement of purpose? What values do we adhere to? What can we offer that can't be found anywhere else?
- What audience are we trying to reach? Is it the same audience we are reaching now?
- What is the information flow for our church? How do events get promoted? Do we have one calendar? One database?

Phase 2: Define

In Phase 1, you got clarity about who you are, what you do and what type of experience you want to create. Phase 2 is where you *define* how you want to tell that story specifically online.

- What audience will we serve first? Who is our secondary audience?
- What are our objectives? What will happen as a result of this new site? How will we measure our success?
- What is our current reality (e.g., budget, staffing, technology platform, etc.)?
- What's working with our current site? What's not working?

These first two phases are the most important, and you should spend the majority of your time and effort here.* In them, you find the answers that morph into your project scope—that blueprint you'll use to stay on track and make ongoing decisions. But, depending on what you find, you may need to take some time repairing your infrastructure before moving to Phase 3.

Phase 3: Deliver

By this point in the process, you've probably figured out that you won't be able to do everything you originally set out to do. But, that's OK. Your action plan has clarity—about not only what you're saying no to, but also more importantly, about what you're saying yes to.

* I was hired to build a new Website in 2002. It took two years to find clear answers to the questions in Phases 1 and 2. It took another year for Phase 3. The new site went live in 2005. True story. The point is, this is a process. Don't be tempted to take shortcuts. It will be worth it in the end.

- List your deliverables by priorities: now, soon, and later.
- There is more to your project than development. Make sure to leave room for concepts, testing and content.
- Remember, "like a house." Make a plan for maintenance (bug fixes), improvements (enhancements) and remodeling (upgrades).

Not only does a master plan provide a good outlet for ideas you can't tackle today, it also reminds people what you agreed to do in the first place.* Your finished document will help manage information across multiple departments, establish a unified vision and prevent unnecessary revisions.**

* Newsflash: People have short memories and define reality by their emotion of the day. Document everything.

** Obviously, there is more to defining your web strategy than I can outline in these few pages. However, this may be just what you need to get started and turn things around.

DON'T COMPLICATE THE SOLUTION

> **Simplicity is the ultimate sophistication.**
> Leonardo da Vinci

Enhancing productivity means embracing simplicity.* Many times, we have the power to "simplify real-world problems by defining them to be simple;"[1] we just don't use it. Steve Smith, world-renowned designer and developer, built an entire company around this concept. He talks about simplifying the complex on his blog:

> **One of my favorite quotes is Simplify the Problem, Don't Complicate the Solution. Before you attack a complicated, real-world problem with an equally complex solution, step back and see if you can't figure out a way to make the problem simpler to start with. Simple problems make for simple solutions.**[2]

Recently, I met with a ministry leader who was under pressure from one of his remote teams for a solution to their current crisis. Their numbers had grown significantly, and they needed help checking kids in at a weekly event.

The only solution they saw was to implement a web portal with check-in kiosks like we used at our Granger campus. The ministry leader entered our conversation a bit discouraged, knowing that while real challenges existed, they didn't have the money to implement the solution they needed. Or, did they?

While their numbers had grown significantly, they were only dealing with seventy adults (thirty to forty-five children) at this remote site.

But, because they had started with no system at all, this number became overwhelming to manage in a hurry. And, because they saw the kiosk system we use at the Granger campus, they assumed that was the best and only answer.

I asked a few questions and listened. After I was sure I understood their objective, I "defined the problem to be simple." Even though the conversation started with the need for a web portal, it ended here: associate children with the person who drops them off at check-in (thus ensuring child safety at pick-up).

For years, we had used a paper-sticker system at our church to check in kids and maintain security. We effectively used the same paper-sticker system for fifteen years and did not integrate check-in with our website until we reached a weekend attendance of more than 4,000 people. That remote team didn't need a web portal after all. They just needed stickers. Simple, cheap and effective.

819
All Stars
Reaching Up. Reaching In. Reaching Out.
Child's First Name
Child's Last Name
© churchnursery.com, 2004

819
Child's First Name:
Child's Last Name:
Special Instructions/Medical Conditions:
Age________ Grade________
All Stars

3185
All Stars
Reaching Up. Reaching In. Reaching Out.
This Is
Diaper Bag!
© churchnursery.com, 2003

Child's Name 3185
Parent's Name
Child's Age:
Special Instructions/Medical Conditions:
Please Check All That Apply:
☐ Visitor ☐ Pacifier ☐ Food Allergies
☐ Nursing ☐ Bottle ☐ Other
All Stars
Reaching Up. Reaching In. Reaching Out.

Our sticker check-in security system.

Keep it simple; it works.

I remember my pastor addressing this matter of complexity at a staff meeting. "There is something bad about size and complexity. The more complex things are, the more fragile they are. If you have a stone, you can bang it. No problem. As soon as you play mousetrap, if any link in the chain is off, the whole system stops."

Remember, simplify the problem. Don't complicate the solution.

JUST BECAUSE YOU BUILD IT DOESN'T MEAN THEY'LL COME

> **Technology makes it possible for people to gain control over everything except technology.**
> John Tudor

Your site isn't for you, it's for the person you want to visit (and hopefully, come back). Remember, you're the host of a public, online gathering space! Too many corporate and church sites are self-centered or self-absorbed. Consequently, it sends the message that the organization is self-centered and self-absorbed. Is yours?

- Is your site map organized by your organizational chart or department list? Consider grouping and categorizing around the tasks people are trying to accomplish and resources they're looking for instead.
- Do you split long copy into multiple pages? Don't make people link to different pages if they don't have to; help them scan. Give them more bullets and fewer clicks.
- Do you have an "under construction" or "coming soon" page? Don't tell people to check back, just turn it on when it's done.
- Do you tell people to follow you on Facebook? Why? What do they get out of it? If you're providing something helpful, they'll follow you on their own. And, when they go to your Facebook page, does it offer anything different than the website? The same holds true for apps. You don't need an app unless it offers something your mobile site doesn't. Why bother?
- Do you make people swim through menus and subpages to find what they're looking for? Give people quick access to a search bar so they can bring what they're looking for to the front, when they're looking for it.

- Is your tagline insider-focused? It's one thing to have a sound, operational mission statement. But, all mission statements aren't guest-friendly. Think about what you're communicating on your site. News site *The Daily Beast* uses the tagline, "Read this, skip that." The tagline for the Zipcar car sharing service is, "Wheels where you want them." At a glance, both taglines clearly communicate what the company websites are all about.[3]
- Is it overdone? Your church site is not Madison Square Garden. Don't overpower because you can. Don't show off your performance quality or creative design chops and neglect the core reasons someone looks to the church in the first place.
- Is *About Us* or *Ministries* the top language people see? Instead, consider guest-focused language like *Welcome, Events, For Families,* etc.
- Is it full, big blocks of controlled, corporate-scrubbed content? Instead of looking for ways to create more to say, consider making it easier for people to find, contribute to and share good information that already exists.

When I was in charge of revamping our church site a second time, I knew I needed a fresh perspective. Something to help me design from the outside in, not the inside out. I knew I was too close to it, so I spent a year interviewing more than 100 people, inside and outside the church, about what they like in an online experience. I asked them to think about the sites they love and use regularly in their lives, and tell me what they like about them and why they keep going back.

It is interesting to me that all answers revolved around clarity, ease of use and authenticity. Nobody ever said anything about cool technology or awesome design. Another fun fact? An overwhelming majority of the people I interviewed said no website is better than a bad one.

This excerpt from an article Tony Morgan published drives the point home with some practical examples. Even though this article was written over decade ago, many of the examples he references still happen regularly.

Ways to keep me from visiting your church because I visited your website:

1. Avoid telling me what's going to happen at your church this weekend. I found churches that had prominent information about upcoming golf scrambles, but nothing about this weekend's service. Why would I come if I don't know what I'm going to experience?
2. Put a picture of your building on the main page. After all, ministry is all about the buildings.
3. List every single ministry you have at your church. Frankly, I don't care what ministries you have. I just want to know whether or not I should visit your church this weekend. My first step isn't the men's Bible study or joining your church's prayer partners ministry.
4. Make it as difficult as possible for me to get directions, services times, or find information about what will happen with my kids. It's important that my kids have a great experience. If you can't convince me that will happen, I'm probably not going to risk visiting your service.
5. Put a picture of your pastor with his wife on the main page. That tells me it's all about a personality, and I see enough of those people on television. I actually found one church that had not one, but two pictures of the senior pastor on the main page.[4]

Technology and design can enhance or hinder the online experience, depending on how much authority you give them.

HOW TO DRIVE PEOPLE ONLINE

We all read the chatter about how our phones are making us stupid. Or, how people need to get a life and turn off the computer. Maybe you don't agree with this point of view, but I'll bet you know someone who does, and you don't know how to convince them otherwise. Maybe you're the other extreme and believe the answer to everything happens through technology. So, where do you fall? Overwhelmed? Underwhelmed? Misdirected?

There's so much advice out there, and nobody's an expert (don't believe anyone who tells you they are). Just like people *offline,* there is no one-size-fits-all approach to people *online.* However, everyone—regardless of skill or style—can learn, leverage and grow if they're willing to take a look at things from a broader perspective. It's not about the form—it's about the function.

> **Newspapers solve problems that no longer exist.**[5]

Keep your eyes wide open to the reality that people are looking for and sharing content in new ways. Even the rules of Twitter have changed multiple times over the past couple of years. If you're not committed and responsive to that reality, you'll be having a tea party with your stuffed animals (and other imaginary friends) in no time.

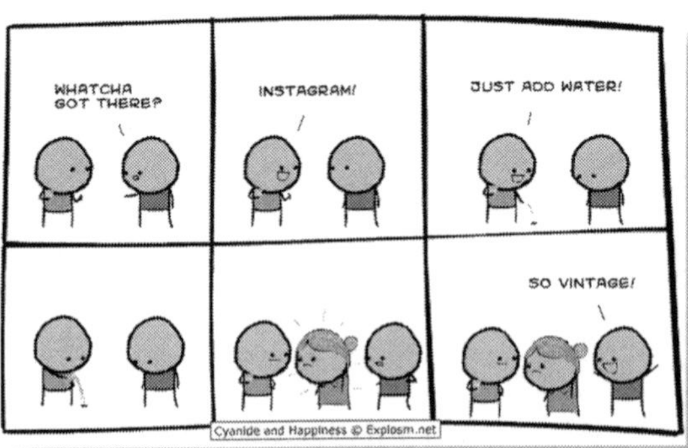

Admit it. It's funny.[6]

I will say this up front: if your audience does not depend on the Internet for life outside your church, these next few pages might not be for you. But, if you live anywhere outside the remote village of Yakutat, Alaska, your audience is paying bills online, using social media, watching YouTube, carrying a smartphone, checking email daily, etc. Even the Amish are online.

If you haven't started making the move, it might be time for you to get going:

- **Use the paper content to drive people online.** For example, replace your paper registration form with a 4x6 postcard that will drive people online to register, print maps, etc. The paper doesn't tell them everything, but tells them where to go to find it. Or, use Facebook as a promo that drives people to your site for the official details.
- **Don't create handouts for your info counter.** Instead, put a computer or iPad at the counter, and train your guest services team to use the website for their source of information. Make it easy for them; condense things on two to four main landing pages so they can quickly find the answers to commonly asked questions (e.g., events, volunteer opportunities, weekend message archive, service times, etc.).
- **Design it once; use it twice.** If your audience is split (half online and half off), you can serve both audiences without duplicating efforts. Create the content and promotions online with the intent of printing the page on-demand at guest services for people who don't go online.
- **Give online users the scoop on content.** Share the weekend series trailer before it's shown in the service. Reveal details not available in the bulletin. Create downloadable resources that extend the weekend service (e.g., discussion guides,

service clips, social media tiles on Facebook, etc.). Create a value for going online, not an online version of what is already available in print.

- **Drive people to the hub.** Print the web address everywhere—service slides, the bulletin, every handout, Facebook, Twitter and Instagram profiles, etc. Make it easy and clear that the one-stop place to visit for all information is this one site. The more web addresses you drive people to, the more confusing it is. Don't make it hard for people to try to figure out where to go for what and to remember which is which. It is more effective and unifying to promote one URL that links to other pages or sites.
- **Eliminate redundancy.** If you make information available in multiple spots, nobody will get used to going to one place to get it. If you have multiple sites for various ministries and departments, make sure they link back to the main site for content that affects 80 percent of the audience. Content that is replicated across multiple sites creates extra work for you and increases the margin for error.
- **Make search king.** With a power search feature, people can bring what they want to the front, when they want it. Ultimately, a simple, search-driven site (versus a hierarchical site) puts the mission within reach for more people by giving each user control of their own experience. If a user is ever feeling lost on the site, search instantly and painlessly gets them back on track. If you can see what people are searching for, even better.
- **Remember tiny screens.** While almost everyone may be going online, not everyone has a computer. A high and growing percentage of people are doing everything they need to do online through their smart phones. Make sure

your site has a mobile version that loads quickly and prioritizes the most in-demand information and features. Since you have less space to convey information, you'll be forced to keep it brief. This is a good thing. Constraints make us better. The whole point—keep it minimalistic and digestible—for you and others.

- **Share the experience.** Give people something to do and invite them into the story. Post quality photos from big events on Facebook so people can tag them and share with friends. Look for opportunities to cultivate common ground with less separation between church and daily life.
- **Create channels for feedback.** Build relational trust with a two-way information exchange. Make sure there's a place for people to ask questions and provide feedback. And, as you read the feedback that comes in, undervalue your own opinions. They may seem rock solid to you, but chances are there's some flawed assumptions just waiting to be discovered. Trust me on this one.

None of this is rocket science. But, it is designed to force you to consider how long you can keep maintaining, resourcing, staffing and investing in old communication channels while the majority of your audience is engaging in other ways. They need your focus and creativity channeled in the places they're searching, connecting and growing.

The goal isn't to stop traditional communication channels, but it might require redirecting energy and resources from some of the things you're accustomed to into new areas of growth.

CURB YOUR ENTHUSIASM

There are some common misperceptions about what makes a great site:

- If I build it, they will come.
- My site is for everybody. Everyone's opinion matters.
- It should include everything so people can decide.
- I just need some stock photos.
- It can be built in a day.
- It worked for somebody else, so it will work for us.
- It just needs to look pretty.

If you really want to know what to include, it starts by knowing what *not* to include. Self-control is the only way to go.

- **Don't reinvent the wheel.** Trying to be all things to all people doesn't work. What is the most important thing? Make that your priority. Why do you need a weather plugin on the church site? People aren't counting on the church for their weather report or local news.
- **It's OK to leave them wanting more.** Your site supports your communications; it is not the communicator. You don't need to tell them everything. Help them find what's happening next and how to be a part of it. Help pull them into the action, instead of assuming they prefer to sit passively on the sidelines reading pages of copy.
- **Online users expect freaky fast.** That cool feature may sound like a good idea, but not if it causes your site to load slowly. People are impatient. They won't wait. They may even assume your site is broken. It's better to leave it out

rather than make people wait. If you can't speed it up, at least give them something to do while they're waiting. Consider rotating captions or a progress bar that keeps them entertained while the site loads.

- **Count the cost.** If you can't maintain it, don't implement it. An outdated site, app or podcast is an outdated church.
- **Give the brain a break.** The brain can only focus on a limited number of stimuli at a time. Organize your site information into categories. This mirrors the way our brains are constantly categorizing new stimuli and helps simplify our thinking. This saves time and increases our attention capacity.[7] Use shorter event descriptions to highlight what matters instead of forcing people to weed through an endless barrage of stuff that doesn't.
- **Don't put the IT or graphics guru in charge.** The designated driver of your web vehicle doesn't function as a webmaster, but as a user-advocate, balancing the needs of the organization with the needs of the audience. They manage the project and set priorities through an all-church filter. Graphics and IT decisions should be supporting players, not the lead character.
- **Be human. Pursue excellence, but not perfection.** Keep close to the messy realities on the ground like a real person, not a censored organization or sterilized avatar. Honesty is more important than genius.

It takes a lot of self-control to limit your online content, but you should be the one working hard at it so the people visiting your site don't have to.

MO MONEY MO PROBLEMS

Maybe you feel the pressure to accomplish much with little, especially when it comes to your digital resources. Well, I'm a big fan of the bright side, and I don't have much tolerance for Eeyores. But, more than anything, I thought you might appreciate hearing how people in a different industry handle the same pressure of doing more with less.

A few years ago, I watched a video panel with six directors on the Oscar circuit talk[8] about the pressures they face. With the exception of one, they were all relatively low-budget (unusual for a Oscar nominees). The lack of big-budget resources forced them to be more creative and focus on the story:

- Boundaries and restrictions create a visual language. Work within the confines and get things done.
- Many times, when we compromise because of cost, the scene ends up being better (because we're desperate).
- Success isn't found in the dollars but who goes with you. Put people on the project who want to be there whether they're paid or not.
- With more money, they would have rolled over local participants in poor form.
- They would gladly give up more money to gain more creative freedom.
- Necessity breeds invention and keeps the egos out.
- You always make better decisions with limitations (even if they are self-imposed).

I've heard it said that scarcity breeds clarity. And, clarity breeds mastery. So, embrace your limits as an advantage and go for it.

SOCIAL MEDIA STARTING BLOCK

The guy who left this comment on my blog is half right: "Pull the computer out of the wall, and go out into your community. Shake some hands, learn some names, invest actual time in people and earn the right to be heard. That's how you minister to your community, not by eavesdropping on what they're saying on Twitter."

But, like I said, he's only *half* right. It's actually a great idea to watch what people are talking about on Twitter.

And, while it's true we can't develop whole and complete relationships online only, we can create great environments online that inspire real people offline. If you boycott the social (intentionally or carelessly), you risk making decisions based on incomplete information and having less impact on the world around you.

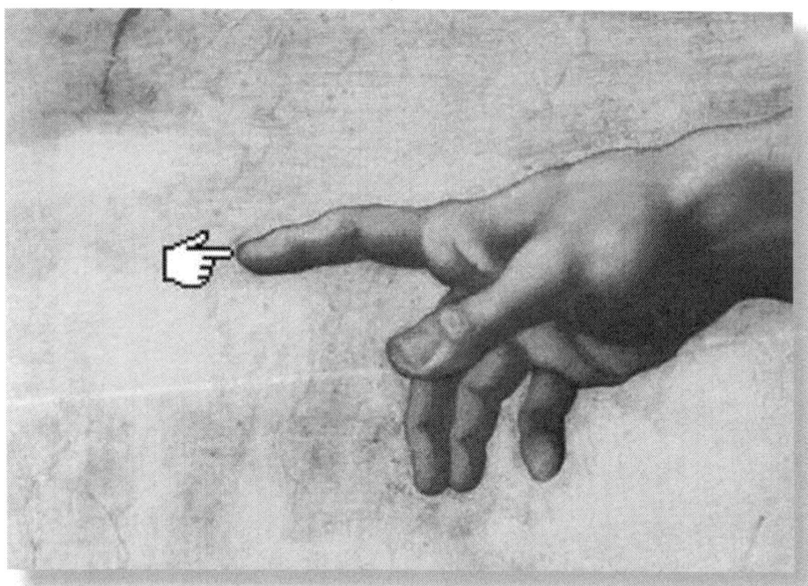

Real community and digital community are not opposites; just different.[9]

Find your center by revisiting the definition of social:

adjective so·cial \ˈsō-shəl\

: relating to or involving activities in which people spend time talking to each other or doing enjoyable things with each other

: liking to be with and talk to people : happy to be with people

: of or relating to people or society in general

Don't panic under the pressure to use and master every social media platform that exists. **Just start with one. Watch, experiment, learn, repeat.** It's that simple.

1. **Pick one.** Before you decide, ask, "Who is it for and why would they care?" Once you decide where you're going to start (e.g., Facebook because you'll get your biggest bang for your buck, or Instagram because you want to learn how to skate with a smaller audience), create your profile. Just include the basics with a friendly caption and link back to your main site. Don't overdo it.
2. **Practice the basics.** Start incorporating your general news feed alerts into social media. Make it part of your weekly pattern, not an add-on or afterthought. It could be as simple as pre-scheduling new event posts and video links for the whole week on Monday mornings. Set it and forget it.
3. **Have fun with the trial and error.** Start experimenting with community engagement. But, remember you're not there to sell. No matter how much you love your church and everything it has to offer, you can't create a desire for it. But, you can figure out what your audience desires, and write to that. Look at your social media peeps as a focus group. Pay attention to how they respond, comment and share (or not). Then, you'll see what resonates and start to refine and

focus your messaging in other areas. It doesn't have to be complex. Try a few things and see what fits. Just because it works for someone else doesn't mean it works for you. But, try it for a while before you decide.

- Switzerland gives their Twitter account to a different resident every week. (If you really want to know what matters to a specific audience, give them the mic and see what they talk about.)
- A third grade teacher asked her students to complete this sentence anonymously: "I wish my teacher knew..." (Create a feedback mechanism to get honest, vulnerable input about real-life dreams, hurts, desires.)
- IKEA gave away the chance to win furniture any time someone tagged one of their showroom photos. If they were the first to tag it, they won the entire showroom. (Incentivize participation; make it worth their while.)
- Online clothing retailer Threadless lets customers vote on the next shirt to be printed. (Let people be part of a process; they want to participate.)
- Guy Kawasaki let his audience compete to design his next book cover. (Co-creation activates different talents in your audience you may not even know are there.)

Once you've experimented long enough to feel out what feels right and what doesn't, it helps to outline your framework* before you start the process over again. Because, you know, since this book was published, there are at least three more social media platforms that have replaced the ones you already figured out. Don't sweat it. You know what to do now.

* I got you covered. There's a sample in the back of the book.

HOW DID WE GET HERE, AND WHAT DO WE DO NOW?

Sometimes it helps to look back at where we've been to make sense of where we're going. And, when it comes to the explosion of digital and social media, a lot of churches are still seeing stars from the changes swirling around them. It's not as chaotic as it may feel, but I know that can be hard to see when you're buried in it. Let's zoom out for a better look at the online church* journey.

- **FIRST** | Content and community was contained to a weekend service or facility. People had to come to us to experience the church service or elements. At best, they could take a message CD home to listen again or share with friends.
- **THEN** | We'd capture our best elements from a service or event and post them on the web afterwards. More people had access to a virtual highlight reel to use as an invite tool or "in case you missed it."
- **NOW** | People start their experience before they come and long after they leave. Our promotions, connection and growth opportunities have the opportunity for a longer shelf life, accessible on the web and mobile devices before, during and after.
- **NEXT** | Instead of crafting one-way productions that "inform and inspire," we create interactive tools that "integrate and elevate." We're not creating more information, but making it easier for people to find, contribute and share good information that already exists.

Now that you've got the bird's-eye view, you might not be as tempted to overthink it.

* Everything your church does online could qualify as online church. Think about it.

PREPARING FOR LAUNCH

When you upgrade your technology (whether it's a new database, app or website launch), there's more to your job than the technical punch list. Many times, the biggest threat to a successful launch doesn't have anything to do with the technology, and everything to do with people who are going to be using that technology.

When your staff or stakeholders aren't aware of the changes coming, what to expect, how it will or won't affect them and when to plan it, they're left to fill in the blanks. This is when the office chatter goes into a dark tunnel and you lose positive team momentum. Without this valuable stakeholder engagement (which is 80 percent emotional and relational), you'll end up creating new and unnecessary challenges for yourself.

Make sure your technology launch includes an internal rollout plan for stakeholders. Unlike the technology project you're implementing, the internal rollout doesn't have to be complicated. Start with a simple conversation tool that reinforces what's normal, what's going to be OK, what to do when you find a problem, etc.

Recently, I was part of a significant web launch where we were prepping multiple leaders and teams across multiple locations for the big change. The closer we got to the live date, the more anxiety levels were rising. We knew we needed to get ahead of wave and design a "freak-out" antidote to use in a variety of settings leading up to, and right after, launch.

Here's the tool we came up with:

5 THINGS TO REMEMBER AFTER LAUNCH

Like we start using physical space before construction is 100 percent complete, we will do the same with our digital space. We're intentionally launching at 80 percent to let traffic start flowing through the space. That last 20 percent is crucial in the development process. We'll get to see how people use it; if things work like we anticipate, what needs adjusting, what bugs are hiding, etc. Extend grace as we keep trucking through the punch list. We're not resting until it's done. Remember to stay positive, advocate the change and celebrate the improvements—this is OUR new space!

- **IT'S DIFFERENT**
  Visually, it is a paradigm shift. Functionally, there will be a learning curve. Exhale. Stuff might not be where you are used to, but once you get used to it, stuff will actually be easier to get to for more people.
- **DISCOVERY IS PART OF THE PROCESS**
  Every day, search results will get better. We will continuously be tagging content so the right stuff shows up. We give up some control on the homepage to gain more control on targeted landing pages that come back in search results.
- **CONTENTS MAY SHIFT DURING FLIGHT**
  We will be scrubbing content as people experience it in a new container. There's content that made sense on our old site that will not fit the new one. We've done our best to scrub as we go, but there are some misfits we won't know about until we start using it.
- **SNEAKY LITTLE GUYS**
  Bugs hide in places we can't see. Won't find them until people use the site. We'll fix them as we go. Don't panic. Let us know when you find one.
- **SPEAK UP**
  We will welcome any and all input from anyone all the time. Don't be afraid to sound off. No idea or question is too small. Send us questions, bugs as you find them and ideas as they come to you. Don't panic. Remember. We're moving into new digs; it takes a few weeks to get things detailed, unpacked, pictures hung on the walls, fixtures installed and clothes put away.

THINK IT OVER
ADOPTING THE BEST PRACTICE: DECLUTTER YOUR DIGITAL SPACES

- ☐ If my website is an environment where people gather and might bring their friends, what am I doing to make it inviting? Why would people want to come back after they visit it once?

- ☐ What percentage of my resources (time and money) am I allocating for maintenance? For upgrades? Which has the bigger impact?

- ☐ What changes can I make to become an audience *advocate* instead of a web *master*?

- ☐ Can I list some of my favorite websites (not other churches') and determine what I like about them and what keeps me coming back? What's the connection?

- ☐ How hard are we making people work on our site? Is information easy to find? Or, is it easy to get lost?

- ☐ Where is my audience searching and sharing?

- ☐ Where do I fit into the social?

- ☐ Have I done my pre-launch flight check? What stakeholders need to be involved? What turbulence do they need to be prepared for? What makes it worth it?

- ☐ Have we designed our online spaces from the inside out? What changes can we make to be more focused from the outside in?

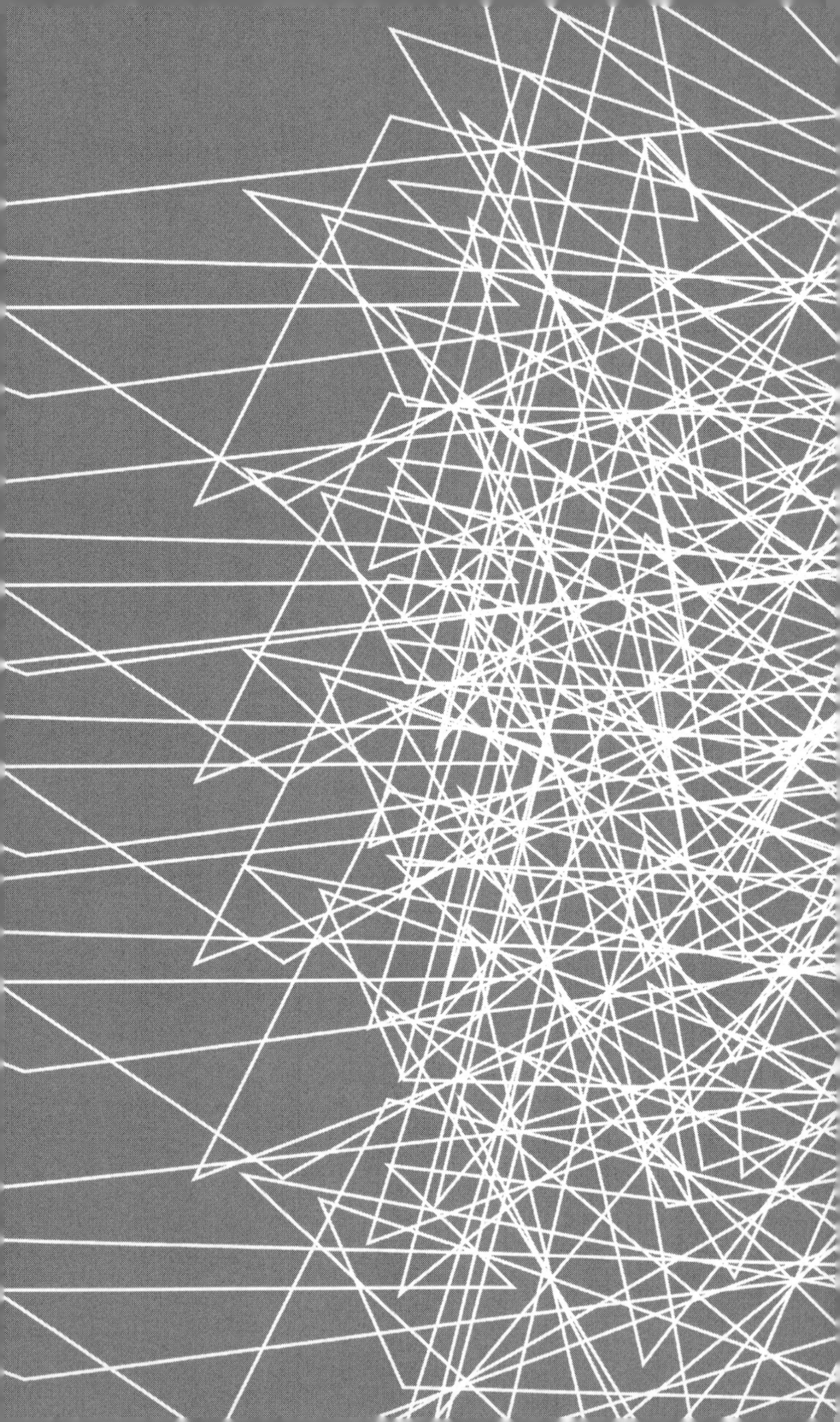

part 3

THE RESPONSIBILITY OF GETTING BUY-IN

It is what we ARE that gets across, not what we try to teach.
Croft Pentz

What starts with the best intentions for leading change often turns to defeat or defensiveness. The candid truth? Most of us are ineffective because we are pushing our own agenda—our way. What we think is the right way. Under pressure to demonstrate results quickly, we have the tendency to skip crucial "soft skills"—the emotional intelligence quotient—of our job. Even with an increased awareness of a better communication strategy, few understand how to get buy-in and manage it. Ric Willmot, a professional executive consultant, paints a great picture of what's at risk when we underestimate the importance of the "people" side of our job: "Without buy-in, strategy remains on the tarmac and the flight remains at the end of the runway."[1]

chapter 11
REWRITE YOUR JOB DESCRIPTION

> **Leaders put their team in the best position to succeed.**
> Colin Powell

Even though you might have all the talent, technique, tools and tricks on your side regarding graphics, creativity, copywriting, etc., you won't get very far if the people you work with think you're an idiot or a controlling bully. I'm not saying you ARE these things, but people might think you are. Do you ever notice your best intentions are met with lackluster reactions from those around you? Not only can you do something about it, you should do something about it. That's the part of this job that is too often ignored.

MY BOSS DOESN'T GET IT

> **Leaders who can't be questioned do questionable things.**
> Jon Acuff, *Do Over*

I've noticed a primary theme over the years as I've interacted with people who ask how to lead change in their organizational communications strategy (or lack of strategy). People are often frustrated and defeated in their jobs trying to get staff to "follow the rules."

There, my friends, is the root of the problem. The challenge typically isn't with a pastor or boss who "doesn't get it," or with an uncooperative staff, but with the person who is trying to get staff to "mind" in the first place.

Many times our M.O.* is the culprit; we take ourselves too seriously trying to get the job done our way. We don't consciously realize that this is often our driving force, but underneath it all, it's there. If we purify and change our objective, we will see a dramatic change in the results—not just for the people who attend our church, but also for the people with whom we work and serve.

Instead of asking questions such as, "How do I convince my boss that we need to run everything through me before we post or print it?" or, "How do I get people to follow the logo guidelines?", the questions should be, "How can I clear hurdles to help people do their best work?" and, "Am I doing what I need to do so others can do what they need to do?"

* Mode of operation.

> **If men could only know each other, they would neither idolize nor hate.**[1]
> Elbert Hubbard

Pause for a minute to let that sink in. That quote should have a significant impact. Its point is key to leading change in an organization. People are attached to comfort zones, and change requires moving from those comfort zones. If we're not sensitive to that reality, it has negative consequences on teamwork and flow. If you want your leaders and peers to care about what you do, first show how much you care about what they do.

- If you are always in the office at 7 a.m., switch up your schedule to see who is hanging around the office late at night.
- If you are a late owl, attend a couple of early morning meetings to see what people do in the daylight.
- Show up at a student gathering just to observe the unique opportunities and challenges for leaders in that environment.
- Attend an event you wouldn't normally attend, just to show support to your peers.

That always means the change is going to take longer than you want it to, but the alternative is failure to launch.

Blaine Hogan published a phenomenally uncomfortable book: *Untitled: Thoughts on the Creative Process.*[2] (Side note: It really should be required reading for every communications and creative professional.) In it, he quotes Dan Allender: "You have absolutely no business taking us to places you're unwilling to go yourself." Ouch. Yep, we've got some work to do. Let's go.

MORE THAN ONE AUDIENCE

I brought a lot of practical and technical experience from the corporate world when I joined the staff team at Granger. But, even with everything I had going for me, it took about two years before I really started making an impact. I was spinning my wheels until I learned some valuable life lessons, and those lessons came to me from a place I didn't expect—my own family.

Ironically enough, I (Little Miss Communications Director) had gone on autopilot and had stopped learning about one of the audiences in my own home—my then-teenage daughter, Erin. She acted out, and dramatic events played out to get my attention. It got ugly and embarrassing during a very tumultuous and eye-opening season. Relationships were strained, and the only way to get through it was to call a time-out.

You laugh, because it's true.[3]

I changed my schedule, cut the fluff and intentionally focused more on Erin. I flip-flopped my approach from talking and teaching (all about me) to watching and learning (all about her). I was able to appreciate and understand her perspective in a whole new light, and it completely changed how I communicated with her. Our relationship improved tenfold.

The lessons I learned at home opened my eyes to why my efforts in the office weren't yielding positive results. Aha. I had been spending all of my time thinking about my message instead of thinking about the people (my co-workers) on the other side of the message. The communications principles I preach about so passionately? Turns out, they apply to external and internal audiences—in the office and in the home. Am I the only one who didn't get that?

DESCRIBE WHAT YOU DO

The generic job description for a communications director varies widely, depending on the environment. I've seen it all: from receptionist to graphic artist, from worship leader to media agent, from videographer to fundraiser, from storyteller to copywriter. The first time somebody asked me about my job description, I answered in two words—**consumer advocate.**

So, what are the job responsibilities of a consumer advocate?

- Embrace the mission, vision and values of the organization. Live it and love it.
- Protect the audience from bad experiences in online, print and media touchpoints.
- Work on behalf of the audience to uncover their needs, and make it easy for them to pinpoint next steps to meet them.
- Identify barriers and distractions and remove them.
- Develop relationships across the organization's stakeholders to develop strategies and tactics for new approaches.
- Develop processes that help cut through the clutter.
- Help people connect with resources and each other without going through a middleman.
- Eliminate information overload.

And, the qualifications for a consumer advocate?

- The ability to stay in touch with audience and management simultaneously, and convey different visions to both.
- Obvious and contagious enthusiasm for the job.
- Access to a network of relevant professionals: writers, designers, creative directors, developers, production managers and filmmakers.

That's a great start. But, what if I only have an elevator ride to explain the job description and qualifications? I would summarize them like this:

Your church has a message. A message of truth, hope and purpose. But, before people in your congregation or community encounter that message, they encounter your church. Your job, as communications director, is to maximize the things in your church that attract people to the message and remove the things that repel them.

The ultimate objective? To deliver a cohesive, unified experience at every place someone comes in contact with your church—the touch-points.

You might be wearing more than one hat, and there's something I don't want you to miss. **Whether you are the receptionist, the senior pastor's assistant, an associate pastor or all of the above, you can take on the role of communications director without any title to support it.** It's not the title that makes any difference; it's the perspective you have in your existing role that makes the difference.

What's stopping you from being a consumer advocate?

COMFORT THE DISTURBED—DISTURB THE COMFORTABLE

I read this one-liner on a t-shirt while I was on vacation. "Comfort the disturbed. Disturb the comfortable." Immediately, I thought, "YES!" Not only is this what we should be doing, it's what we need. I adopted it as my secondary mantra.*

We—human beings and churches—have the tendency to present things from our side of the table—our perspective only. We'll seek out resources that support our viewpoint and avoid things that don't.

It's uncomfortable and messy when we expose ourselves to perspectives that swing outside our lines. And, people don't like being uncomfortable. Especially people in church. **If we're too comfortable, we need to be disturbed.**

When we're too comfortable, we're smug and quick to judge. This is why the rest of the line is so important. I've heard it said it this way: "Don't live out your faith by calling the police when people need an ambulance." **If people are disturbed, we need to comfort them.**

I'm as guilty as the next guy, and it takes work in my personal life not to live in my own "bubble." One way I try to learn about what's disturbing others is to read books that fall outside the lines I've drawn for myself. Last year, I read a few that I probably wouldn't leave out on my desk; one was counter to my core belief system, and the others were explicitly vulgar at times. One of the books I read was about a subject I have absolutely zero interest in, but I read it anyway because it's of interest to someone I work with.**

* If you don't know my first mantra by now, you're just not paying attention. Less chaos, less noise!

** Because sometimes, the person that needs the most comforting is the one sitting at the desk right next to us.

I can't say these books will necessarily show up on my recommended reading list, but I can say I learned from every one of them, and that not a single one of them was a waste of my time. Each book revealed a condition of human nature or culture to which I was blind.

"Comfort the disturbed. Disturb the comfortable." Let it sink in. Then, figure out what you're going to do about it.

YOU DON'T NEED A TITLE TO BE A LEADER

> **All leaders are leading language communities.**
> *How We Talk Can Change the Way We Work*

It bums me out when I hear people say, "I can't do anything about it because I'm not in charge." Lack of power in an organization doesn't always equate to lack of influence. Have you ever heard of "leading up"? It is how to get things done and motivate others without formal authority.

Mark Sanborn wrote a book about it: *You Don't Need a Title to Be a Leader.* In it, he listed a few ingredients to leading without the virtue of power or position:

- **Self-mastery.** Develop your competence, character and connection. Focused attention on your sphere of influence beats brains, brawn and technology every time.
- **Power with people rather than power over people.** Don't strive to be likeable or capable, but a balance of both.
- **Implementation Quotient.** This is the ability to execute. Don't just talk about what needs to be done; take ownership, and make it happen.
- **Persuasive Communication Skills.** Influence others; don't force-feed your agenda.
- **Giving.** Giving of everything—yourself, your time, your knowledge.

According to the latest research, IQ accounts for only 4 percent to 10 percent of career success.[4] More important are the "soft aptitudes"—the qualities tougher to quantify such as imagination, joyfulness and social dexterity. You may know your stuff, but until you expand your toolbox and master these qualities, you're not going to stand out.

WHAT HAPPENS WHEN YOU GO VIRAL?

Everybody talks about how to create buzz* and go viral. But, nobody talks about what to do when it actually happens.

I remember the first time it happened to us. It was February 2006. And, we were in the middle of a five-week message series shooting it straight about sex. It was not what people were expecting from a church.

To help promote the series, we used billboard advertising around town that featured one image and one line of text. Curious onlookers who visited mylamesexlife.com saw a brief movie asking questions that commonly surround the topic of sex. At the end of the movie, viewers were redirected to our website with more details about the upcoming weekend series called PureSex.

The unintentionally scandalous billboard.

* Buzz is the excitement, energy, anticipation and conversation around a product or service. It's the best type of marketing—when "people are buzzing."

It sparked controversy and conversations around our community and got national attention. The response—positive and negative—was overwhelming. It created a stir. But, I'm not going to talk about the advertising we did or the media attention that resulted from the series. I'm going to answer the question nobody's asking (but should): what did we do with the attention once we got it?

That's the hidden land mine in creating buzz and going viral. Everyone is so busy trying to manufacture it, but few are prepared for it when it comes.

When the media gets hold of something, it can take on a life of its own. It takes intentionality to avoid getting caught in the momentum of a distorted reality.

What happens when you get what you were hoping for? What happens when the crowds come in droves, or the phone is ringing off the hook, or every media outlet is wanting a sound bite? Things can go sideways before you realize it, and then you start feeding the frenzy around you. In the process, you can lose sight of what you came to do in the first place. It's dangerous for anyone, especially if you are in the church.

We didn't set out to create a flurry of activity, but to create a helpful series about sex for people who weren't hearing the truth from anyone, anywhere. We tried a few things that people don't expect from a church, hoping people would be curious enough at least to come check it out. And, that is what created a flurry of activity.*

* But, really, between you and me, we didn't come up with anything that shakes the core of culture. I still can't believe it got the media attention it did. A church teaches what the Bible says about sex and advertises the series with bare feet on a billboard. Is it really that newsworthy? I still don't get that part of it. Anyway, back to the story.

I'll admit, it even threw me off when we started getting calls from the national media. My mind automatically short-circuited into figuring out ways to manipulate a new message with an expanded platform positively. It's easy to freeze like a deer in headlights when you are in the spotlight, but it's just as easy to avoid being surprised if you've prepared for it and stick to your original goal. If you can't say what that goal is, then you're not ready.

When I asked our senior pastor if he was nervous about the television anchors on their way over with a camera crew, here is how he responded. He remembered the original goal:

> **"This is not new for us; it's what we do all day, every day. People matter to God, and we're just loving people one at a time. I'm not nervous. Reporters are people, too. They matter to God, and they matter to us. It's just another day at Granger Community Church."**

Even with a flurry of buzz—local, regional, national—communication isn't complicated. The old rule still applies: less is more. Were we expecting Fox News in New York or Mancow in Chicago to call us about the series? No. But, when they did, our senior pastor was prepared. You see, he knew the message never changed. It wasn't about the billboards, the website, the media or the sex. He started and stayed with the same message from beginning to end: "People matter to God." Plain and simple.

THINK IT OVER
GET BUY-IN: REWRITE YOUR JOB DESCRIPTION

- ❑ What am I doing to show my co-workers I care about what they do?
- ❑ How do my actions portray a different me from the one I want people to see? What "soft aptitudes" do I need to develop?
- ❑ Do I recognize the multiple audiences I serve? Or, am I focusing on one at the expense of all the others? Am I living by the same rules with my co-workers as I do with church guests and members?
- ❑ What am I doing to get uncomfortable to learn about the people who need my comfort?
- ❑ How can I put my own best interests aside to foster a collaborative environment? What gifts can I give others—even if the "gift" is humor, understanding or knowledge? What else can I give?
- ❑ Am I asking questions such as, "How do I convince my boss that we need to…" or, "How do I get people to follow the guidelines?", when I should be asking, "How can I clear hurdles to help my boss do his job?", and, "Am I doing what I need to do so others can do what they need to do?"
- ❑ How can I describe what I do? What am I an advocate for? What change will I make if I am successful?

chapter 12
ASK, DON'T TELL

> **Be curious, not judgmental.**
> Walt Whitman

Effective communication depends on a common vocabulary. Do you know the vocabulary from other departments in your organization, or just yours? Knowing how to carry on a dialogue is more important than forcefully proclaiming what you know. The people in charge are supposed to have all the answers, right? I am going to assume you are smart enough to know that the answer to that question is no. One size does not fit all. The most effective team builders make time to hear from others about their unique audience needs, department hurdles, system problems and team pain points. You will gain insight and credibility by leading your conversations and running your projects—big or small—with more questions than directives.

GET AN IMAGE CONSULTANT

I read somewhere the top three reasons people don't want to work with the corporate communications (or marketing) department are:

1. They're controlling.
2. They don't have a clue as to what I do in my job.
3. They make things harder and get in the way.

Do you know how you come across to others? What are people saying about you when you are not around? Do they think you are controlling, clueless and make things harder? Don't feel bad. Sometimes, it comes with the territory.

But, there is good news in all of this. Perception is reality for some people. And, when you are aware of what that perception is, you can do something about it.

I wanted to know what people were saying about our team, so I had a friend set up a camera at our staff meeting and ask people to answer the question, "What was your first impression of the communications department?" We gave people permission to be candid and assured them the feedback would be helpful. It was an intentional step to demonstrate we care more about how our actions make people feel than how to get them to do what we want.

That exercise proved to be more valuable than I anticipated. I was able to draw upon the wisdom of others with diverse perspectives. When I heard from people who think differently than me, my blind spots were revealed to me.

Here are some of the things that were said:

- "Why do we need them?"
- "Trouble."
- "A force to be worked around, overcome and ignored."

Right then and there, I decided I needed to figure out a way to get helpful feedback like this on an ongoing basis.

For many years, I leaned on two trustworthy friends and co-workers as image consultants at the office: Tim and Jami. They really knew me and my tendencies. I processed with them before I acted—tested my theories, previewed my plans, shared my frustrations and pitched my solutions. **They helped me anticipate problems, offered advocacy when needed and put professional guardrails in place to save me from me.**

Everybody should find at least two image consultants in the workplace: one who helps process *your effect on individuals* and another who helps process *your effect on the crowd.* It's good to have a boss and a peer on your image team—two honest people who are on your side with a front row seat to your strengths and weaknesses. They'll save you from you.

LEADING THE WITNESS

A friend of mine had the title of Communications Director but said it should be changed to Communications Redirector because he spent 50 percent of his time redirecting people and projects. I think it is a fair perspective and good example to follow, regardless of what your role or job title may be.

But, there is tension in that, isn't there? Sometimes there is tension because people are coming to you to get something done. They really aren't interested in being "redirected" or processing more questions with you. Other times, the tension is there because what they're asking you for isn't going to help them. In fact, it might even hinder them—and you know it. But, they didn't come for you to tell them they're wrong. You can't sell what they're not looking for.

Every conversation and project has different dynamics, but if you can find a system that helps you avoid spending too much time creating or too much time regulating, it's a win. **It's never a win if you consistently find yourself playing the role of the communications police.** One way is to start every project with a healthy skepticism and simply ask questions.

Somebody smart told me about the three areas they evaluate for everything they do. I don't remember the *who,** but the *what* stuck, and it helped define a system we used for years at Granger.

* Whoever you are, I'm sorry I forgot about you.

Here are the three areas we filtered to evaluate everything we did and some of the questions we asked along the way:

- **Is it appealing (*context*)?** Are we focusing our energy from the "inside out" or from the "outside in"? Do we know why people will spend their time and attention on us? Does it apply to their life in a practical way? What makes it worth the hassle? Do we know the comfort zone?
- **Is it engaging (*presentation*)?** Are we unifying our message or diluting it? Are we reducing the noise in people's life or adding to it? Are we removing the barriers to entry? What problem is this solving? Does this support or compete with the intended experience for our audience? Are we making things easy for them to find? Easy to understand? Easy to do?
- **Is it helpful (*content*)?** Are we giving people what they want, when they want it? Or, are we answering questions they haven't asked yet? What expectations are we setting that are unrealistic or out of our control? Are we promising something we can't deliver on? Are we making statements as if they were facts, when in reality they are subjective and left to personal interpretation? Are we baiting people with exaggerated benefits?

Sometimes, you are leading the witness with your questioning; other times, the two-way collaboration comes naturally. Either way, the results are breakthrough thinking and new insights from everyone being on the same page.

TEST ASSUMPTIONS

I read an article that reminded me how completely unnatural it is for us to actually get out of our own way. You don't have to read the whole article. Here's an excerpt:

> The human eye has a blind spot in its field of vision. The human mind has something similar. Sometimes you can't "see" new information because you are bound by filters and lack the mental framework to make sense of what your eyes take in. People often see what they want to see and ignore information that doesn't fit their preconceptions. We default to the shortcut of seeing things the same way. People seek stability and security, so seeing things in a way that confirms their beliefs gives them both.[1]

We revert to autopilot, and it takes intentionality and practice to disable that habit of

↓

filling in the blanks

↓

which causes us to make assumptions

↓

which leads to bad information

↓

which leads to bad decisions

↓

which, ultimately, leads to bad consequences.

Those consequences could be a missed opportunity, a damaged relationship, an ineffective outreach, a dying church, a broken life or a fractured community.

Did you remember when the Mount St. Helens live webcam was blocked by a fly?

What an image![2]

The big picture (a massive volcano) is lost because of the speck (an itty bitty insect) on the lens. This happens personally and corporately. The closer we are to the "fly," the harder it is for us to see around it. We lose effectiveness in our perspective, our judgment and our communication when we lose sight of the big picture.

It is our responsibility to acknowledge that nine times out of ten, there is more to the story. Before we leap to conclusions—about a person, a method, a decision, a program—we should learn about it. When we are deliberate about doing our homework, it is amazing the new wisdom, impact and connection that opens up to us.

Untested assumptions, preconceived notions, wrong conclusions—they all impair your sight.

Is there a fly in your environment that is blocking your view? Marcia Connor said, "Help yourself see more by looking past your beliefs." What have we fallen in love with that is not as effective as it used to be? Where are we working hard with little return? What are we doing out of habit without remembering why? Where are we manufacturing energy? Why does my mom cut the ends off her pot roast?*

Of course, the biggest consequence of a clouded lens is the absence of varying perspectives. In her book, *Yes, And,* Kelly Leonard talks about how to generate better ideas and foster more effective communication by incorporating the techniques of improvisational comedy into the business world. She draws on her experience from working with leading talents such as Tina Fey, Stephen Colbert and Amy Poehler.

> When you have a great idea, are you usually open to letting other people tweak or change it altogether? Most people certainly aren't. While it's understandable to want to retain ownership of your idea, controlling your ideas too tightly can deter co-creation and stifle creativity.

* If you don't get this reference, this story might be helpful. You can find a variety of versions on the Internet, but here's the gist: a mother was preparing pot roast for Sunday's big family dinner. Before placing it in the pan, she carefully sliced the ends off. Her five-year-old daughter asked, "Mommy, why do you cut the ends off?" She answered, "My mom taught me to do it that way, and it's delicious, so it must be a good idea." When everyone sat down for dinner, the daughter remembered the question and asked, "Grandma, why did you teach Mommy to cut the ends off the roast?" Grandma smiled and said, "It's the only way I could get it to fit in my small pan."

When working collaboratively, it's essential to be open to allowing others to change or build upon your ideas. This might mean your idea gets entirely transformed, but this is not a crisis. What's ultimately important is not finding your idea, but the best idea!

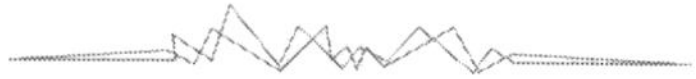

Test your assumptions, dig in with some questions and clean your lens.

> **When there is too much to know, having the right question may be more important than having a ready answer.**
> Liz Wiseman, *Rookie Smarts*

MY TEAM DISAGREES WITH ME

I believe the best team members are the ones who communicate what they think. There is no penalty for disagreement. And, for the record, any team I lead has people who frequently disagree with me. I am often wrong.

But, I don't take that personally. And, neither do they.

I believe in (and thrive in) a culture that promotes honesty with each other about everything. Not honesty in the context of negativity, irrelevant advice or directionless opinions, but honesty in an environment that allows people to express what they see, even if that means they see something different from what I see.

No. Make that: *especially* when they see something different from what I see.

When my team members feel free to be honest about what they see, it allows me to see the entire picture—the sum of opinions—to make decisions about what needs to be done.

I remember one time I asked one of my team members to complete a project. Twenty-four hours later, that team member came back to me and said, "I don't think we should do this. I don't think it will be helpful, and here's why." After I had the chance to ask a few questions, it turns out—they were right.

This only works when the team starts with a unified vision. Because, let's face it—every dysfunctional team out there disagrees all the time. That makes it hard for team members to agree at the end of the day on what needs to be done for the success of the team because the "success of the team" has never been defined. There is no shared agreement that "we are all pulling in the same direction." People only focus on their own part or opinion.

Once you have that unified vision of the big picture, keep the unity by leaving room to disagree about how to get there. This type of culture allows everyone to wrestle with each other over an idea, to see all sides and land on our feet to move forward better, faster and stronger* together than they ever could alone.

You know who else likes a team that's not afraid to disagree with him? Ed Catmull, co-founder and president of Pixar Animation Studios. His successful gig** was built not from telling people what to do, but by inviting opinions from the people around him.

Wouldn't you agree? It's OK if you don't. I won't take it personally.

* Shout out to Proverbs 27:17! Just like iron sharpens iron, friends sharpen the minds of each other.

** 15 Academy Awards and an average worldwide gross of over $600 million per film.

TREAT PEOPLE AS IF THEY'RE SMART

The need for control is a challenge that nearly all of us wrestle with. That impulse kicks in and before we realize it, we tell people how they should think. Just ask my husband if I can ride silently in the passenger seat.* We all have fallen victim to the tendency, and every time we allow the impulse to take over, it magnifies stress and works against us, especially in the workplace.

Nobody likes to be controlled. They like it when you get them thinking, but not when you tell them what to think.

This quote by author and entrepreneur Guy Kawasaki ought to get you thinking:

> "I believe that people are inherently smart. If you provide them with the right information, they are the best judges of the suitability of your product or service. I don't believe you should—or can—bludgeon people into becoming a customer. My recommendation is that you enable people to test drive your product or service in order to make their own decision. Essentially, you are saying, "I think you're smart. Because I think you're smart, I'm going to enable you to try my product to see if it works for you. I hope that it does and that we can do business."[3]

How does this affect your agenda? In essence, you are selling yourself and your ideas as a service product, right? Remember,

* I asked him for you. He said, "Sometimes," which is a major improvement. A few years ago, his answer would have been, "Never."

products and services are "bought," not sold. You can't sell what people aren't asking for. **It's worth asking, do you hear your co-workers saying, "Thank you!", or, "Why do we have to do this?"** The difference between treating people as if they're smart and as if they don't have a brain is the difference between placing blame and sharing, forcing and encouraging.

What a novel idea: treat people as if they're smart, and ask them what they think. They will champion what works and reveal what doesn't.

THINK IT OVER
GET BUY-IN: ASK, DON'T TELL

- ❑ Do I know how I come across to others? Are there times when my message comes across cold and harsh when that is not my intent? Do I act as if I have all the answers, or do I leave room for non-consensus?

- ❑ Am I afraid to hear full perspective from others, or are others afraid to share with me because of my argumentative reaction?

- ❑ People are better art critics than they are artists. How can I give them the ability to comment without having to make them create?

- ❑ Am I so close to the mechanics that I've lost sight of the big picture? What speck on my lens is getting in the way of the big picture? What fly do we have in our organizational environment blocking the view of the mountain? Do we have fly swatters on our team?

- ❑ What opportunities do I have to redirect communications—in my department or for my organization? Do I have a healthy skepticism toward every project until we're able to process the context, presentation and content? Do I evaluate things to make sure they are appealing, engaging and helpful? Or, do I just create things without running them through any filter?

chapter 13
FIND THE YES BEHIND THE NO

> **A man should look for what is, and not for what he thinks should be.**
> Albert Einstein

When you are asked to think differently or change the way you have always done something, does it tend to evoke some type of emotion? Especially when we are already under pressure, it's hard not to react to unexpected directives with anger, defensiveness, alienation or frustration. What do you think happens when we come at others with some new policy, system or restriction? Yep. Like you, they have a hard time not taking it personally. So, try a different approach. When you do find it necessary to introduce a new process or guideline, find ways to implement it as a helpful framework with room to move, not a rigid policy. Instead of coming at people, come alongside them.

FREEDOM WITHIN A FRAMEWORK

One of the guiding principles I champion is "Freedom within a Framework." The "freedom" means we don't boss people around with a list of rules. The "framework" is the guidelines we give them to work within. Or, as my friend Jason Powell calls it in his IT work, "maximize empowerment and minimize liability."* Our job is about harnessing the power of a message and enhancing the experience, not about the do's and don'ts. **There is a balance between centralizing efforts that maximize excellence and creating a bottleneck for the things that don't matter.** Do you know how to evaluate that contrast?

Let's use an example from my early days at Granger as an example. Before social media took off, I was asked to write some blog guidelines for our staff handbook. I looked to IBM, Yahoo, and Sun, as well as a few other churches for inspiration, and wrote my first draft; it was several pages long. Feel free to scan it, but don't spend too much digesting it. Trust me.

Granger Blogging Policies

Some Granger Community Church employees who maintain personal websites and/or blogs, or who are considering beginning one, have asked about the church's perspective regarding these sites. In general, we view personal websites and blogs positively, and respect the right of our employees to use them as an avenue of self-expression and outreach.

As an employee of Granger Community Church, you are seen by our members and outside parties as a representative of the church. Therefore, as in all areas of daily life, a church staff member's personal website or blog is a reflection on the church, whether or not the church is specifically discussed or referenced. If you choose to identify yourself as a Granger Community Church employee or to discuss matters related to the church on your website or blog, please bear in mind that, although you may view your site as a

* Jason Powell is director of Tech Ops for Granger Community Church and one of the founders of the Church IT Network. There are lots of good resources and help to discover at churchitnetwork.com.

personal project, many readers will assume you are speaking on behalf of the church.

In light of this possibility, Granger expects our staff to observe the following important guidelines:

Notify Your Supervisor. If you currently have a personal website or blog, or are considering starting one, be sure to discuss this with your supervisor.

Include a Disclaimer. On your site, please make it clear to your readers that the views you express are yours alone and that they do not necessarily reflect the views of **Granger Community Church.** To help reduce the potential for confusion, we recommend you prominently display the following notice, or something similar, on the homepage of your site:

I work at Granger Community Church. Everything here, however, is my personal opinion and is not read or approved before it is posted. Opinions, conclusions and other information expressed here do not necessarily reflect the views of Granger Community Church.

We recommend a disclaimer if your site is published under your name, even if it is entirely personal and does not mention Granger Community Church or your employment, as readers will inevitably connect your personal life to your professional life.

Respect Confidentiality. You must take proper care not to purposefully or inadvertently disclose any information that is confidential or proprietary to Granger Community Church. Be sure that what you are announcing has been in the weekend bulletin, on the website, or announced from the stage before posting it. Otherwise, check with your supervisor. Any employee who violates our policies regarding confidentiality will be subject to serious discipline, up to and including immediate termination of employment.

Respect the Church and Its Staff. Since your site is a public space, we expect you to be respectful to the church and our leaders, employees, volunteers and members. Any employee who uses a personal website to disparage the name or reputation of the church, its practices, or its pastors, officers, employees, volunteers or members will be subject to serious discipline, up to and including immediate termination of employment.

Respect Your Audience. Don't use ethnic slurs, personal insults, obscenity, etc., and show proper consideration for others' privacy and for topics that may be considered objectionable or inflammatory. Don't pick fights; be the first to correct your own mistakes. Try to add value. Provide worthwhile information and perspective.

Respect Your Time. All time and effort spent on your personal site should be done on your personal time and should not interfere with your job duties or work commitments.

Respect Our Beliefs. When working for a church, it is important to remember that employment decisions will be made based upon our Christian beliefs. If your personal website displays inappropriate images or reflects personal opinions or lifestyle choices that are contrary to Granger Community Church's beliefs, you may be subject to discipline, up to and including immediate termination of employment. For this reason, we encourage you first to seek guidance from your supervisor if you have any questions.

Respect Copyright. You may provide a link from your site to GCCwired.com or WiredChurches.com, if you wish. Contact a member of the communications group for graphics. Please do not use other church trademarks or logos on your site or reproduce material without first obtaining permission.

Follow the Staff Handbook. Consult your staff handbook and staff statement of ethics for guidance. As with other forms of communication, do not engage in personal, racial or sexual harassment, unfounded accusations or remarks that would contribute to a hostile workplace.

Use Common Sense. Use common sense in all communications, particularly on a mass communication vehicle like a website that is accessible to anyone. What you say on your site could potentially be grounds for dismissal. If you would not be comfortable with your manager, co-workers or the executive team reading your words, do not write them.

If you have any questions about these guidelines or any matter related to your site that these guidelines do not address, please direct them to your supervisor or the communications department, as appropriate.

For the record, this is a bad example of freedom within a framework. It went overboard with all of the "discipline" and "immediate termination" references—not to mention that it goes into exhaustive detail with a condescending tone that doesn't really foster a workplace that says, "I think you're smart and believe in you." It's a good thing I ran this first draft by my image consultants.* They sent me back to the drawing board.

Here is the final draft. One page.

* Remember, we talked about this in Chapter 12? Get an image consultant. No, seriously. Do it.

Personal Blog Best Practices

We've developed this document to help equip staff team members who maintain personal blogs and/or post on other people's blogs. These recommendations provide a roadmap for constructive, respectful and productive dialogue between bloggers and their audience (whoever that may be). These are not "rules" and can't be broken. There is no hidden meaning or agenda. We consider these to be "best practices guidelines" that are in the spirit of our culture and the best interest of the church, whether you blog or not. We encourage you to follow these guidelines, but it is not mandatory to do so. It's your choice. We really mean that.

Be Respectful. Be thoughtful and accurate in your posts, respectful of how others may be affected. Even if your site is published under your name, is entirely personal and does not mention Granger Community Church or your employment, readers will inevitably connect your personal life to your professional life. It's a good idea to include a disclaimer on your home page that states your opinions are personal. And, just to avoid any surprises, think about giving your manager a courtesy heads-up about your blog's existence.

Engage in Private Feedback. Not everyone who is reading your blog will feel comfortable approaching you if they are concerned their feedback will become public. In order to maintain an open dialogue everyone can comfortably engage in, welcome "off-blog" feedback from colleagues who would like to respond privately, make suggestions, or report errors without having their comments appear on your blog. Bloggers want to know what you think. If you have an opinion, correction or criticism regarding a blog post, reach out to the blogger directly. Whether privately or on their blog, let the blogger know your thoughts.

Legal Stuff. When you choose to go public with your opinions on your blog, you are legally responsible for your commentary. Individual bloggers can be held personally liable for any commentary deemed to be defamatory, obscene (not swear words, but rather the legal definition of "obscene"), proprietary or libelous. In essence, you blog (or comment on other people's blogs) at your own risk. Outside parties actually can pursue legal action against you for postings. It's probably not a high risk in our line of work, but we thought you'd like to know.

Use Common Sense. Take care not to disclose any confidential or proprietary information.

Press Inquiries. Blog postings may generate media coverage. If a member of the media contacts you about a church-related blog posting, we've got trained back-up available to help you in the communications department.

This would be a good example of freedom within a framework. Notice the difference in tone? The new version communicates, "We believe the best in you and want you to succeed," versus, "We think you're an idiot, so follow this overbearing list of do's and don'ts."

We get ourselves into trouble when we take the top-down approach and prioritize policy over people (unless safety is at risk). Author and executive coach Larry Little says simple language can help you avoid all kinds of emotional disconnects. Likewise, a change in tone can encourage everyone's best, which is what we're going for in the first place. Google's founders created a staff document outlining guiding principles using phrases like, "Don't be evil," and, "Make the world a better place."[1]

I was even caught off-guard recently at how a simple twist on the standard "DO NOT ENTER" or "STAFF ONLY" sign can improve my disposition on the spot:

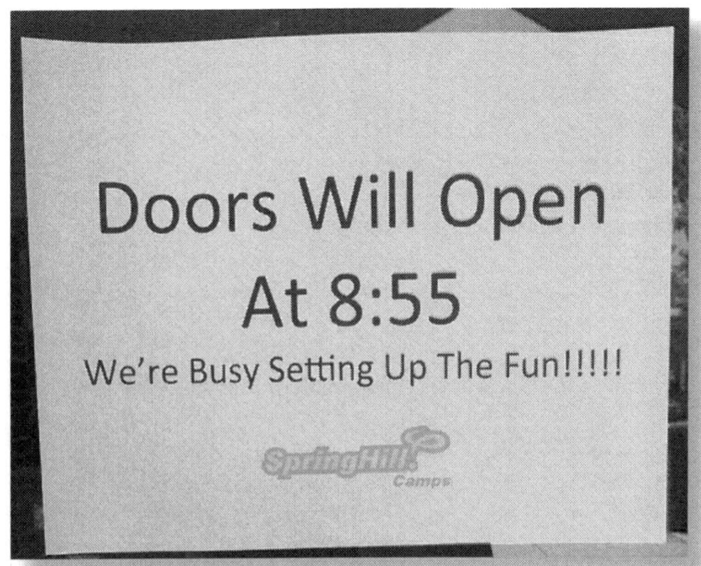

This sign actually made me happy the doors were locked. Who can be annoyed when they were busy setting up the fun?

So, look for where you can throw out a policy and replace it with guidelines. Minimize the list of do's and don'ts. Replace hard lines with soft where and when you can. Assume the best, keep it simple for everyone and champion the value, not the how-to. There's no need to censor or edit someone unless there's a problem.* A heart softened, even in the paperwork, is a two-way street.

* When you do experience the rare and occasional problem, handle it with the individual instead of making an office-wide policy. It's more effective for everyone.

FOCUS ON YOUR SPHERE

Focus on your "sphere of influence." Like Stephen Covey wrote in *Seven Habits of Highly Effective People*, you should have passion for all that you do, but spend the bulk of your energy on the things you can influence and change, instead of the things over which you have no control. (There's that "control" word again.)

The secret of harnessing the power of a message and unlocking maximum effectiveness in an organization is figuring out how to synchronize communication efforts without creating a bottleneck—to coordinate without control. This can be tricky when you have a message of which everybody owns a little piece, with so many delivery channels at their disposal (i.e., mass mailings, email blasts, text updates, blog posts, postcards, social media sites, etc.).

Governing every communication channel is impossible, but synchronizing communications is very possible if you stay balanced and realistic. The yes behind the no? You can't control everything, but if you focus on what you can control—and you're good at it—you'll influence others by your example.

This "focus on your sphere of influence" principle doesn't just apply to people in charge of communications—it applies to anyone who communicates. So, that means everyone. And, practical examples always help. So let's have some fun with a few practical examples.

Let's say you're responsible for communicating ongoing women's ministry news. Don't send mass mailings or email blasts to the entire church mailing list to get the word out. Your mailing list should only include people your news affects. For the record, that list is not every female in your church—just those who have expressed interest.

I speak from the audience perspective on this one. It's counter-productive when I get blasted with mailings and emails for every scrapbooking, dessert tea, retreat or mom's day out because I was born female. Because, when I do, I end up throwing away your mailing, tuning out your announcement and deleting your email without ever reading what it's about because I feel targeted. I don't know about you, but being in someone's crosshairs* is not a good feeling.

So, how do you get the word out to me about events that apply to women without tipping the scales? Relax, and let go. Don't tell me about everything—just the biggest, coolest stuff. I'll care about what you have to say because you're showing me you care about me by putting down the rifle. You'll gain my trust. I'll like you.

But, what about the other 1,000,000 opportunities you think I just HAVE to hear about? Don't worry. I'll learn about them from others. Invest all news in the people you have relationships with, and let them feed me the news through the relationships they have with me. They know my likes, dislikes, struggles and hurdles. They know what applies. If it doesn't, then I don't need to know about it. It's just noise.

Because I worked for a church and know a lot of people who work for churches, my social media feed is flooded with weekend series promos on a regular basis. After so many "best weekend ever" or "don't miss this series" or "must watch" videos, it starts to turn into white noise for me. Not bad promotions—just invisible. But, that all changes when an unpaid endorser speaks up. That jumps off the page and stands out from all the rest.

Just this past week, I was scrolling through the usual feed when this stood out:

* Think "scope of a rifle."

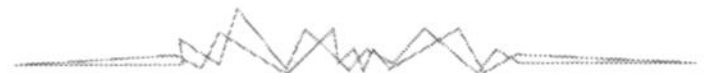

"I spent some time listening to messages tonight while walking. This series by Pete Wilson is spot-on! If you deal with any sort of fear in your life—and come on, who doesn't—you NEED to listen to all the messages in this series! Some things he said have completely made me re-think my thought patterns! I will be having my teenage girls listen to this series as well—it is some of the most applicable stuff I have heard in a while."

It wasn't the church, the speaker or the promo that cut through the noise on my feed (even though they all are top-notch). It was a friend who was sharing her story. You know, I went and listened to that entire series.

Netflix focused their sphere to parents this past New Year's Eve when they created a series of on-demand fake countdowns to help get kids in bed before midnight. Parents (or kids) could even choose their favorite host.

Recently, our church promoted a women's event by targeting the men in the crowd. I thought it was brilliant. If they could sell the benefits to the men, the men would sell (or surprise) the women. It was a creative approach to bring new life to a tired event. And, it worked.

I hope by now that you're picking up on the truth that the responsibility of getting buy-in applies to focused external audiences (i.e., women's retreat promotions) as much as the internal ones (i.e., all-staff email).*

There was a colleague of mine at Granger who hated email. Inbox zero was not one of his life goals. Consequently, I had a hard time getting a response from him whenever I emailed him. If I could text, call or walk to his office, I would. But, that wasn't always possible. Sometimes, Jason—err, uh, I mean this *colleague*—needed to respond to his email. I knew I needed to crack the code, but berating him with more email reminders or nagging him as we crossed paths in the hall was not effective. So, I put my thinking cap on and came up with my money play. I found the key to get him to open and reply when my email hit his inbox. What was my secret?

I changed the subject line. You see, Jason loved his dog, Jack, more than anything. So, if I had an important message that needed his immediate reply, I'd change the subject line to "Jack," or anything about Golden Retrievers. It worked because 1) I took the time to personalize the message to him, even if it was a joke, and 2) I only pulled this stunt for important messages. The rest, I could wait for.

The principle of focusing on your sphere of influence applies as much to the internal audience as the external ones. These habits are interchangeable and necessary with anyone you are trying to communicate with. Focus on your sphere. Figure out what you have control of and look for ways to narrow your focus and personalize your message.

* Your external audience is the public, guests and church members—your mass audience. Your internal audience includes your boss, peers, volunteers—the team you work with. The best practices and principles throughout this book apply to both. You have to be conscious of your overloaded audience on both sides and remember people are people.

WHAT DO I GET OUT OF IT?

A centralized system can free up resources across an organization by routing information and functions through a main hub. Whether it's for your communication channels (online and off), data entry, technical support, ticket tracking or something else, the benefits of a centralized system are:

- Increased accuracy; bad content leads to poor service.
- Better accessibility; easy-to-find resources and easy-to-run reports.
- A seamless flow; no conflicts or dead ends, start-to-finish distribution.
- Continuity; a consistent experience across multiple touchpoints.
- Reduced costs; automated manual processes and no duplicate efforts.

All of this should be a good thing, right? Right. Except, many times, anyone outside the central "hub" perceives the system as a bottleneck for his or her work and a loss of control over his or her job. The average person doesn't associate "systems" with "good times." And, you won't motivate anybody to replace what they're used to with a new policy or rule.

If you're looking for buy-in to generate momentum for a new system across your organization, you have to figure how to communicate what people get out of it, as well as what's at stake if they don't. Be conscientious about the way you say or don't say things to help express your pure intent of collaboration, not control.

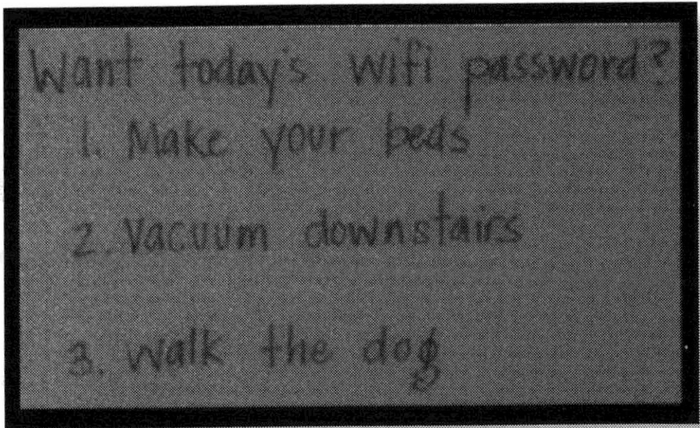

Well played, Internet mom. Well played. She gets the "yes behind the no" concept.[2]

> **If you believe that people hate change and that it is your job to change them, they will hate it. If you believe that people thrive on change and that your job is to unleash it, you will tap into a limitless source of ingenuity, energy and drive that will allow you to take your big ideas into big results.**[3]
> Michael Kanazawa

Say this:	Instead of this:
Connection	Intimacy
Group	Small Group
Volunteer	Fellowship
Team	Committee
Community	Ministry
Guest	Target Audience, Unchurched and Visitor
Volunteer Expo	Ministry Fair
Next Steps	Go Deeper
Invite	Recruit
Opportunity	Need to Help
Experience	Attend
Explore	Commit
Growth	Maturity

Here's an outline to help you organize your thoughts before you roll out that new system:

- **Current reality:** Use practical examples and stories to describe the situation.
- **Solution:** Introduce one item of change and a timeline for the next couple of steps. Transitions will go so much smoother when everyone knows when and where the change is happening. Keep it simple. Allow room for questions. There is a chance you may have missed something.
- **Benefits:** Don't take anything away without giving something back. Either identify a tangible pain point that will be eliminated or a value that will be gained because of the new system.

See how easy that is? "It's not that people hate change...they just hate how you're trying to change them."[4]

WHAT ABOUT THOSE STYLE GUIDES?

Mismatched communications from any organization look sloppy. Using the same logos, fonts, terms and punctuation rules gives your materials a more cohesive feel and professional look. I think a style guide* can be a good tool everyone can benefit from in the end, but it's primarily a hands-on tool for people who coordinate the bulk of your mass communications.

Here are a few things to keep in mind if you are creating a style guide:

- **Make it friendly.** Keep it less intimidating by just covering the basics and keeping it brief.
- **Use examples.** Do's and don'ts side-by-side provide a helpful contrast/comparison.
- **Give rationale.** Don't just give rules without the reasoning behind them.
- **Include at-a-glance pages.** At-a-glance pages add value with things such as a list of commonly misused or misspelled words, five things you need to know for everything we do here, where to go for help, and so on.
- **Don't recreate the wheel.** Use existing published style guides for your foundational reference book.** Your style guide is only a supplement to address the exceptions or specific elements for your environment (e.g., proper names of ministry teams).
- **Allow yourself room for exceptions.** Remember it is a guidebook, not a law book. On occasion, the appropriate thing to do is bend a rule rather than sacrifice a relationship. Consider the scope of the piece (how many people it will affect) to determine whether you need to issue a citation.

* I've included a few sample pages in the back of the book from the Style Guide we created.
** We use the Associated Press Stylebook for English/Grammar and the Wired Style Guide for the Web.

Now the worst thing you can do after creating a style guide is to force-feed it to your staff and volunteers as the "rulebook they have to follow, or else." I'm not saying you would do that. But, it is a mistake made by many well-meaning people. Like, for example, me.

It was an ineffective practice I carried into Granger from the corporate marketing world. I look back and laugh. I actually distributed the style guide to every staff member (and thought he or she would love me for it). That is funny. What was I thinking?

TRANSITIONS: REDEFINING CORPORATE AND INDIVIDUAL WINS

Recently I was facilitating a coaching network, and the leaders in the room seemed to have a lot on their shoulders with the change they were carrying for their organizations. I asked our executive pastor, Mark Waltz, to spend a few minutes with us talking about transitions. I jotted down some notes and am sharing them with you now. Helpful as ever.

Remember, you are the most qualified person to set yourself up for the win. Nobody knows what's best for you better than you. And, most importantly, the relationships inside any transition are the hardest to protect. Bearing down and focusing on the task alone is when people get hurt.

Don't skip these crucial steps:

1. **Sequence.** Pay attention to sequencing. It matters. Don't let go too early. The hand-off is on you. Are you setting up the baton pass so the person running the next leg will win? You were not hired to juggle–you were hired to move the ball down the field. If you are juggling with no sequence, it's a circus act.
2. **Embrace.** Change is happening; embrace it. Don't play the hero role. Don't play the victim. ("I keep my cape tucked." Yeah, right.) When you play the hero or victim, you discount your own ability to work smart and balance well. You also diminish your team's confidence in leadership.
3. **Empower.** Work with and empower team around you. Avoid the two extremes: holding too tightly and throwing it away too fast. Don't power up and take it all on yourself. Don't isolate and put other people at a distance with the attitude of, "I'm going to prove I can do this without anyone's help."

THINK IT OVER
GET BUY-IN: FIND THE YES BEHIND THE NO

- ☐ How am I helping people do what they need to do without going through me?
- ☐ Am I falling into control-freak traps such as top-down attitudes, prioritizing policies before people and dictating mandates as if I have all the answers? How can I relax and let go to give people the room to move?
- ☐ Can I identify the balance between maximizing excellence and creating a bottleneck for the things that don't matter? Do I know the difference between the two?
- ☐ What am I enforcing company-wide that may be more appropriate for a smaller group of people? What is my sphere of influence? What people should I be intentionally pouring into individually, rather than trying to address corporately?
- ☐ Do I operate as if it is my job to change people, or to unleash the change already inside of them?
- ☐ Am I paying attention to the relationship side of the transition as well as the task? How can I minimize the emotional disconnects?

chapter 14
BRING THE GLUE

> **As human beings, we like to operate in small tribes. If there's not someone creating and communicating the overarching, simple plan for the larger organization and getting every-one to pitch in, people start breaking down into small tribes and pursuing their own goals and agendas.**
> Dan McGinn, *Quick and Nimble Culture*

One of the most important keys to the success of any organization is to have all parts working and pulling together, independently aligned to the same vision. This is easier said than done. Focused on their tasks, individuals have a hard time understanding how their daily decisions affect the bigger picture, and how their actions have a domino effect (good and bad). Even when everyone starts in the same place, by the end of one busy day with normal demands, vision drift starts to happen. When you bring the glue, you can more easily keep people connected to the same vision, fostering collaboration and cross-training that move people from spectator to participant. Find ways to create mirrors that show the parts what the whole is doing. That is the glue.

MISPLACED LOYALTIES

I purchased a Roman shade and found it damaged when I opened the package. I had the receipt. I had the original packaging. I had the product. But, the store wouldn't let me exchange it. They said that since it had been more than ninety days, they "couldn't help me."

I explained that the shade was purchased for a remodeling project that was just completed. It sat unused in the box until I decided to return it. All I needed was an exchange.

"Sorry, that's our policy."

Again, I showed my receipt.

"Sorry, your receipt is expired." (Since when does money expire?)

"We don't carry that product anymore. It has no value to us." (Yes. They really said that.)

"Sorry. That's our policy." (This should be illegal. Really.)

They tried to brush me off and told me to go home and call the toll-free customer service number. I asked them to call it for me while I was standing at the desk. Surprise, surprise. After twenty minutes on the line, even they couldn't get through to a live person. Uh, huh. That's what I thought.

Here's my point. This business was more concerned and more loyal to their "policy" than they were to the customer. When I heard the customer service representative say, "That product has no value to us anymore," it was obvious to me they could care less about customer service. Never mind the fact they sold me damaged goods. After ninety days, it's not their problem—it's mine. No matter what. Happy trails. How is that for customer service?

That experience, and others like it, make me wonder why more businesses don't empower their employees to champion customer satisfaction. The Roman shade was just over $60 with tax. If I were in charge, I would allow employees to make judgment calls under a certain dollar amount to retain happy customers.* I would teach them about the common sense of spreading goodwill and making a better store experience that makes people want to tell their friends—and come back.

Do we keep this in mind when we deal with our teams? Do we say things such as, "That's our policy," "Sorry, I can't help you," or, "That's not the way we do things here"?

Do we empower our staff and volunteers to use common sense and break protocol to create great experiences? How many "Do Not Enter" or "No Drinks Permitted" signs are in your lobby? Are your greeters coached on how to smile, read body language and make people feel welcome?**

I once read about a great service-centric policy at Griffin Technologies:

> **"Some companies make you jump through hoops to get a replacement for a malfunctioning device. Griffin Technology takes a rather different approach to the process by issuing replacements right away and asking only**

* Someone told me the managers of each Enterprise Car Rental shop have the authority to quote their own rate to an individual customer even if it means a lower quote than what is advertised. That's a great example of empowering a staff to deliver customer service.

** In his book *First Impressions*, Mark Waltz has a whole chapter of "wow-busters." I think it should be required reading for every church.

> **that the customer destroy the non-functioning device 'in a creative manner' and send photographic evidence. One customer took the challenge to heart and decided the only sane thing to do would be to take the obvious route: blow it up with model rocket engines."[1]**

Griffin Technologies gets it. And, typically, this model works from the inside out. It's how superiors treat their employees and co-workers treat each other that ultimately affect how a staff treats the customer.

If you make this your mode of operation, you'll have the insight to use rules in context and develop relational collateral. If you don't, people will do everything they can to work around or ignore you.

Here's how you can avoid advocating rules over people:

- **Lead with the listen.** Give leaders, peers and subordinates the space to be heard. See what you can learn from their feedback before you push the policy.
- **Drop the hall monitor badge.** It is all about relationships. Show people you are human and for the team—not for your-self.
- **Be available.** Open your door, come in the office, take off your headphones, walk around and don't hide behind email or voicemail.
- **Smoke what you're selling.** If you want other people to care about your job, show others you care about theirs. Support what they're doing—with nothing to gain, no strings attached.

Guidelines and rules are good when they bring people together. Remember who you're serving.

SAVE MONEY ON ASPIRIN

Have you defined the communication "win" for your church yet? If you can't identify the one, shared win that applies to everyone, you'll end up swimming in chaos with a headache from the noise of insatiable, individual desires. Sound familiar? I thought so. So, start by defining your communications "win."

Before you start, a few guidelines might help save you some hassle. Many times when I walk people through this exercise, it takes a while to get the hang of it.

At first glance, you may think any of these are worthy definitions of a shared communication win:

- A noticeable increase in overall community;
- More engagement during specific events, campaigns or ministry opportunities;
- Increased attendance, giving and social media engagement;
- Unchurched people connect with God.

In reality, they are great wins. But, they aren't exclusive to communications. When you're outlining your shared "communications" win, try to avoid connecting it to anything connected to a single event, department or output you're not in control of. Instead, identify the win you can land, no matter the channel or scope size. Think *more operational* and *less aspirational.* And, again, *more outcome, less output.*

When I led the communications team at Granger, we defined our win as this:

> **To simplify everything our audience sees, to make their life easier and more rewarding in every interaction with our church and ministries.**

Sounds good, doesn't it? I still believe in it. It's good stuff. While it's not something we could measure externally with precision, it was the perfect internal filter to make good decisions and get all players working together (instead of against each other).

When you have a shared definition of the win, you can start streamlining your work toward that win with less noise, less headaches and less aspirin.

CONSTANTS YOU CAN COUNT ON

If you've already defined the overall communications win for your church (see page 182), your next step is to write down the communications constants; the values you live by. In other words, document how you communicate with each other (internally and externally) to bring the *what* to life.

A communications constants list might look something like this:

- **Clear.** It's not what you say; it's what people hear. Remove distractions to simplify everything your audience sees or touches to help them effortlessly connect with Jesus and others. Eliminate the fluff and get to the point. Answer the essential questions: who, what, when, where and how.
- **Portable.** Put the mission within reach for everyone. Make it shorter, visual, specific, scanable, searchable and categorical.
- **All Access.** Easy to find. Easy to use. Easy to share. We use universal language and avoid insider jargon (and acronyms). We focus on the needs of our guests, not the needs of our ministries.
- **Well Done.** If it's worth communicating, it's worth getting it right. When you're trying to enhance the experience and harness the power of a message, every detail and touchpoint matters, up front and behind the scenes.
- **Guide.** We use communications not as a final destination, but as an effective vehicle that helps people find their way from A to B. We treat our deliverables as way-finding tools that help people navigate their way to what's next in the process, not everything at once. We draw people into the content we have to offer—allowing them to absorb and seek on their own terms.

- **Whole.** The whole is greater than the sum of its parts. We are a unified church working toward one common vision we all own, not a federation of sub-ministries working for our own agenda and goals. We don't strive to be fair, but rather appropriate based on scope.

Once you're done, abide in those values like your own little personal quality control department. Whatever you do, don't check the box, file it away and forget about it. After we documented our values at Granger, the team unified and time marched on. Old staff rolled off the team, new staff rolled on, volunteers came and went and ministry ebbed and flowed. A few years went by and those carefully crafted values had settled their way into the background of all the activity we were trying to keep up with.

When did we notice? When the noise started to increase again. Not only did we stop feeling the win, we started feeling more pain. It was then that we looked around and said, "Hey! What happened to our values?"

Remember, your values are the rules you live by daily. Keep them in front of as many stakeholders as possible to make sure there's more than one person, or one department, with their eye on the ball. Don't let them settle into the background.

YOU ARE REPLACEABLE

What is the number one way to get the word out about your church (and keep people coming back)? This is for everyone—ready? Set. Go!

- Flyers? No.
- Website? No.
- Social media? No.
- Banners? No.
- Advertising? No.
- Free stuff? No.

None of these things are bad. They all can help. But, they are supporting characters. They become ineffective when you give them the lead role in your story.

The number one way to get the word out about any organization is through the words and actions of the people in the organization. Every person in your church is like a walking billboard. How they act, work, talk, respond and treat people represents you and leaves a lasting impression on others.

It doesn't matter if your music is great. Or, if you've got fantastic design skills. Or, if your pastor is the most charismatic person on the planet. If your customer service is average or bad, your church is replaceable.

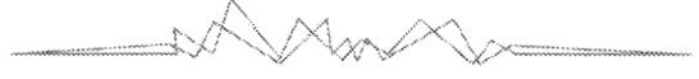

Author and blogger Andy Sernovitz explains why:

> "Sooner or later, most customers will leave you for a company that treats them better (even if the price is a bit higher or the product is a bit worse).

> "I've had an eFax account for almost ten years. It works great. But for the third year in a row, they raised the price—without telling me or even sending a receipt. I just noticed the bill on my credit card. It wasn't an issue of price. It was an issue of trying to sneak something past me. The first time was annoying, the second time I got angry. This time I walked."

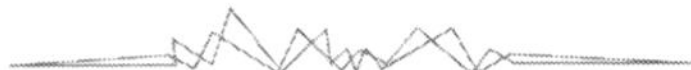

I will boldly go here: **before you spend money on marketing, spend money improving the people skills of your people.**

Making somebody a better artist or writer isn't really what I'm talking about here. It's the human communication behavior issues such as:

- How to treat others under pressure.
- How to turn negatives into positives.
- How to redirect rather than issue a "smackdown."
- How to deal with difficult people.
- How to focus and capitalize on people's strengths rather than complain and get aggravated by their weaknesses.

Your people might need the most help with these social graces. The return on investment will blow your mind. The sustainability can't be challenged. People skills count more. And, some of your people might need help with those skills. A little shared training goes a long, long way.*

* Looking for a place to start? Read some books together. I've included my current must-read list in the back of the book.

TOUCHY-FEELY DATABASES

I watch organizations treat their database like a technology add-on when, in fact, it should be treated as the central lifeline for customer care. It's the digital "turnstile" for a person's connections, history, growth, safety, milestones, relationships as well as a place to find trend indicators and organizational health reports. Contrary to popular belief, the database is very "touchy-feely."

That is why we didn't assign a technology guru or someone with mad data entry skills to be in charge of our database. We handpicked a representative from each department to form a SuperTeam.

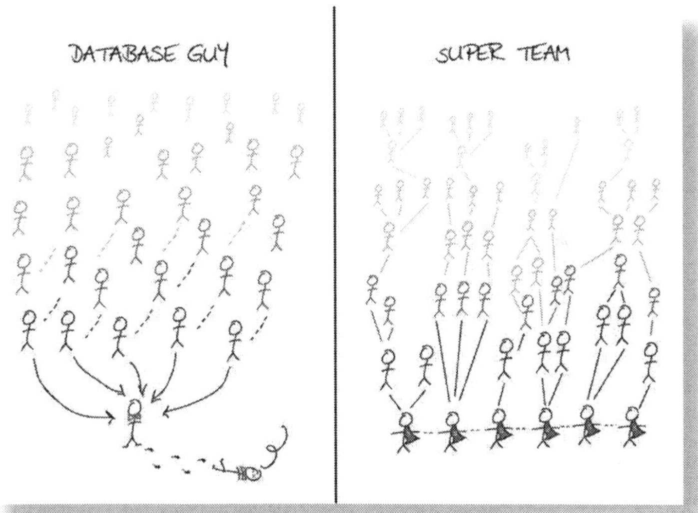

Eliminate the bottleneck and empower advocates across the entire organization.

As our organization grew, we found ourselves in a place with multiple community touchpoints—each serving up a different experience, off and running in its own direction, capturing (or not capturing) its own data. When individual teams track data their own way—using systems unique to their team only—critical information gets lost or isolated. People and projects proliferate, as does confusion. This creates real liabilities for the organization as a whole.

Here are just a few examples:

- People with preschoolers or who no longer had children at home consistently received letters addressed, "Dear Middle School Parent."
- A family in our church lost a child. For several weeks in a row after that horrendous loss, a check-in tag for their deceased son would print at the kiosk when they checked in their other children.
- We had volunteers with serving restrictions due to moral or security reasons who would move from team to team repeating their offenses because there was no central filing or flagging system to alert team leaders.
- We had several people flagged as core covenant members who had not been active in the church for over six years.
- We had people who had moved out of state still flagged as attendees.
- We mailed sensitive and confidential contribution statements to the wrong addresses.
- A widow in our church continued to receive correspondence addressed to her deceased husband.

Each event was not only discouraging and painful for the members affected, but also for us as a staff. We wanted to reinforce how much the church really "cares" with our customer service, not just with our words. The only way to resolve the issues was to connect the multiple areas to operate as part of a larger family.

Management guru Peter Drucker makes the best case for it:

> **"The successful company is not the one with the most brains, but the most brains acting in concert."**[2]

Getting our database in order and assembling a SuperTeam to protect it was the only responsible thing to do.*

While there is one central champion for the database, the one champion doesn't carry the entire workload. Currently, our Tech Ops director pulls the SuperTeam together on a regular basis (for an hour or less) to share stories that provide the needed people background for data decisions and the systems that support them. They ask questions, clarify intentions and learn the benefits of relevant functionality. With a "shared ownership" mindset, they help discover how the pieces fit together and determine next steps to maximize operations church-wide, not just for one department.

Most conversations are about topics of shared impact such as volunteers, staff responsiveness, event registrations, sensitive data, lists, reporting, check-in, and so on. When the SuperTeam isn't meeting, each member operates as a power-user for his or her area of ministry. They watch for and address inconsistencies in data and reporting. They champion the team approach to increase the effectiveness of our whole organization, in every department.

Is somebody flying solo with your database today? Your database will only be as effective as the communication between departments. Set the stage for your SuperTeam strategy sooner rather than later. Ask that person flying solo to partner with just one other champion and operate as a team unit to put technology to work for you, not the other way around.**

* Our SuperTeam includes at least one person from each major ministry unit. Think about including one key stakeholder from arts, family, administrative support, IT, facilities, connections, counseling, finance, communications, missions, etc.

** It's not an exact science. Our SuperTeam is in a constant fluid state, learning and adapting as we go. Your SuperTeam may only start out with two people. Ours did.

NO MAN IS AN ISLAND

Like John Donne said, "No man is an island." In an organization, inter-dependencies exist among team members, resources and assets. We thrive when we have the ability to negotiate among these dependencies and find a middle ground where empowerment and decision-making align. To pull it off, though, we need to be clear about what we need from each other and realistic about the challenges that come with it.

This is an easier task if you start out by sharing the same mission across your organization. If we are all working toward the same goal, there will be less territorialism and more teamwork. Every ministry, every team, every employee, every volunteer leader should be looking at the same mission statement. Multiple, unique mission statements across a single organization create chaos and conflict.

Besides that, it breeds an environment where people operate in ministry silos. You know what I'm talking about, right? The connections department runs its own campaign and doesn't see what's being communicated by the volunteer areas, the missions area, the student ministry area, the children's area, the men's and women's ministry teams, the pastor, and others. The missions department does its own thing. The student leaders do their own thing. And, the pattern repeats throughout the whole church.

The result? **Individual departments end up competing against each other with a carnival communication style, trying to out-yell or out-explain.**

One mission statement transcends specific departments to unify the whole. Our mission statement at Granger is, "Helping people take their next step toward Christ...together." That mission statement applies to every ministry. It doesn't mean the mission statement action steps can't be tailored to a specific audience. But, everybody is working toward the same goal, like-minded, maintaining alignment. "Helping students take their next step toward Christ...together." "Helping women take their next step toward Christ...together." "Helping people afraid of dogs take their next steps toward Christ... together."

We are all on the same page. No man is an island.

> **If you want to go fast...go alone. If you want to go far...go together.**
> David Gergen

WHO IS IN CHARGE OF WHAT?

One of the most common questions I get from people trying to organize their communications departments is about what a communications department "controls." People want to see how the boxes and lines are drawn. It is a hard question to answer because it's not the hard lines and boxes that make a communications department succeed. While a traditional org chart hierarchy is necessary for obvious reasons, it's not what drives daily operations. Communications is more dynamic than a flowchart or assembly-line format.

The best team cultures are all about shared ownership. Through the years, the creative, production and communications functions at Granger have never been segregated departments, nor have they ever been morphed into one department with one person in charge. It has always been something between the extremes with continuous conversations happening between key stakeholders who were intentional about collaboration and cross training.

The lines between communication, creative and production arts can be blurry. Although it might be easier if everyone stayed in his or her own area, or just one area, it just wouldn't be as effective. Sometimes you have to trade efficiency for effectiveness.

I'll use a *very* loose football analogy to paint a picture of how our teams divided up supporting communication responsibilities:

- The Creative Arts team executes the plays on the auditorium platform. That affects the live performance arts, technical arts and service media.
- The Connections team executes the plays for the best environments. That affects events, guest services, retail, etc.

- The Communications team executes the plays for anything you read, touch or click beyond the auditorium stage. That affects promotions, print materials, the website, etc.

Each department has a coach to help carry the vision, call the plays and keep the ball moving down the field on a daily basis for his main area of responsibility (think offensive line, defensive line, special teams). The rest of the staff team has specific positions to play in the game but can be moved around, depending on the situational landscape.

There's a lot of overlap between the teams, but each team has special skills, disciplines and rhythms they play by. Even when there are differences of opinions, every player is for the same team, with the same mission, vision and values.

For big-picture direction, the executive team speaks into a creative brief* for each series. Individual jobs are easier and group efforts more unified because team members aren't left to operate independently, trying to "define" what is communicated. Everything ties back to the creative brief—it unifies promotions, the service production, the scheduled programs out of the weekend, and so on.

Once that message on the creative brief is complete, each coach has what they need to guide their respective teams to protect, support and extend that message.

Of course, at any time, the players on the turf may make mid-play course corrections, yielding to the direction from the team owners (the senior and executive pastors). They care about the team running the plays as well as the fans.

* Of course there's a sample for you in the "back of the book." I can't believe you even asked.

I told you it was a loose analogy. But, it paints a picture that might help you see how a cross-functional team approach could work in your environment, too. While sometimes it may take longer, the end result yields more inter-departmental collaboration, helps champion values over projects and communicates ideals over events.

> **I tend to think of organizations as eight-cylinder engines, and in every organization you ask: 'How many cylinders are actually firing?' If the answer is five or six, then you think, 'How awesome and powerful would it be if we could unlock those two or three extra cylinders?'**
>
> Adam Bryant, *Quick and Nimble*

FIVE MISSING INGREDIENTS IN GREAT TEAMS

I've had the chance to work with and be a part of many great organizations over the years in a variety of sectors: local advertising, regional business consulting, national technology products and global financial services. Along the way, I've had the privilege of working with outstanding leaders and talented professionals who continue to impact who I am and how I do things to this day. But, the twelve years on staff at Granger Community Church was where I learned the most about being part of an enriching team culture.

While there's no secret to success, there are a few ingredients I've observed that are consistently missing in successful, healthy teams:

- **Superstars.** There are no lone rangers and no individual heroes. As a matter of fact, when I was hired at Granger I was told that I would not be celebrated for or held accountable to my own personal success, but for the success of the team around me. That's how important team is to the culture.

  It's a no-ego-fly zone.

- **Games.** All roads are closed to the whambulance and complaining is as fashionable as PalmPilots and mullets. We assume the best in each other and make sure all talk stays about the issues, not people. If there is something that needs to be worked out, it's handled simply and directly.

  It's a no drama zone.

- **Posers.** There are no boxes to fill, but roles that are shaped around individual gift sets. Sure, there are tasks to be done, but it's not for the goal of assembly line production or identical thinking. Individuality is a good thing and comparisons are a waste of time. Strengths are celebrated. Weaknesses are starved.

  It's a no clone zone.

- **Failure.** Creativity, progress, growth and risk are encouraged. When mistakes happen, I might get coached to try it different next time, but I am never in trouble.

  It's a no fear zone.

- **Put-downs.** Value is communicated in different ways to different people. And when the focus is mission, not mirroring, the whole culture changes. Harry Firestone said, "You get the best out of others when you give the best of yourself."[2]

  It's a no superiority zone.

THINK IT OVER
GET BUY-IN: BRING THE GLUE

- ☐ Where are my loyalties misplaced? What changes can we make to prioritize people over policy?

- ☐ Are we ineffectively trying to get the word out about our organization because we fail to equip the people in our organization? What tools and coaching can we provide to help unify words and actions?

- ☐ Do we have people in place who can effectively balance individual needs and corporate needs? Are we maximizing that skill set to maximize the benefits of a team?

- ☐ What things are we promoting as an organization that foster silo ministry? Individual mission statements? Separate budgets? Individual marketing plans? What can we do with our systems and conversations to eliminate a competitive "us versus them" spirit between departments?

- ☐ Are there opportunities in our structure to replace efficiency with effectiveness? Can we blur the lines to open lines of communication between departments and stakeholders?

- ☐ What ingredients do I need to add or remove from my team culture?

chapter 15 GETTING FROM HERE TO THERE

> **Form a common bond to help you carry on through the maze and mash of days where maps have not been drawn.**
> Dallas Clayton

Implementing a communication strategy happens through a series of steps that build on each other. But, the concept is all-encompassing, and the task at hand is so big it's hard to know where to begin. After all, you have a job to do, and the ministry around you will not allow for a hard reboot—you can't just stop the bus and rearrange everything. However, you could use some handles, next steps and tools to help evaluate and organize the internal chaos. Some places to start and some early wins can help.

MAKE TIME FOR CONVERSATIONS

> **The key is not to prioritize what's on your schedule, but to schedule your priorities.**
> Steven Covey

If your job has anything to do with communications, then you need to look at your schedule and see how much space you are leaving for conversations. (Hint: everybody's job has something to do with communications.)

Now, I'll just bet there are a few of you out there who just read that, and now have this in the thought bubble above your head:

> That's just great, in theory. But, how am I supposed to get anything done if I'm wasting time having conversations?

If you're not leaving time on your calendar—the white space—for impromptu conversations with the people you work with, then don't expect to see organizational and relational change any time soon. You see, momentum advances over time through a series of conversations; it is not a one-happy-chat or email event.

If you're still thinking to yourself:

> I can't afford the time for that.

I say, you can't afford not to. Every conversation you invest in on the front end makes the next project go smoother. At the end of the day, it's all in our perspective, isn't it?

If you want to promote forward movement, progress and next steps as an organization, it begins with your own personal habits, not your tasks. In other words, you can't get what you *could* have until you let go of what you *do* have.

I listened to Mark Beeson share with a group of leaders feeling the pressure of leading change. He outlined five key areas of individual work that most impact organizations. I took notes. If you're feeling stuck, focus on these areas—it could be your turning point:

- **Attitude.** Without this, you will hurt yourself.
- **Relationships.** Without these, others will hurt you.
- **Persistence.** Without this, problems will defeat you.
- **Priorities.** Without these, the insignificant will hamper you.
- **Credibility.** Without this, no one will follow you.

You in? I thought so. I know you can do it. Just be prepared. There will be times when you lose momentum and experience reversal of hard-won gains. Along the way, some days you will feel strong, and some days you will feel defeated. Stay the course and keep working on your personal habits. It's a "give up to go up" moment.

LEADING CHANGE

People need people. They bring out the best and worst in us, don't they?

When it comes to our jobs, our neighborhoods, our communities and the lasting impact we make on this life, significance cannot happen without people. And, growth can't happen without change. But, change makes people whickety whack.*

Author Eric Hoffer said, "Every new adjustment is a crisis in self-esteem." Have you ever been there? Quit lying. I know you have.

Awareness of this reality is where successful change management comes in. To lead change, you have to be conscientious about leading up, sideways and inside. And, that's where the advice I got from a very smart leader** about this topic comes in.

I've taken what he shared with me and added some ideas of my own to create the following list:

- **Build alliances.** Add some people to your trust pool who have not always agreed with you. Adopt a no-turf policy and treat people as partners.
- **Be realistic.** Old habits and existing problems are not easily solved. Don't give yourself or others false hope by pretending they will be.
- **Go to the source.** Rather than making grand assumptions and quick decisions, make a point of visiting others where they work. See how they operate. Judge first-hand what the problems are before you attempt to develop solutions.

* You can quote me on that. Go ahead. W-h-i-c-k-e-t-y w-h-a-c-k.
** Ladies and gentlemen, meet my husband—Mark Meyer. He has more smart insight that provokes personal and group excellence at maximeyer.com.

- **Go unrecognized.** Look for ways to help others succeed. Find ways to make them look like rock stars, even if that is not in your job description.
- **Be different.** It's normal to blame, complain and let others worry about fixing problems. Don't be normal. Make it about others, not yourself.

If you are trying to lead change in any organization and influence any group of people—students, churches, businesses, communities, a family—in today's uncertain times, this list applies to you.

FIVE THINGS TO REMEMBER ABOUT WINNING PEOPLE OVER

The toughest thing about fresh insight, new strategies and a personal passion to see it through is waiting for others to catch the wave! Am I right!?

Here are five things to help you stay the course as you try to champion a dream, win people over and lead change of any kind:

1. **It's a trip, not a destination.** (Play on words intentional.) If we're focused on the outcome, we'll constantly feel the frustration instead of the win. But if we focus on the people over the project (or the process over the event), relationships will gradually strengthen and each little step will feel like a win on the way to our ultimate goal. Remember, it's less about technique than it is attitude.
2. **It's not "all or nothing."** We can't change everyone and everything at once. There will be several steps forward and a couple steps back along the way. Don't let that discourage you if it's more of an exception rather than a rule. It's like a golf game. You're going to have some good holes and some bad ones. When you have a bad hole, move on to the next one. It's not game over.
3. **Focus on a few rather than many.** Rarely, if ever, is a one-size-fits-all rollout effective. We are going to have to spend more time with some leaders than others. And what works to get buy-in from one person won't work with the next. It takes time to navigate through the personalities to discover what motivates and builds trust for each person. Invest in constant and ongoing conversations with your leaders all along the way. Not to get things done, but to keep process-

ing the wins, the struggles and the cost of standing still. And then pick one or two leaders to invest in to build trust and create some key, visible wins. It will attract others to the cause and you'll gain momentum and speed.

4. **It takes time.** God isn't just using this change to help improve others, He's using others to help change us. Whatever time you think it's going to take to roll something out, multiply that by at least three. It's not linear, but multidimensional. There is more at play than we can see. With faith, persistence and a commitment to self-awareness, the stars will start coming into alignment down the road. It took me about three years to start to see a tipping point for some initiatives I've led in the past—*not* three months.
5. **You're never done.** While you will build more advocates in your camp along the way, it will never be a 100 percent consensus. You will need to keep refining your vision casting, coaching and redirecting skills. There will always be new team members or difficult personalities unwilling or unable to change. What you can look forward to, though, is the hard part being 20 percent of your job instead of 80 percent.

ARTISTS AND LEADERS NEED EACH OTHER

With all the progress we have made in the church around our creative efforts, there seems to a companion to that growth. I see and hear about mounting frustrations between "leaders" and "creatives" as they try to understand each other.

I pulled two lists from separate sources to help show what the two groups have to learn from each other:

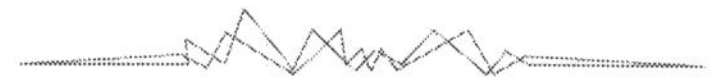

How leaders should act like artists:[1]

1. **Artists constantly collaborate.** It's a common occurrence for artists to host exhibitions together—the so-called "group show." Even in the context of a solo show, the artist works with the gallery owner, the curator, the framers, the installers, the lighting person, and the publicist to bring their vision to life. Every exhibition is a collaboration to the nth degree.
2. **Artists are talented communicators.** The whole point of a work of art is to communicate something—a thought, an idea, a feeling, a vision. More explicitly, the artist frequently gives a talk to explain the thought process behind the artwork. Engaging the audience in a meaningful, expansive dialogue is often critical to the exhibition's success.
3. **Artists learn how to learn together.** Perhaps the reason why artists collaborate and socialize so well is that they learn in the studio model: ten or more students in the same room for hours on end. Bonded together in a personal space of intimate self-expression, they come into their own through the familial ties of the studio setting. When interviewed recently about the differences in her education at Brown and

at RISD, one student who is getting a dual degree from both institutions said, "At RISD there's a lot of learning from your peers. Brown (in the classes I've taken so far, anyway) is about listening and note-taking in class."

How artists should act like leaders:[2]

1. I speak my mind and fight for ideas but refuse to play the "victim" when my idea doesn't win out.
2. I do what's in the best interest of the team and the project, even when it costs me something.
3. I do the little things that matter even when I could feasibly cut corners.
4. I stretch myself to see things from new points of view.
5. I think strategically, even when I don't have all the information I want.
6. I don't point fingers, talk trash or assign blame behind closed doors.
7. I have something that guides my creating beyond comfort and preference.

WHERE DO I START?

"We don't have excellence in church communications because we don't have the money for it." That is not a reason; it's an excuse. I hate it when I hear people say that. And, I hear it often.

A small budget is not a hurdle to jump. It does not prevent you from WOWing your guest and it does not restrict you from adding value.

I read* about the budget restraints Steven Spielberg faced when he was shooting *Jaws*. He was just getting started in the business and didn't have a dream budget. He wanted to film an incredibly lifelike, mechanical great white shark attacking and consuming weak humans en masse. The problem? An incredibly lifelike, mechanical great white shark was incredibly expensive.

So what did he do? He didn't make a bad movie and blame lack of money for it. He had to think of something else. Something creative. Something cheap. He decided to shoot the unsuspecting swimmers from the shark's point of view (with scary music), and it resulted in a classic.

Resist the temptation to blame the reason you can't make improvements on the lack of financial resources. Here are some things you can do right now to improve your church communications with no additional budget:

- **Have conversations.** Lots of them. Ask questions and spend time listening to peers and leaders to build relational equity. Help coach the people you work with to stop thinking about more output, and start thinking about desired outcomes. Invest in brand handlers by finding ways to overlap with other

* I first read the story in Biz Stone's book. I bet you didn't know Biz is one of the co-founders of Twitter.

departments. Cheer them on and support their efforts relationally. Find reasons to meet that have nothing to do with a logo, e-newsletter, platform announcement or deadline.

- **Create a style guide.** A consistent stylistic approach will have a positive impact on the overall excellence of your church.
- **Identify your specific audience.** You need to know who you're talking to before you know how to say it. Learn about people's worldviews and draft a personality profile that describes the demographic and psychographic of the type of person you're tailoring your content and design for.
- **Document your communication values.** Define your win and how you work together to get there. What is the method and context of your environment? Find out and write it down.
- **Outline a promotions framework.** Determine what is communicated, in what priority, using what channels. Not all news is appropriate for everyone.
- **Reduce emotional overload.** Create less and say more. Look at everything you're creating and find something to cut. Look at the number of words (or pages) in your bulletin. Look at the amount of content you're asking people to trudge through on your website. Edit it all down.
- **Tell your story like one family.** Look at the materials you're printing and the content you're posting online. Do you use a common vocabulary? Create a "voice" tool that all stakeholders use as a guide so you're speaking with one voice.
- **Implement an official proofing team and process.** Have a group of volunteers review everything for accuracy and consistency before it's printed, posted or distributed.
- **Assemble a group of consumer advocates (or secret shoppers).** This team of critical thinkers and advisors can experience your materials from "the shark's perspective" and provide input into what's working and what isn't. Have them attend the service as an outsider and provide feedback

about the things you can't see yourself. Have them test drive your website or scan your social media to find ways to improve flow and ease of use.

- **Revisit legacy communication vehicles.** Just because they were top priority before, doesn't mean they're top priority today. Take inventory of all your print and online materials. Evaluate whether people are still using the materials the way they used to. Make changes to what's included, how it's organized, how often it's distributed, etc. Start revising and improving by biggest scope first.
- **Create conversation tools (not policies).** Create pre-emptive checklists to cut down on busy, or reactive, work. Practice finding the yes behind the no with templates people can use, timelines people can see and pre-defined channels that cut down on subjectivity and streamline activity.
- **Rewrite your job description.** Look for ways to help people do what they're already trying to do. Look for ways to nurture and encourage. Look to implement empowering tools or advice that leaves people saying, "Thank you," instead of, "Why do I have to do this?"
- **Be social.** Use Facebook, Twitter and Instagram (in that order) to leak series themes early, new volunteer job openings and the inside scoop about new event opportunities. Think less broadcast and more access.

Pro tip: Courtesy is easy on the budget. Treat others the way you would like to be treated.

Everything on this list works in a church of ten or ten thousand. Budget or broke, this list is a great place to start. You have resources. You just need to use them in better ways.*

* You can find samples for the audience profile, communication values, promotional priorities and a few sample pages from our style guide in the "back of the book."

AS CHAOS SPIKES, THE CLUTTER DOESN'T HAVE TO

Sometimes with ministry and life, things are going to get chaotic. It's not always bad and it's not always in your control. My pastor once talked about the chaos you'll experience in any delivery room when a baby is being born. He was telling the story to help train us up in how to manage the seasons of chaos and noise that come with change, growth and life. He said, "If you're looking for quiet and calm all the time, go live in a funeral home."

OK. I got the point. And, it did help me recognize *all* chaos is not *all* bad. (But, less chaos is always good.)

So, if it's not eradicating chaos, what are we supposed to be working on? Our *response* to the chaos. When we react to the chaos with panic, that's when the wheels come off the bus and we add to the problem with *more* noise and *more* chaos.

Wait! What's the difference? For this exercise only, chaos can be good and clutter is bad. See if this helps:

Chaos	Clutter
Influence	Control
Movement	Institutional
Outside	Inside
Less concerned with telling the whole story than the same story. Embraces different expressions bound by common objectivesand values.	Cannot make rational decisions about what is useful and what is not. Unaware anything is wrong with piling more on, as long as the client likes it.
Committed, engaged groups of activists motivated by common values, unquenchable passion and innovative agility that seed personal social change.	Obsesses about every piece and is compelled to fix it. Structures of order that tend to compete for resources, resist collaboration and bind creativity with control that hinders growth.

My friend, Rob, once talked about the "Sumo-ninja" church. He even had a bad graphic to drive the point home:

Obviously he was having some fun with it, but the whole challenge for us was to aim to be a sturdy and agile organization. I like it. **And, now, the tension I feel from one day to the next makes more sense. It's supposed to be this way.**

As chaos increases around you, it's tempting to hold things tighter, but better to let things go. Work toward harnessing the power of a message and enhancing an experience instead of creating a list of do's and don'ts. There's a balance between centralizing efforts that maximize excellence and creating a bottleneck for the things that don't matter.

See, the more you think about it, sumo-ninja works, doesn't it? **Respond to chaos with agility and precision.**

PICK UP YOUR BATON

Several years ago when I was on vacation, I had the opportunity to hear speaker Christine Caine[3] from Australia deliver a message at Healing Place Church in Louisiana. How is that for a blending of cultures—a girl from Indiana listening to a girl from Australia speak to a group of people in the Bayou? The message struck a chord, and it has set off a continued reverb in me that hasn't stopped since I heard it. It keeps coming back to me. I think it was important, so I'll do my best to paraphrase.

She talked about how, in relay races, it doesn't matter how fast, how big, how strong or how fantastic you run your leg of the race—an entire team can be disqualified because one person doesn't hand the baton over right.* To drive the point home, she replayed how the American team lost their race in the 2004 Athens Olympics. They had the fastest qualifying team in the women's 4x100 final. They should have won. Everybody knew they were going to win. But, guess what? They lost. All because of the baton exchange.**

God uses your life as part of a bigger plan. This race is not an individual sprint. The church is interdependent—running together on a relay team. So what are we to do?

- **Strip down.** Runners strip themselves of any unnecessary weights so they can run unencumbered. What do we need to strip? The baton exchange between Saul and David should have been seamless, but Saul didn't deal with issues of his heart, so it became a complex affair.

* In case you forgot, remember Paul likens our life to a relay race in 1 Corinthians 9:24–27.

** There's a twenty-meter exchange zone where it's legal to hand over the baton. If you don't hand it over the right way, the whole team gets disqualified. During the race, between runners 2 (Marion Jones) and 3 (Lauren Williams), the race was lost because of a bad exchange.

- **Look at the team.** Don't forget that others have come before you. You had better remember this because if you don't, you just might forget there are still others to come after you. It's not just about the here and now, but about your part of something bigger that God's been doing throughout all of eternity. We can lose sight of what's going on if we forget that we didn't just arrive. A whole generation that came before you paid a massive price for you to be here. And, others will come after you, counting on you to pass the baton to them.
- **Take your place.** Everything will take longer than you think. In a relay, runner #4 doesn't get his nose out of joint when he doesn't get to run with a baton when the gun goes off. He understands there is a process that happens before he gets the baton. In churches, in life, God sees beyond what we do. He sees runner #4 in position years before he or she is ever there. Too often though, we get out of place, and we will never be in position for the baton because we didn't take our place at the beginning.
- **Play it out daily.** It is not the responsibility of politicians, the media or educational systems to carry the baton and leave a legacy for this generation. It's our responsibility, and God is trusting us to carry the baton. What does this look like every twenty-four hours in our seemingly insignificant life? It doesn't matter if you're a full-time homemaker, a corporate CEO, in manufacturing, a teacher, a student, a librarian or a doctor. Every normal daily decision counts. Don't cheat, quit or give in to shortcuts others accept—don't drop the baton.
- **Endure.** Things get hard. You'll get tired. The heat will turn up. You'll want to give up. Though we are confronting great obstacles and hurdles as a church (and individuals), this is not a time to give up. It's a time to endure and get our eyes

off our temporal circumstances because there is a bigger picture. It only takes one generation to drop the baton and sever the next generation. Don't be surprised when a generation ends up living as if they came from nothing and live for no reason, and they're going nowhere when that's all they've been taught.

- **Go back and pick up your baton.** We are all interdependent on each other. It doesn't matter if you can run like Marion Jones because unless you run your 100 well, cross the line and exchange the baton successfully, the whole team loses. Get back in your lane, take your place and start running your race to finish your course. If you dropped a baton, go back and pick it up yourself. Don't wait for somebody else to do it. Jesus gives us forgiveness for our past, a brand new start today and hope for our future. So, don't waste time feeling like a loser if you dropped a baton. Just go back and pick it up.

We are here for a purpose. The baton is in our hands.

THINK IT OVER
GET BUY-IN: GETTING FROM HERE TO THERE

☐ Is something holding me back from the change I need in me, so I can change my team? Is it unresolved heart issues: anger, fear, insecurity, jealousy and so on? Or, is it another type of weight: culture, tradition, expectations or outdated habits?

☐ If God looks at the 21st century and says, "Who was the church?" what will be my reply? What will happen to this nation on my watch? What personal and organizational habits are status quo that I am willing to change?

☐ What could I have if I let go of what I do have?

☐ Am I conscientious about leading up, sideways and inside? How can I improve? Am I reacting to my own self-esteem crisis or helping others through theirs?

☐ Do I use lack of money as an excuse not to do better?

☐ Do I approach problems like a hit-and-run car accident—only identifying the problem without following through with the possible solutions and approaches to get there?

☐ Who is the one person I need to meet with right away? Who do I need to enlist to help me?

☐ Am I a leader that needs to act more like an artist or an artist that needs to act more like a leader?

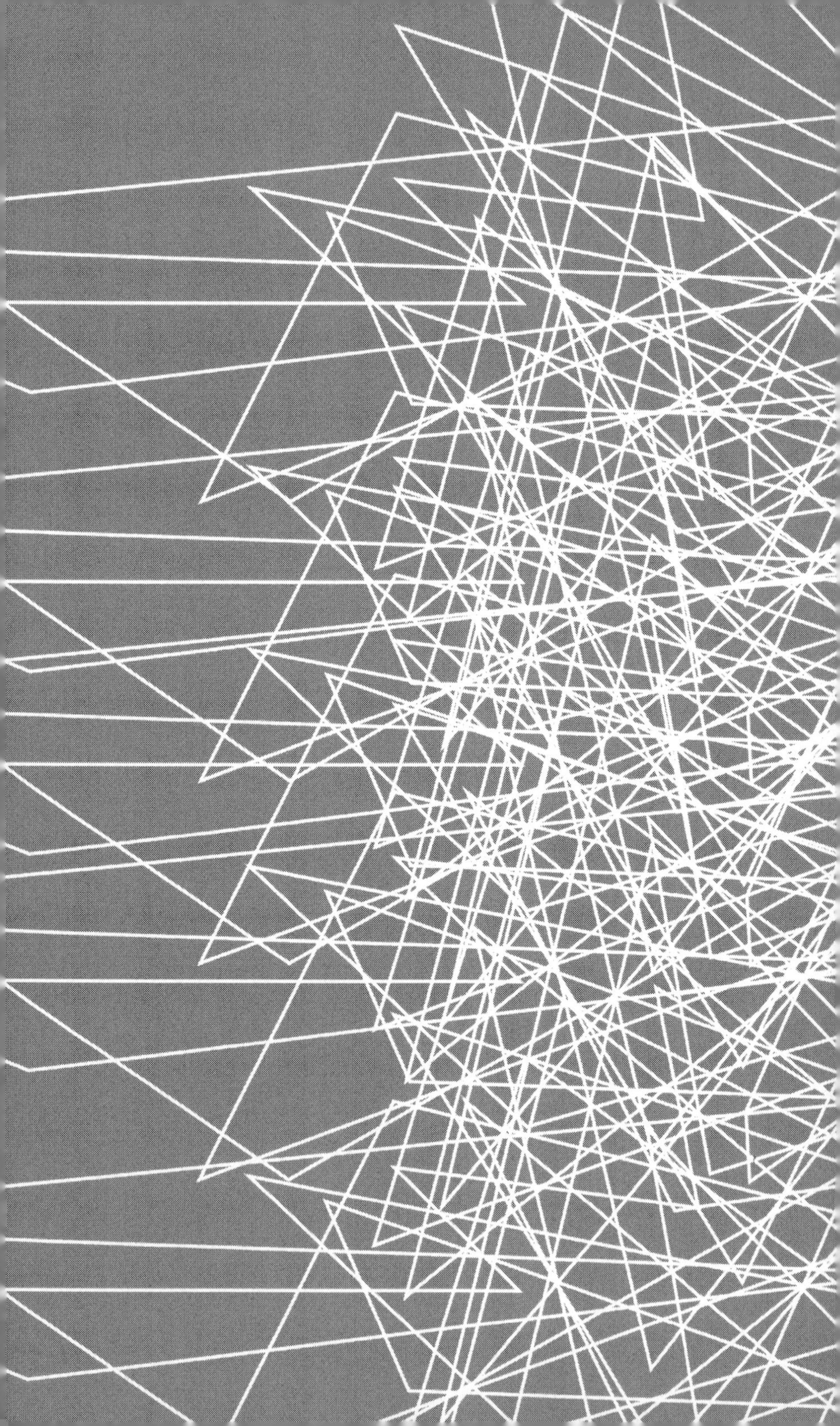

BACK OF THE BOOK

I believe the world is one big family, and we need to help each other.
Jet Li

The following pages include sample communication team documents from my own toolbox, as well as a few examples from other churches and trusted sources. Thank you to these churches and organizations for sharing their work to offer additional inspiration, help and support.

The idea here is to share a few of this book's concepts in practical applications. My hope is that you can customize and improve upon these examples in your own work and setting.

KEM'S MUST-READ LIST

These are some of my favorite reads. Personally, these titles (some old and some new) have been the most influential and helpful sources for me in leading others, setting expectations and organizing a strategy around communications. I assure you this list is incomplete and out-of-date, because I'm always reading and always learning. But, this is a good list of some greats.

- *Generational IQ*, Haydn Shaw
- *Simple Rules*, Donald Sull and Kathleen M. Eisenhardt
- *Untitled*, Blaine Hogan
- *Coherence*, Richard H. Bailey
- *The Brand Gap and The Brand Flip*, Marty Neumeier
- *Fairness is Overrated*, Tim Stevens
- *Traction*, Gabriel Weinberg and Justin Mares
- *Be Our Guest*, The Disney Institute and Theodore Kinni
- *Stuck in a Funk*, Tony Morgan
- *How to Wow Your Church Guests*, Mark Waltz
- *All Marketers Are Liars*, Seth Godin
- *Unique*, Phil Cooke
- *Orbiting the Giant Hairball*, Gordon Mackenzie
- *Don't Make Me Think*, Steve Krug
- *Make a Difference*, Dr. Larry Little
- *Necessary Endings*, Henry Cloud

DIY EFFECTIVE COMMUNICATION CHECKLIST

- ☐ What's redundant or unnecessary? What can I cut? Or, save for later?
- ☐ Has my messaging acknowledged real-life circumstances to motivate a next step? What do I want to happen as a result of this communication? What is the one thing I am asking people to do? Is it clear?
- ☐ Who is the one person I'm writing this for? Am I tailoring my content for them? Am I answering the questions they would ask, or am I subjecting them to the information I think they need to know?
- ☐ Have I made the essentials easy to find: who it's for, what it's about, when and where it happens and how I get in? Have I included basic contact information?
- ☐ Does my communication pass the "so-what" filter? Can it simply and honestly answer the ultimate question in my audience's mind: "What's in it for me?"
- ☐ What's redundant or unnecessary? What can I cut? Or, save for later?
- ☐ Have I asked someone to proof this for accuracy as well as meaning? Am I saying what I mean to say?
- ☐ Would someone who is new to my church understand the words and names I've used?
- ☐ How will people use this communication? Does my method fit the context of where and how people will read and experience the material? Are they on the go? Sitting still? Distracted? Focused? In a hurry? Relaxed?
- ☐ Is it easy for people to take action on this information? Are there too many options that make the next step hard to find or hard to use? Is the most important information at the front?
- ☐ Have I thought about all the areas this communication will affect? Have I included the right stakeholders in the loop for awareness, advocacy, registration, follow-up, guest services, etc.?
- ☐ What's redundant or unnecessary? What can I cut? Or, save for later?

A CHANGE IN APPROACH STARTS WITH A CHANGE IN MINDSET

Not this...	But this...
publicize	connect
control	cultivate
push	personalize
censor	coach
capture	liberate
prescribe	influence
conform	channel
send	release
broadcast	listen
output	outcome
educate	motivate
inform	transform
fairness	strategy
react to imagined urgency	respond to real needs
varied expectations	shared win
information	action
perfection	progress
calendar driven	values driven
task vantage point	holistic vantage point
design drives excellence	flow drives excellence
efficiency	effectiveness

FREE MARKET RESEARCH

- bea.gov
- nielsen.com
- barna.org
- census.gov
- milkeninstitute.org
- knowthis.com
- censusscope.org
- factfinder.census.gov
- zipwho.com
- fedstats.sites.usa.gov
- personapp.io
- ubersuggest.org
- sba.gov
- bls.gov
- ssa.gov
- federalreserve.gov/releases
- ftc.gov
- dol.gov

SIMPLE SOCIAL MEDIA FRAMEWORK

There are different components to a social media strategy; all posts are not treated the same. Sometimes it helps to organize social media efforts around a grid that outlines the purpose of each channel, who is responsible for what/when, etc.

A simple framework goes a long way; it doesn't need to be over-complicated. As you can see, there is not one "staff owner" of the strategy, but rather a team approach for maximum impact. In this example, Bonnie is the only staff person. David and Amanda are both volunteers.

WHAT	Communications	Community	Promotions
WHY	Information, Event & News Stream	Relational, Guest Services, Live Support	Marketing &Advertising
WHEN	Weekly, heavy M–F	Daily, heavy on the weekend	By campaign or project need
WHO	Staff Led	Volunteer Led	Staff & Volunteer
HOW	Routine Process, Pre-Scheduled	Realtime	Pre-Scheduled
POINT	Bonnie	David	Amanda
WHERE	Facebook/Twitter	Facebook/Twitter	Facebook/Twitter/ Instagram

PROOFREADING CHECKLIST

There's more to proofing than grammar—accuracy and context are just as important in the review process.

1. Accuracy. Cross-reference dates and days of the week with a calendar and with what's listed on our website.

2. Audience. Do you answer the most important question our audience asks: "What's in it for me?" Leo Burnett, leading advertising executive of our generation, says, "Don't tell me how good you make it. Tell me how good it makes me when I use it."

3. Basics. Does it include the necessary basics of: Who, What, Where, When, Why and How (call to action)? Did you include contact information?

4. Consistency. Check punctuation, style and formatting to make sure it's consistent throughout the piece. Compare to the Style Guide to review capitalization, indents, type size, typeface, leading, alignment, page breaks, hyphens, etc.

5. Names. Double-check accuracy on names, phone numbers and extensions; cross-reference with more than one proofer. Test URLs to make sure they work like you say they will.

6. Spelling. It's critical. A single misspelling can convey the information or audience is not important or valued. Do not rely on your computer's spelling and grammar checkers. Sometimes it helps to read backwards. You'll catch the mistakes you normally miss.

7. Terminology. Step into the shoes of a new guest and consider what their reactions may be to certain phrases and the appearance of the piece. Do certain words sound "cliché" or "too implied?" If so, it is likely the message may not be understood by our audience. Don't be lazy. Be clear.

8. Tone. Are we accurately representing the intended meaning? Question anything that may raise a red flag to you. It's better to address the potential problem than to allow it to go unchecked. Don't assume someone else will do it.

BIG PLANS AND NEXT STEPS

The following page includes a sample of a working grid I created to help me to look at our plans and decisions across the life of the church at a higher level. It covered the five purposes of our church, as well as major venues and campuses for one year. I used it as an at-a-glance resource to manage my workload and project weighting appropriately, as well as a conversation tool in leadership meetings about our balance in programming. It's not fancy. But, it got the job done. And, the 30,000-foot view helped us lift our focus beyond one calendar event at a time to answer the big-picture questions, like:

- Are we leveraging cross-departmental / cross-functional opportunities?
- Are we planning ahead for vision casting and storytelling?
- Are we balanced as a church in our programming / purposes?
- Are we prioritizing the right thing, at the right time, across every campus?
- Are we keeping the main thing, the main thing?

BIG PLANS & NEXT STEPS

JANUARY					
Worship/Series	*Growth*	*Outreach*	*Connect/Serve*	*Vision*	*Kids & Students*
LET HOPE IN	• Communion 4-5	• Food Drop 25 • Penn Snowball 19 • Family Mission Mtg	• Men Connect 31 • Women Connect 30 • VolunTOUR	• Year in Review • Kids/Students • Generosity	• Summer Missions Mtg
FEBRUARY					
Worship/Series	*Growth*	*Outreach*	*Connect/Serve*	*Vision*	*Kids & Students*
ONE OF A KIND	• Life Foundations 5 • Financial Peace	• Community Center • ELC Open House	• Couple Connect 28 • Discover GCC	• BAR Project Update	• Superbowl • HS Retreat • Seniors/Parents
MARCH					
Worship/Series	*Growth*	*Outreach*	*Connect/Serve*	*Vision*	*Kids & Students*
I DON'T WANT	• Life Foundations • Marriage Foundations • Parenting Foundations	• Workshops • Magazine	• Volunteer Expo • Family Event	• The Table • YouVersion Plans	What's going on 28

Early Learning Center LaPorte Elkhart All-Skate

Big Plans & Next Steps Page 1 of 4

AUDIENCE MINDSET

Here is just one iteration of an audience profile we used for a season to help teams plan and brainstorm. The profile helped get beyond static demographics to the psychographics of their target customer to define and prioritize message series, graphics, music, furniture, promotions, copywriting and everything in between.

- Primarily unchurched
- Educated
- Likes his/her job
- Enjoys what is "different" and "unique;" innovators on the edge
- Values creativity
- Likes the "buzz" of a big crowd, but the intimacy of friends
- Searching for truth; for something more in this life
- Doesn't want all the answers; "get me thinking, but don't tell me what to think"
- All about the "experience"
- Skeptical of institutions, government and organized religion
- Independent thinker; values individual expression and personalization
- Prefers the casual and informal over the formal; "be who you are"
- Over-extended in time and money
- Consumer mindset; accustomed to being served
- Wants to do the right thing, on their terms

PRIMARY CUSTOMER VALUES

gcccreative

PRIMARY CUSTOMER VALUES

- **MAN**
- **MARRIED**
- **CHILDREN AT HOME**
- **EDUCATED**
- **SUCCESSFUL**
- **SPIRITUALLY THIRSTY**
- **FRIEND OF SOMEONE ALREADY HERE**

EXCELLENCE
- Clean
- Organized
- Well Prepared
- Tech Savvy

EXPERIENCE
- Fun
- Customized
- Consumer
- Relationships/Friends

TRUTH
- Authenticity
- Cares That The Church Is Real, Even If He Is Not

FREEDOM
- Free From Burdensome Debt
- Free Time
- Choice
- Options

SIGNIFICANCE
- Life Has Meaning
- Kids Find Success

COMMUNICATIONS ARTS TEAM BIG PICTURE

It's important to provide people with good information, so they can make good decisions about where to serve with their time and talents. And, making a decision like that is a process, not a one-time conversation or print piece transaction. When people start by browsing all opportunities to choose from, they don't need detailed documentation about every department, every team in that department and every role on that team. What they need are some big-picture tools that help them scan and move toward a general area of interest.

The following page contains a sample overview we used for a season as the introduction to what happens on our Communications Arts team. The purpose of this tool isn't to "close the deal," but to provide a tool for tier 1 fact-finding and self-sorting.

BIG PICTURE | COMMUNICATION ARTS

What we do:

- Proofing, copywriting, editing and content coordination
- Graphics, design, page layout, project management
- Digital, web and mobile technologies and statistics
- Online church and social media advocacy and strategy
- Story chasers, curators, scoopers & spillers
- Customer care, product support and special events that resource and encourage other church leaders
- Wayfinding—online and off

Who we are:

- Group of teams who lead and leverage design, language and digital media to eliminate information obesity and simplify complexity across departments and campuses.
- Resourcing people, nurturing community and encouraging spiritual growth with insanely excellent usability and flow—online and off.
- A unique and inspiring culture full of workhorses who are energized, demanding, encouraging and a little weird—we have a deep appreciation for a serious sense of humor under tight deadlines.
- Fast, focused and high interactive people with a passion for building "WOW" experiences with no office hours or geographic boundaries.
- Team oriented. No matter how great the talent, this is a no-ego fly zone.
- Passionate, heated, diverse and competitive in our brainstorms, observations, ideas and opinions. But, at the end of the day—the *why* trumps the *what* and we work as one—every time.
- Dual platform with love for both mac and PC users. We are a bi-partisan team with no annoying fan boys.
- Super talented in a general way, empowered to bring our own unique blend of skills to the table to get a job done.
- Leaders of people or projects—working together to rally the troops or the tasks.
- Self-directed, driven people who love being out on the cutting edge—finding new ministry and connection opportunities through new technology and communications.
- Initiators who have a healthy degree of impatience with idleness and consistently push ideas and projects forward.
- Servants committed to supporting and fulfilling the mission, vision, values and goals of the church.

COMMUNICATION VALUES

How we communicate with each other brings the *what* to life.

Rules of Engagement (Communication Constants)

How we communicate with each other and our audience brings our values to life. By protecting these constants, we are able to help people take their next step towards Christ and each other. **Abide in these Communication Constants like your own little personal quality control department.**

Simplicity is the ultimate sophistication.
Leonardo da Vinci

The win? To simplify everything our audience sees, to make their lives easier and more rewarding in every interaction with our church and ministries.

- **Guide.** Communications isn't the final destination but a vehicle that helps people find their way from A to B. Our deliverables are wayfinding tools people use to navigate their way to what's *next* (not everything at once). We draw people into the content we have to offer allowing them to absorb and seek on their own terms.

- **Clear.** It's not what you say, it's what people hear. Remove distractions to simplify everything your audience sees or touches to help them effortlessly connect with Jesus and others. Eliminate the fluff and get to the point. Answer the essential questions: who, what, when, where and how.

Stay alert. This is hazardous work I'm assigning you. You're going to be like sheep running through a wolf pack, so don't call attention to yourselves. Be as cunning as a snake, inoffensive as a dove.
Matthew 10:16

- **Portable.** Put the mission within reach for everyone. Make it shorter, practical and actionable.

- **All Access.** Easy to find. Easy to use. Easy to share. Make things searchable, scannable. Avoid insider jargon (and acronyms).

- **Well Done.** If it's worth communicating, it's worth getting it right. Every detail matters, up front and behind the scenes, when you're trying to harness the power of a message. Think about the whole flow before, during and after the experience.

- **Whole.** The whole is greater than the sum of its parts. We are one church with a common mission, not a federation of sub-ministries. We don't strive to be fair, but appropriate based on scope. "Equal time" is not valued or considered. We focus on the needs of our guests, not the needs of our ministries.

ALL CHURCH VALUES: BEFORE AND AFTER

Over the years, our church values never changed, but they did expand. We "improved" by adding values that were missing, applied an attractive layout and enhanced each value with clever copy and corresponding scripture for each. It had grown to a solid piece we were all proud of and happy with. All stakeholders were in agreement that "this covers everything."

Before:

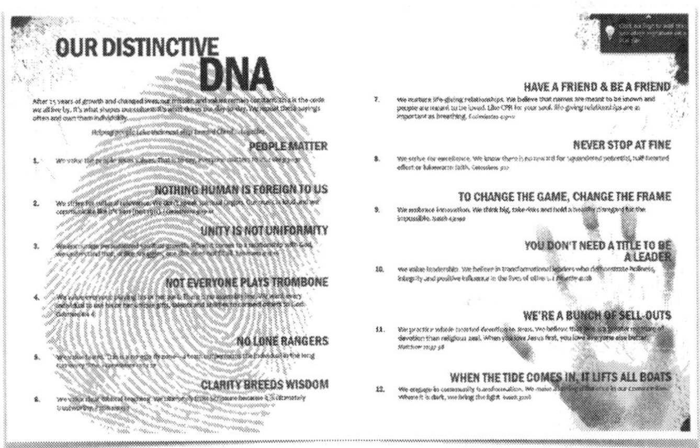

OUR DISTINCTIVE DNA

1. PEOPLE MATTER
2. NOTHING HUMAN IS FOREIGN TO US
3. UNITY IS NOT UNIFORMITY
4. NOT EVERYONE PLAYS TROMBONE
5. NO LONE RANGERS
6. CLARITY BREEDS WISDOM
7. HAVE A FRIEND & BE A FRIEND
8. NEVER STOP AT FINE
9. TO CHANGE THE GAME, CHANGE THE FRAME
10. YOU DON'T NEED A TITLE TO BE A LEADER
11. WE'RE A BUNCH OF SELL-OUTS
12. WHEN THE TIDE COMES IN, IT LIFTS ALL BOATS

Here's the problem. None of us could recite our values from memory. Even though they made us feel really good about ourselves, our values weren't at work in our daily lives. Real values aren't aspirational, they're operational. And, when they're easy to remember and recite, people own and live them—corporately and individually.

After:

COMMUNICATION PRIORITIES

Promotional Layers

As individual departments operating as part of a larger family, here's the filter we use to help triage for promotion emphasis and methods.

HIGH	MEDIUM	LIGHT
• All skate! • Church-wide • Applies to 80% of the congregation.	• Many • Large venues and demographics • Applies to 50% of the congregation.	• Limited • Small • Targeted by location, life-stage or sensitivity.
• Champion: Communication Arts crafts & drives the promotions • Stakeholder: Ministry leader or event owner collaborates with direction and context	• Joint Effort: Communication Arts drives the conversations and crafts the promotions in partnership with the ministry leader (or event owner)	• Champion: Ministry leader or event owner • Stakeholder: Communication Arts works in supporting role with coaching and resources

WHERE PROMOTIONS SHOW UP BY EMPHASIS

Promotional Aids

	HIGH	MEDIUM	LIGHT
GCCwired.com home page	X		
GCCwired.com other pages	X	X	X
Weekend program	X	X	
Calendar	X	X	X
Atrium table	X		
Banners	X		
Signage	X		
Social media	X	X	X
Media release	X		
Bulk mailings	X		
Pre- & post service loop	X	X	
Video	X		
Invitations	X	X	
Print piece	X	X	
Platform announcement	X		
Check-In	X	X	X
The Feed	X		
Reporting	X	X	X
Live stream	X	X	
Graphics	X	X	
The Table	X	X	X

This framework is typical, but actual methods may change on a case-by-case basis.

WHAT GETS COMMUNICATED

How To Decide What Gets Communicated

	Applies to Large %	Applies to Small %
Big Potential Impact	A	B
Small Potential Impact	C	D

Communications Tool	A	B	C	D
Stage Announcement	●			
Promo Video	●			
Email	●			
Text Notification	●			
App Push Notification	●			
Brochure/Flyer	●	●		
Sign Up Table	●	●	●	
Social Mention	●	●	●	●
Web Site	●	●	●	●

ChuckScoggins.com | CFCClabs.org

BIG IDEA WORKSHEET

This tool was used for a season as a comprehensive snapshot around each series. It helped equip the teams who write copy, execute creative concepts, build promotion campaigns, create themed environments, prepare for next-step follow-up, etc. Eventually, we moved the tool online, but it all started here, in a simple document:

REELDATING

Week	Title	Big Idea	Next Steps (in bulletin)	Key Promotions—from platform (No more than 2 each weekend)
Aug 26/27 Beeson	**Hitch** *When do you make a commitment, and what does it look like after you do?*	*A commitment should be based on your values. Once you make the commitment, your behavior should change.*	◦ *Core classes: Sept 5* ◦ *Starting Point for Singles Only: Sept 11* ◦ *Baptism: Sept 10*	◦ *Core 101-401: Saturday, Sept 5* ◦ *Baptism: Sept 10* ◦ *Singles Starting Point: Sept 11*
Sept 2/3 Beeson	**Meet the Parents** *In today's crazy world, how do you prepare your kid for dating?*	*Prepare your kids well so they will have great relationships leading toward a great marriage.*	◦ *Core classes: Sept 5* ◦ *Baptism: Sept 10* ◦ *Starting Point for Singles Only: Sept 11* ◦ *Second Saturday: Sept 9*	◦ *Core 101-401: Sept 5* ◦ *Baptism: Sept 10* ◦ *Singles Starting Point: Sept 11*
Sept 9/10 Beeson	**A Lot Like Love** *We're just friends. Or are we? How do we start dating without letting things get out of hand?*	*Principles that will take you from a friendship toward marriage without messing up. (Includes appropriate boundaries).*	◦ *Baptism: Sunday!* ◦ *Starting Point for Singles Only: Sept 11*	◦ *Baptism: Sunday!* ◦ *Singles Starting Point: this Monday, Sept 11*
Sept 16/17 Beeson	**Mr. & Mrs. Smith** *Just because you are married doesn't mean you should stop dating.*	*Dating gives you the time that is required to maintain faithfulness in your marriage.*	◦ *Starting Point for Married Couples Only: Oct 2*	◦ *Married Couples Starting Point: Oct 2* ◦ *Next series: (Fall Launch)*
Sept 23/24 Laurent	**How to Lose a Guy in 10 Days** *What are the signs that you are in a relationship that is taking you down?*	*Don't enter a relationship thinking you can change the other person. Determine your non-negotiables and don't compromise.*	◦ *Starting Point for Married Couples Only: Oct 2* ◦ *Men's Retreat: Oct 13/14*	◦ *Married Couples Starting Point: Oct 2* ◦ *Men's Retreat: Oct 13/14* ◦ *Next series: (Fall Launch)*

Let's face it—everyone has either been on a date or will be soon. Yes, even you married couples. Isn't it about time that the church starts a conversation on this topic? After all, the Bible is incredibly practical and has so much to help us in our relationships. How do you recognize Mr. Right? How do you see past the first impression to discover who's really behind that smile? Or how do you find a mate when you can't even find a date? And if you're married your dating reality may seem as elusive. How do you keep the romance alive? And how do you help your kids avoid some of the same mistakes you made in your dating days?

Join us at Granger Community Church for some straight talk about sex, dating and romance – whether you're married, single, single again or a student. For five weeks, we'll look at the advice of Hollywood and compare it to the teachings of the Bible.

SERIES BRIEF

gcccreative

WEEKEND SERIES BRIEF

SERIES: Fight | WEEKEND: What are You Fighting For

5 words describing the series/wknd:	1 sentence or question describing the series/weekend:
• Purpose • Grit • Resolve • Pro-active • Challenge	There is a battle and you're in it; how will you respond?
What do we hope people say? • I can do this • I must do this • I need help • I need training • I'm not alone • I'm not going to lose another fight • It's worth living and dying for • I have to come back next week	**What cultural references apply?** • Game of war • ND Football • Cinderella Man • New Star Wars • UFC • Cancer • Work/life balance • Political fights • Fight song - Platten • Fight the new drug • Violence against police
What scriptures could we use: • Ephesians 6 • Nehemiah 4:14 • Joshua 1:9 • Luke 22 • 1 Timothy 6:12 • Jude 3 (MSG) • 1 Peter 5:8-9 • Hebrews 11	**What stories could we tell:** • Boater stuck in a current • Prashan NBC video • Wake-up call • Adam & Jen El-Benni (Josh) • Historical Christian wake-ups (Amazing Grace)
What is the tone/mood of the delivery and environment? • Urgent • Ignited • Dynamic build • Energized	**What props could we use:** • Gloves • Ring • Punching bag
What do we want to avoid: • Endorsing culture warrior mentality • Silence the opposition • Condemnation	**What are possible next steps or resources:** • Memorize 1 Timothy 6:12 • Small boxing glove (write your fight on it) • Marriage Foundations • Christmas Offering • Next weekend (invite a friend)

SERIES TIMELINE

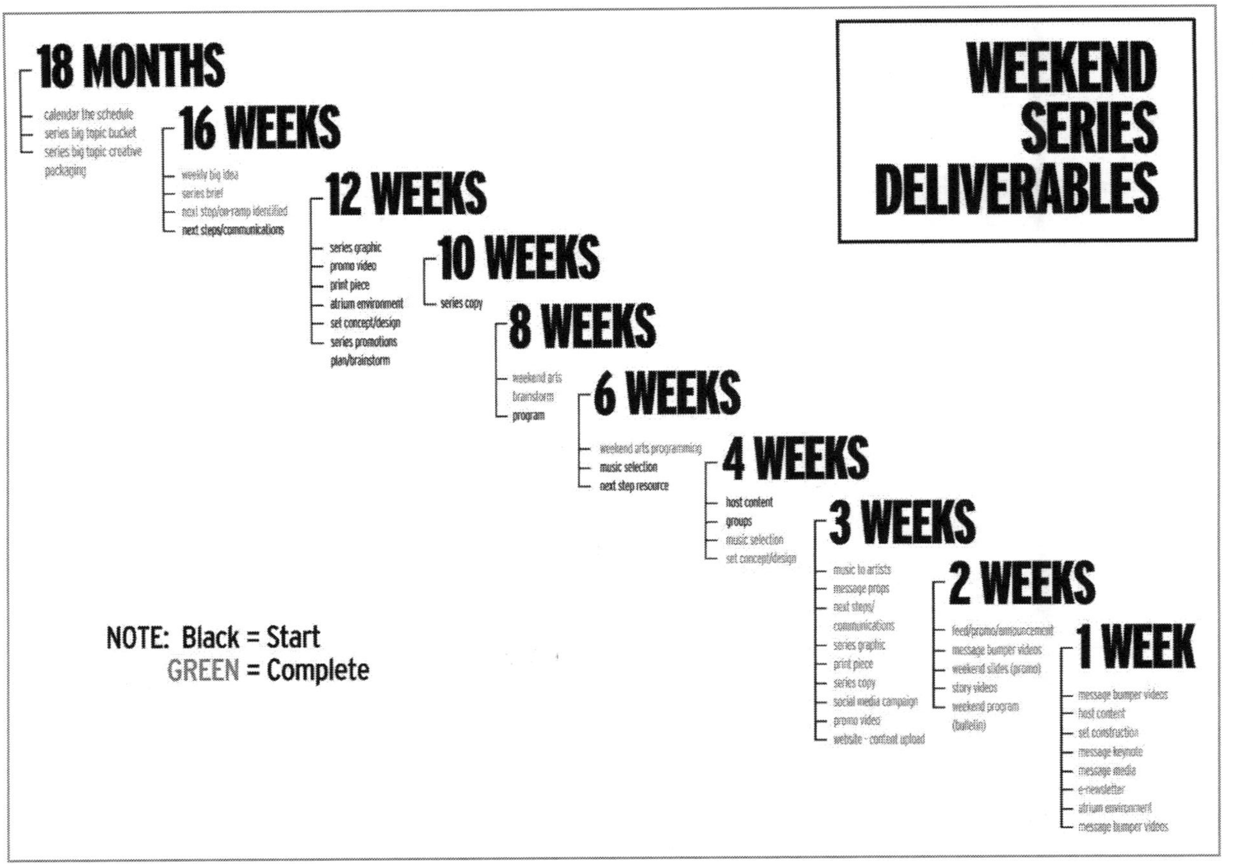

BRAND PERSONALITY PROFILE

A few years ago, PlainJoe Studios walked us through a pretty thorough personality process to align our brand with our mission and vision. Here is one tool we gained as a result of that experience. If you are in the early stages of clarifying your identity, you may not be ready for something this comprehensive. But, you can begin to ask yourself some simple questions in these areas to take early steps toward strengthening your brand (which is more than a logo).

CHARACTER (creates value)	RELATIONSHIP (transfers value)	IDENTITY (embodies value)	VOICE (expresses value)
Purpose — Heroism Remove barriers to help people get out of their seat and into God's story	**Roles** of: Volunteers IF: Leaders LR: Senior Management Team	**Physical** Creative	**Vision** Raise the bar by 20% for what's conventional
Mission — Management Mobilize teams and leverage resources to move beyond inspiration to action	**Goal** Be the church where you are	**Emotional** Encouraging	**Opportunity** Make a kingdom impact with others
Offer — Experience Opportunities to personally experience Jesus	**Measure** Baptisms, attendance, giving, participation, stories, start-ups, community health	**Intellectual** Unpredictable	**Insight** Don't wait around for someone else to do what only you can do
Cause — Reform Change the way people think about their Creator, themselves and others	**Effort** Create environments to share ageless truths with inventive approaches	**Social** Relatable	**Commitment** It's a lifestyle not a destination
Effect — Power We are catalyzed to transform our surroundings.	**Outcome** Reproducing churches that reproduce followers of Jesus.	**Spiritual** Empowering	**Experience** 25 years of consistency, integrity and changed lives
WHO YOU ARE	WHAT YOU DO	HOW YOU ARE KNOWN	WHY IT MATTERS

Personality™ plainjoestudios

Essence: Holistic community transformation

Brand Logic

BRAND EXPERIENCE TOUCHPOINT WHEEL

Brands are built through the total experience they offer. A good experience is authentic and consistent. It doesn't contradict itself. And, neither will a good brand. The first time we audited our brand experience was when the team at AspireOne walked us through the following exercise:

- In the center of the wheel, list the unifying values that rise above demographic lines. Think of the constants that don't change with time and are hardest to imitate. This is *who you are.*
- In the surrounding circles, list all of the places someone comes in contact with, or "touches" your brand experience. It's *what you do.*
- Ask yourself at each touch point: "Does *who we are* match *what we do* here, here, here and here?"

AspireOne.com

Fragmented identity equates to lost identity. Everything that touches your audience contributes something; the key is to make sure it positively reinforces the message you want to send. Deliver on your promise to build a brand that bonds and gets people talking.

TOUCH POINT EXERCISE

Put It In Practice :: Touch Point Exercise

Brainstorm all the different ways your ministry communicates today. Are they in alignment with who you say you are? Here are some ideas to get you started:

On Campus

- Signage (Indoor & Outdoor)
- Parking attendants
- Greeters/ushers
- Congregation
- Printed materials
  - Bulletin/weekend program
  - Guest/visitor information card
  - Ministry brochures/postcards
  - Welcome booklet (Or the overview of what to expect at your church)
  - Guest/visitor gift
- Children's ministry check-in
- Restrooms
- Sanctuary/auditorium
- Lobby monitors/side screen promotions
- Table tents
- Bookstore/cafe (Environment & staff)
- Pulpit/platform announcements
- Church name/logo
- Online campus/live streaming

Before Arrival

(External Communications)

- Website
- Social channels
- Pastor/Ministry leader blogs
- Word of mouth & your reputation (e.g., What are you known for today?)
- Billboards
- Advertisements (Such as newspapers, community bulletin boards, etc.)
- Weddings, funerals, & community serving or outreach events
- Holiday promotions (Christmas, Easter, etc.)

Post-Weekend/Ongoing

- Volunteer & small group sign-ups
- Member newsletter (Printed and/or e-newsletter)
- Text messaging
- Ministry-specific emails/postcards
- Membership next steps
- Guest/visitor initial follow-up

★ **Pro Tip ::** Don't forget to include what a guest might experience BEFORE & AFTER a weekend service in addition to what they may encounter when they arrive

Questions? We'd love to help—Hit us up:
info@AspireOne.com or visit AspireOne.com

AspireOne.com

CAUSE CALENDAR

OAKHILLS | CHURCH

2015 - 2016
Calendar of Causes
We are the Body of Christ, called to be Jesus in every neighborhood in our city and beyond.

This schedule was developed with the intent to bring consistency, focus and structure to giving/serving opportunities. The structure of the schedule allows for church-wide initiatives that bring maximum impact. The causes listed support both Community Life and Campus Life. Scheduling was intentional to provide seasons of rest and allow the congregation to breathe between each-call to-action.

Definition of "Cause":
A unifying missional call to action to meet a physical or spiritual need by giving time, talent or financial resources for God's glory.

Month	Church-Wide / Campus Specific	Campus/ Community	Cause	Ministry Lead	Promotion Dates
September	Church-Wide	Campus Life	Manos de Cristo (Shoebox Gifts) Global Outreach	Global Outreach / Family	9/1/2015-10/31/2015
October	Church-Wide	Community Life	National Night Out Community Outreach	Community Life	9/1/2015-10/2/2015
November	NONE	NONE	NONE	NONE	NONE
December	Church-Wide	Both	We Are Called Vision Campaign End of Year Offering	Executive	12/1/2015-12/31/2015
January	NONE	NONE	NONE	NONE	NONE
February	NONE	NONE	NONE	NONE	NONE
March	Church-Wide	Community Life	BLESS My 5 (Neighborhood Initiative)	Community Life	3/1/2016-3/31/2016
April	NONE	NONE	NONE	NONE	NONE
May	NONE	NONE	NONE	NONE	NONE
June	Church-Wide	Community Life	Bible Clubs Community Outreach	Community Life	6/1/2016-6/30/2016
July	NONE	NONE	NONE	NONE	NONE
August	NONE	NONE	NONE	NONE	NONE

OakHillsChurch.com

MONTHLY ANALYTICS CHECKLIST

Monthly Analytics Checklist

EVERY MONTH WHEN YOU LOOK AT YOUR ANALYTICS, WE RECOMMEND YOU DIVE INTO THESE AREAS:

GOOGLE

- [ ] Audience > Overview
- [ ] Mobile > Overview
- [ ] Acquisition > All Traffic > Channels
- [ ] Acquisition > Social > Network Referrals
- [ ] Behavior > Overview
- [ ] Behavior > Behavior Flow

FACEBOOK

- [ ] Posts
- [ ] People > Engaged

TWITTER

- [ ] Top Tweet
- [ ] Top Follower
- [ ] Top Mention

For more free resources, visit fishhook.us

EMPLOYEE HANDBOOK

INTRODUCTION

This handbook is designed to provide important information about working at Granger Community Church. Though we realize many of the policies and procedures within are quite boring, they are still important to communicate and we hope you find we've written them in such a way you won't fall asleep while reading.

While we've worked around the clock on this document, we have not been able to think of everything. And many of the things that did occur to us we chose not to include. Remember, we don't want you to fall asleep.

So, if you have questions not answered in this manual, don't be alarmed. Just ask your boss (if you don't know who that is, ask the person in the next cubicle) or the office administrator. We'll warn you in advance there are some things in this handbook we're encouraged by law to include. It's really hard to make those interesting, but we've done our best.

Have fun reading!

6 Granger Community Church Employee Handbook

PAYDAY

Hooray, it's payday. Employees who desire to be paid are normally paid every two weeks on Fridays. (Aren't you glad it's not once a year?) Direct deposit is required. Pay is in U.S. dollars only. Sorry, no rupees, euros or monopoly money available.

Certain deductions from your paycheck may be for elective options, like insurance and 403(b) investments. Other deductions are required by law, like taxes.

The Administrative Council determines compensation packages for the Senior Pastor and the Executive Pastor. Compensation packages for all other staff are determined by the Senior Pastor and the Executive Pastor (in consultation with supervisors) and approved by the Administrative Council. All compensation packages are reviewed annually based on scope of the job description, performance and attitude.

Other changes in pay or benefits are based on a number of factors including overall budget, financial condition of the church, cost of living considerations, performance and value to the church. Normally, raises are not given until the beginning of the calendar year following the first entire year of employment (e.g., Waldo is hired in July 2008, he will probably not be considered for a raise until January 2010).

Hourly staff are required to record work hours on a weekly time sheet. Time-and-a-half will only be paid for hourly wage staff working in excess of 40 hours in a given week if those hours have been approved by their supervisor.

Shhh...Keep Your Lips Sealed

Compensation packages are personal and confidential. Employees should never discuss their compensation package with anyone, unless they are a member of your family. This is something we take very seriously. Sharing compensation information with others could cost you your job. It's that serious.

STYLE GUIDE SAMPLE PAGES

In addition to logo guidelines, color palette options and brand design elements, a style guide should also include some basic style cues so the organization operates as one family in their voice, grammar and punctuation.

The Details

Nitty-gritty things that matter

Style Guide

This section is all about the little things. A simple look over this part of the Communications Playbook will help us stick together and will prevent us from making some common mistakes.

1. Station Identification

The Bare Minimum. Always include the Granger Community Church name or contact information on every public piece you distribute (even in your own ministry).

Example:
Granger Community Church
630 E. University Dr.
Granger, IN 46530
GCCwired.com

Or:
Granger Community Church – GCCwired.com

Or:
Granger Community Church
2701 East Bristol Street
Elkhart, IN 46514
GCCwired.com

Granger Community Church
GCCwired.com/Elkhart

Communication Arts Playbook 11

2. Core Content

Every piece should cover the most important question our audience asks: "What's in it for me?" Then follow up with the necessary basics of: Who, What, Where, When, Why and How (call to action).

Example:

WHO:
This is an all-ages, family-friendly event.

WHAT:
Do you want to help people, but don't know where to start? This is a great opportunity to serve our community, with your friends and family by your side.

The Church is commonly known by what we're against—but we want to be known by what we are *for.* All three GCC locations (Granger, Elkhart and MC3 in South Bend) will come together to make a positive impact in one of our communities. We'll have three types of opportunities: Heavy-duty, light-duty, and family-friendly.

Please be sure to wear closed-toe shoes and clothing you don't mind getting dirty.

WHEN:
Saturday, May 16, 9 a.m.-12:30 p.m.

WHERE:
Meet at the Granger Campus Auditorium and serve throughout Michiana.

REGISTRATION
Browse the full list of serving options, then choose the best one for you and your family when you register.

REGISTER

Things To Watch

Instead of striving to be right we strive to be consistent. This section contains our grammar, style and punctuation best practices.[3]

- ☐ **Abbreviations**. Avoid in general, particularly when referring to events or groups.
  - *Example:* Granger Community Church (not GCC or Granger) – GCC is acceptable in second reference. Granger is acceptable in second reference for WiredChurches.com pieces.
- ☐ **Dates.** Drop reference to year when appropriate. Don't abbreviate.
  - *Example:* Tuesday, March 9 (not Tues., Mar 9 2014)

[3] We choose to use *The Associated Press Stylebook and Briefing on Media Law* (primary resource) as well as *Wired Style: Principles of English Usage in the Digital Age* as reference materials.

FOUR PHASES OF CHURCH COMMUNICATION

This basic training tool helps campus admin teams see what a healthy process could look like for each communication planning step, and where the baton gets passed between those steps.

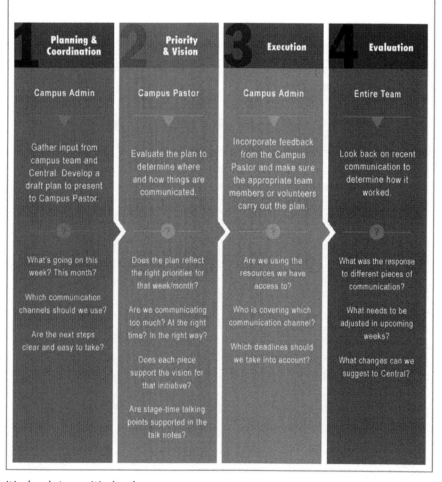

life.church | open.life.church

FOUR PHASES OF CAMPUS COMMUNICATION

1 Planning & Coordination

The **Campus Admin** gathers input from campus team members and from the Communications Team to see what needs to be communicated during the current and upcoming weeks. With that information, the Campus Admin can pull together an initial plan to present to the Campus Pastor, noting what will be communicated through different communication channels.

Key Questions

- What's going on this week?
- What's coming up in the next few weeks?
- Which opportunities are best suited for which communication channels?
- Are people being presented with a manageable amount of information to digest?
- Will people be able to clearly see and take their next steps?

2 Priority & Vision

The **Campus Pastor** evaluates the plan to determine where and how things are communicated.

Key Questions

- Does the communication plan reflect the right priorities for that week/month?
- Are we communicating too much? Does something need to be deleted, delayed, or changed to a different communication channel?
- Does each piece of communication support the vision for that initiative?
- Will people be able to clearly see and take their next steps?
- Is everything I'm mentioning from stage also in the talk notes?

3 Execution

The **Campus Admin** incorporates feedback from the Campus Pastor and makes sure the appropriate team members or volunteers carry out the plan.

Key Questions

- Are we using the resources we have access to?
- Who is covering which communication channel?
- Do we have everything we need to communicate in each channel?
- What deadlines should we to take into account?

4 Evaluation

The **entire team** looks back on recent communication to determine how it worked.

Key Questions

- What was the response to different pieces of communication?
- Did anything have an unusual response–either more or less than expected? Why?
- What needs to be adjusted in upcoming weeks?
- What changes can we suggest to Central for current or future resources?

TIPS FOR ESTABLISHING A COMMUNICATION REVIEW PROCESS

In a multi-campus environment, each campus carries a set of responsibilities to ensure excellent written and visual communication. The Central Communications and Creative Media teams resource and equip Campus Admins as point people for all-church standards. They also are the go-to people for questions about the quality or origin of campus-created materials. Leveraging responsibility and accountability, this guide helps Campus Admins establish an empowered and collaborative campus review process.

Tips for Establishing a Communication Review Process

Campus Admins/Admin Leaders should monitor written communication without being a bottleneck - working more like a consultant than a content creator. Talk to your Campus Pastor about what that would look like ideally.

Focus primarily on things that people will be seeing on their first or second touch with Life.Church. For the insider communication (like special-focus blogs, ministry leader emails, etc.), work on a spot-check basis asking to check things periodically.

Things that should definitely be reviewed: talk notes (each week), campus emails, potty pub, mailers, and anything else with a broad audience.

Some Specific Ideas to Consider:

- Give your team the Communications Values & Best Practices document. It's a great resource for anyone who uses words. Really.
- Let your team know what sort of pieces you'd like to review and when you'd like to review it. Have them send you their final draft for review.
- Set expectations for a turnaround time from you – can you get to everything that day, need a couple days, etc.
- Let them know what you can and cannot do for them. Point them to resources they can pull from when creating content and focus on reviewing.
- Identify and work closely with other skilled proofreaders and editors on your team including volunteers. Share the communication resources, guides, and standards with them. Consider having different people review for different things – one for grammar and spelling, another for context/message, another as a newcomer, etc.
- Consider setting up a proofing volunteer team. Just a handful of volunteers who you can send materials out to.
- When someone brings you something to review – ask who, what, when, where, why, and how. Have them tell you the goal of the piece.
- If the piece will be printed – review it printed. If it's an email or online material – review it electronically.
- Don't just point out what's wrong, but what you like and what they did right.
- Teach them along the way – you're the one with the communication standards in mind not them.
- If you routinely see "bad" communication from a team member or ministry, take some time to work with them or have standard pieces and content they can pull from when needed. Be sure to give them examples of good writing.
- Above all be flexible and let the team know that you'll be working out a process and things could change – but it will be for the better!

PLAN IN CIRCLES NOT GRIDS

When planning annually or semi-annually in a calendar grid, an open date can look like the perfect spot for another activity! It is easy to let a calendar get too full because there are so many little boxes waiting to be filled. But with a large planning team, it is much easier to see when the circle is simply getting too full.

We take the approach of planning in monthly circles. We fill the space with the ideas that are central to that month. We estimate together how much voice, time and resources it will require.

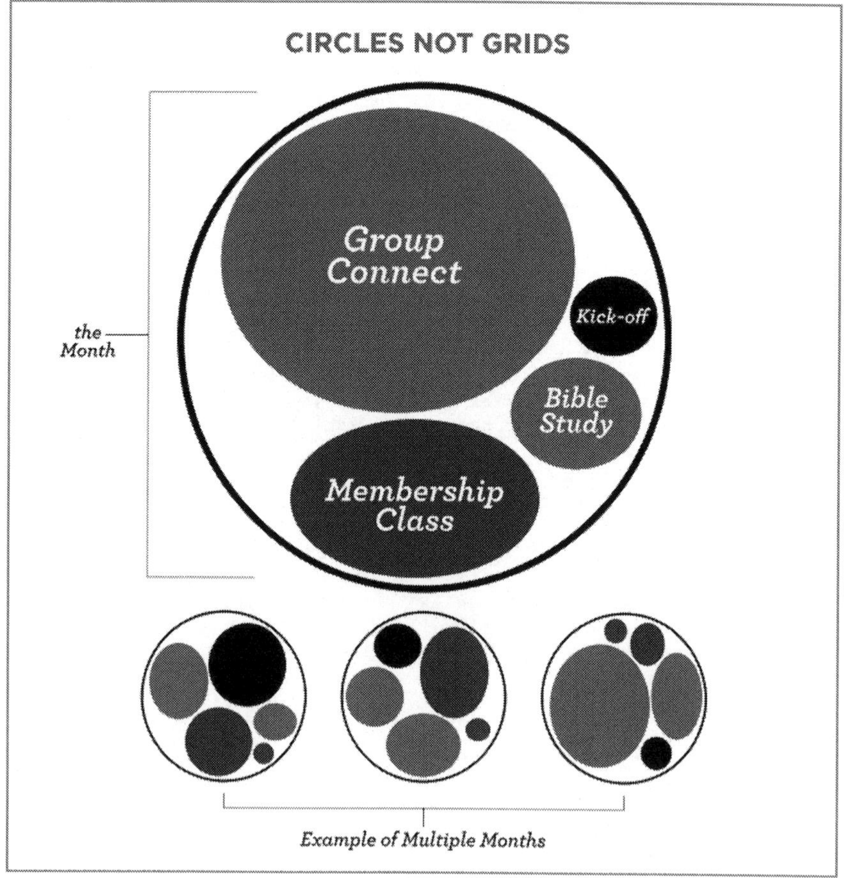

MOVING FROM REACTIVE TO PROACTIVE

A small change in structure can turn organizational behavior from a reactive environment to one that values advance planning and collaborative dialogue. The result? A sustainable workflow and a clear message on a large scale.

Before:

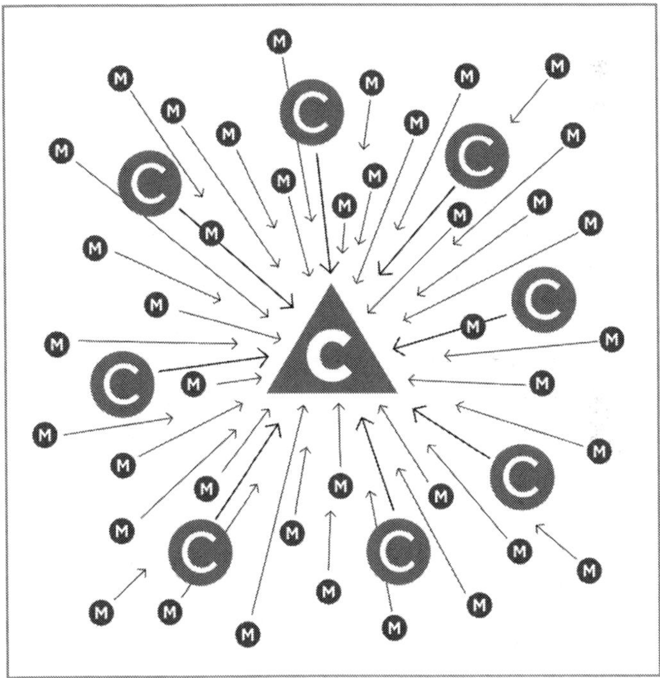

hillsidewired.com

This visual shows a common structure, with the communications function sitting in the center of a circle with everyone firing projects and request their way*. Unbridled input and direction from every angle feels as bad as it looks.

* C (Center) = Communications   C (Circled) = Campus   M = Ministry   ML = Ministry Leader

After:

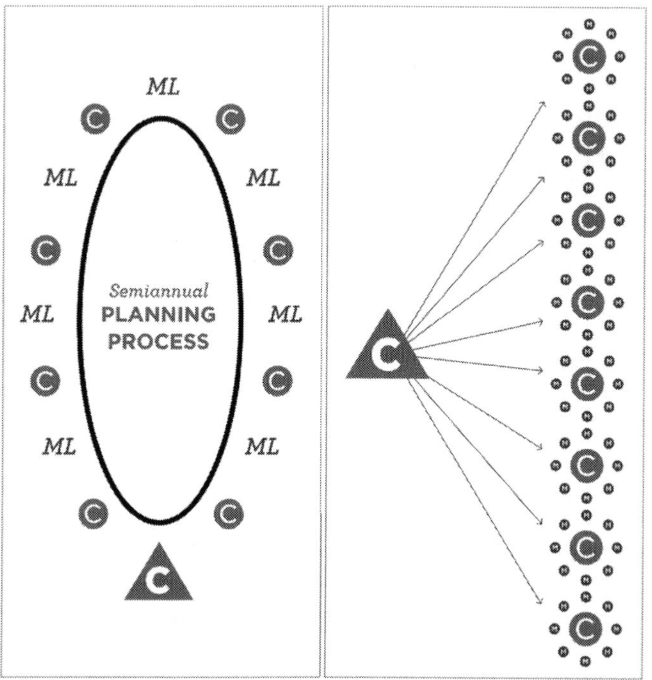

hillsidewired.com

A small investment of time up-front to talk through the vision and purpose of the approaching ministry season saves countless frantic hours of wasted effort. The communications team can listen to big-picture plans from stakeholders across the life of the church, look for cross-promotional opportunities, organize resources and present a strategic communication plan for each campus (or ministry) season, not just one calendar event at a time.

WEEKLY COMMUNICATIONS CHECKLIST

Weekly Communications Checklist

THE 10 TASKS TO DO EVERY WEEK EVEN IF YOU DON'T HAVE A COMMUNICATIONS DIRECTOR

☐ **1. CONNECT WORSHIP AND COMMUNICATIONS.**
Consider if you have clear lines of communication between preaching/worship and those who are producing your communications tools (bulletin, worship announcements, building displays, website, social media, etc.). When communications tools align with the messages in worship, newcomers and church members know what to do next to engage or move forward in their faith.

☐ **2. OPEN UP THE VALVE AND MAKE SURE INFORMATION IS FLOWING FROM YOUR LEADERSHIP TEAM TO OTHER KEY LEADERS AND IMPLEMENTERS.**
As your executive team plans, regularly ask, "Who else should be a part of this conversation?" Make sure your staff and leaders know about upcoming initiatives, sermon series, strategic plan objectives, church-wide events, etc.

☐ **3. REVIEW WHAT IS COMING UP IN THE NEXT 7-10 DAYS AT YOUR CHURCH.**
What rises to the top as a church-wide priority? Feature it on your website, app, bulletin, eNews and in your video announcements.

☐ **4. TAKE NOTE OF WHAT'S HAPPENING IN THE NEXT 30 DAYS.**
These opportunities are nearing the final countdown when it comes to communications. Consider who would benefit most from these items and list ways to connect with these audiences.

For more free resources, visit fishhook.us

- ☐ **5. KEEP A MASTER CALENDAR THAT GIVES YOU AN OVERVIEW OF THE NEXT 6-12 MONTHS AT YOUR CHURCH.**
  What are the top priorities as you invite folks to participate in ministry opportunities? How can you encourage teamwork? Any major initiatives/events that would benefit from a specific planning team? Talk about these calendar items in your staff meeting to help avoid scheduling conflicts.

- ☐ **6. FIND THE STORY.**
  Life change is taking place through the ministry of your church! How can you share the stories from individual ministries, small groups, families, etc.? Think videos, print or online articles, photos and social media. Pick a few stories and make a plan to let the congregation see how others are living out the mission!

- ☐ **7. SCHEDULE WEEKLY SOCIAL MEDIA POSTS.**
  What are you currently using? Facebook? Twitter? Instagram? If you're just getting started, try investing in one option and do it well! This will help you create a community online and avoid feeling overwhelmed. Try posts that go beyond sermon series and events. Ask questions. Invite people into conversations.

- ☐ **8. UPDATE YOUR CONTENT.**
  When newcomers visit your website, help them find current, interesting and engaging photos and content!

- ☐ **9. EVALUATE AND ANALYZE.**
  What recent event, series or ministry opportunity could you learn from? Who participated? What was their response? Consider your web analytics. Use available stats to find out who is visiting your website, engaging with you on social media and opening your weekly eNews. These facts can help you learn more about what you are doing well and where you should invest more resources.

- ☐ **10. CONSIDER HIRING A COMMUNICATIONS DIRECTOR!**
  Even a part-time staff member can make a significant difference in keeping information flowing among staff and leaders as well as to the congregation and community.

For more free resources, visit fishhook.us

ENDNOTES

Introduction

1. "2015 Sees Sharp Rise in Post-Christian Population," Barna Group, August 12, 2015, barna.org/barna-update/culture/728-america-more-post-christian-than-two-years-ago#.Vmw0yWQrJhB.

Chapter 1

1. PepsiCo. Inc.
2. Image source: "Oneify," boygirl, flickr.com/photos/70411511@N00/72753726.
3. "It's the Conversation Economy, Stupid," David Armano, BusinessWeek.com, April 9, 2007, bloomberg.com/bw/stories/2007-04-09/its-the-conversation-economy-stupidbusinessweek-business-news-stock-market-and-financial-advice.
4. Nelson Books, *New Rebellion Handbook: A Holy Uprising: Making Real the Extraordinary in Everyday Life* (Nashville, TN: Thomas Nelson, Inc., 2006).
5. "Do You Google?" Google Official Blog, October 25, 2006, googleblog.blogspot.co.uk/2006/10/do-you-google.html.
6. "Fair Play," The LEGO Group, lego.com/en-US/legal/legal-notice/fair-play.

Chapter 2

1. Richard Saul Wurman, *Information Anxiety* (New York: Doubleday, 1989, 32).
2. "Email Statistics Report, 2013-2017," The Radicati Group, April 2013, radicati.com/wp/wp-content/uploads/2013/04/Email-Statistics-Report-2013-2017-Executive-Summary.pdf.
3. Internet Live Stats, internetlivestats.com/.
4. "App Store Metrics," PocketGamer.biz, pocketgamer.biz/metrics/app-store/.
5. "Google Search Statistics," Internet Live Stats, internetlivestats.com/google-search-statistics/.
6. "Death by Information Overload," Paul Hemp, *Harvard Business Review*, September 2009, hbr.org/2009/09/death-by-information-overload.
7. "Information Overload-When Information Becomes Noise," Steve Nguyen, Ph.D., *Workplace Psychology*, May 18, 2011, workplacepsychology.net/2011/05/18/information-overload-when-information-becomes-noise/.
8. "How to Reduce Information Overload," Tina Su, *Think Simple Now*, thinksimplenow.com/productivity/how-to-reduce-information-overload/.
9. Sara Martin, "Our health at risk," *The American Psychological Association Monitor* Vol 43, No. 3 (2012): 18.
10. "Stress," American Psychological Association, apa.org/topics/stress/index.aspx.
11. "Your 'new' is not news," Katya Andresen, *Network for Good*, August 30, 2007, networkforgood.com/nonprofitblog/your-new-is-not-news/.
12. "Recommendations from friends remain most credible form of advertising among consumers; branded websites are the second-highest-rated form," Andrew McCaskill, Nielsen, September 28, 2015, nielsen.com/us/en/press-room/2015/recommendations-from-friends-remain-most-credible-form-of-advertising.html.
13. Philip Kotler and Joanne Scheff, *Standing Room Only* (New York: Harvard Business School Press. New York, 1997).
14. Denise Lee Yohn, *What Great Brands Do* (San Francisco: Jossey-Bass, 2014).

Chapter 3

1. "Justin Timberlake No Soliciting vinyl decal," amazon.com/Justin-Timberlake-Soliciting-vinyl-decal/dp/B00MN1T668.
2. "Starbucks is Just Like You," Stephen Denny, *Note to CMO*, October 17, 2007, stephendenny.com/note-to-cmo-starbucks-is-just-like-you/.
3. "Careers: Work Among True Believers?" Rusty Weston, *Fast Company*, October 10, 2007, fastcompany.com/661017/careers-work-among-true-believers.
4. "A Friend Told Me About It," Jessica Hagy, *Indexed*, September 9, 2008, thisisindexed.com/2008/09/a-friend-told-me-about-it/.

Chapter 4

1. "It's the Conversation Economy, Stupid"
2. Marshal McLuhan and Lewis H. Lapham, *Understanding Media: The Extension of Man* (Cambridge, MA: The MIT Press, 1964).
3. Haydn Shaw, *Generational IQ* (Carol Stream, IL: Tyndale House Publishers, 2015).
4. "Perspective," DOGHOUSE, thedoghousediaries.com/4564.
5. "Humans have shorter attention span than goldfish, thanks to smartphones," Leon Watson, *The Telegraph*, May 15, 2015, telegraph.co.uk/news/science/science-news/11607315/Humans-have-shorter-attention-span-than-goldfish-thanks-to-smartphones.html.
6. "Memory of a goldfish? Actually fish can recall events 12 days ago." Raziye Akkoc, *The Telegraph*, July 1, 2014, telegraph.co.uk/news/science/science-news/10937888/Memory-of-a-goldfish-Actually-fish-can-recall-events-12-days-ago.html.
7. Photo: @esmith_images/Instagram, "Humans have shorter attention span than goldfish, thanks to smartphones."
8. "The 5 Metrics You Need to Know to Give a Great Presentation," Noah Zandan, Prezi, April 10, 2014, prezi.com/zg1cutjilff5/the-5-metrics-you-need-to-know-to-give-a-great-presentation/.
9. "Mind Over Mass Media," Steven Pinker, *The New York Times*, June 10, 2010, nytimes.com/2010/06/11/opinion/11Pinker.html?_r=0.
10. "The web shatters focus, rewires brains," Nicholas Carr, Wired, May 24, 2010, wired.com/2010/05/ff_nicholas_carr/all/1.
11. Shaw, *Generational IQ*. Sourcing "The State of The Bible," Barna Group, 2014.
12. "What Captures Your Attention Controls Your Life," Kare Anderson, *Harvard Business Review*, June 5, 2012, hbr.org/2012/06/what-captures-your-attention-c.
13. "Rela-tech-ship," Kelley Hartnett, *Blue Is a Circle*, September 30, 2008, kelleyhartnett.com/.
14. "The Pace of Modern Life," xkcd, xkcd.com/1227/.

Chapter 5

1. "The One Simple Secret that Will Help You Reach More People," Chris Forbes, December 27, 2006.

Chapter 6

1. Robert K. Cooper, *Get Out of Your Own Way* (New York: Crown Business, 2006).
2. Nancy Hoft Consulting, world-ready.com/.
3. Gary Ferraro, *Cultural Dimension of International Business*, 5th ed. (Upper Saddle River, NJ: Prentice Hall, 2005).

4. Richard L. Reising, *Beyond Relevance*, beyondrelevance.com/.
5. *Relevant Magazine*, March 2008.
6. Mark L. Waltz, *Lasting Impressions* (Loveland, CO: Group Publishing, Inc., 2008).
7. Disney Institute, *Be Our Guest* (New York: Disney Editions, 2001).

Chapter 7

1. "About Modern Toilet Restaurant," Modern Toilet, moderntoilet.com.tw/en/about.asp.
2. Image source: yeinjee.com/taiwan-modern-toilet-restaurant/.
3. Robert Kegan and Lisa Laskow Lahey, *How the Way We Talk Can Change the Way We Work* (San Francisco, Jossey-Bass, 2001).
4. Dennis Fletcher, *Leadership Journal*, 2008.
5. "[On writing] Marketing madlibs," Matt Linderman, *Signal v. Noise*, February 4, 2008, signalvnoise.com/posts/814-on-writing-marketing-madlibs.
6. "Gobbledygook Manifesto," David Meerman Scott, *ChangeThis*, August 8, 2007, davidmeermanscott.com/documents/3703Gobbledygook.pdf.
7. "Disney's Mission Statement," The Walt Disney Company, disneycompanyprofile.weebly.com/.
8. Disney Institute, *Be Our Guest*.

Chapter 8

1. "Are Our Schools Going Green?" Michelle Wegner, MichelleWegner.com, August 26, 2010, michellewegner.com/2010/08/26/are-our-schools-going-green/.
2. "Communications Revolution Part 3: The Death of the Weekly Program/Bulletin/Newsletter," Tim Schraeder, TimSchraeder.com, July 31, 2008, timschraeder.com/2008/07/31/communications-revolution-part-3-the-death-of-the-weekly-programbulletinnewsletter/.
3. "What is Getting Real?" 37signals, LLC, *Getting Real*, 2006, gettingreal.37signals.com/ch01_What_is_Getting_Real.php.
4. Image source: thisisnthappiness.com/post/113723968214/take-one.
5. "List of virtual communities with more than 1 million users," Wikipedia, en.wikipedia.org/wiki/List_of_virtual_communities_with_more_than_1_million_users
6. "Which Social Media Accounts Really Matter and Why," Neil Patel, Kissmetrics Blog, June 05, 2014, blog.kissmetrics.com/which-social-accounts-matter/.
7. "Facebook's War Continues Against Fake Profiles and Bots," James Parsons, *Huffpost Business*, May 22, 2015, huffingtonpost.com/james-parsons/facebooks-war-continues-against-fake-profiles-and-bots_b_6914282.html.

Chapter 9

1. John B. Priestley, *Thoughts in the Wilderness* (New York: Harper and Bros., 1957).
2. "Victim of the great garbage patch: Turtle is just one of thousands left deformed or dead by Pacific Ocean plastic," *UK Daily Mail*, July 15, 2011, dailymail.co.uk/sciencetech/article-2014849/Victim-great-garbage-patch.html.
3. Image source: dailypicksandflicks.com/2012/07/12/daily-picdump-517/rust-oleum-stops-rust-the-irony/.
4. "3 Easy Ways to Lose Your Identity," Jeremy Scheller, JeremyScheller.com, February 20, 2008.
5. Andy Sernovitz, *Word of Mouth Marketing: How Smart Companies Get People Talking* (Chicago: Kaplan Publishing, 2006).

6. Image source: 41.media.tumblr.com/tumblr_m9u87vH9Zg1qasthro1_500.jpg
7. "The Art of Reframing," Mark Batterson, MarkBatterson.com, October 23, 2006, markbatterson.com/uncategorized/the-art-of-reframing/.

Chapter 10

1. "Don't Complicate the Solution," Steve Smith, orderedlist.com, November 14, 2007.
2. Ibid.
3. Steve Krug, *Don't Make Me Think, Revisited: A Common Sense Approach to Web Usability* (New Riders, 2014).
4. "10 Easy Ways to Keep Me from Visiting Your Church Because I Visited Your Website," Tony Morgan, TonyMorganLive.com, May 14, 2005, tonymorganlive.com/2005/05/14/10-easy-ways-to-keep-me-from-visiting-your-church-because-i-visited-your-website/.
5. Anthony D. Williams and Don Tapscott, *Macrowikinomics: Rebooting Business and the World* (New York: Portfolio Penguin: 2010).
6. Kris Wilson, "cyanide and happiness," explosm.net, June 14, 2012, explosm.net/comics/2829.
7. Daniel Levitin, *The Organized Mind: Thinking Straight in the Age of Information Overload* (New York: Penguin Group, 2014).
8. "Directors on Directing," Lynda.com, lynda.com/player/popup?lpk4=80161&playChapter=False.
9. "Social media starting block," *tastefully offensive,* tumblr.tastefullyoffensive.com/post/28099740796#.VusPK5MrJBw.

Part 3 Intro

1. "Getting Buy-In," Sue Bushell, CIO, September 8, 2005, cio.com.au/article/7954/getting_buy-in/.

Chapter 11

1. "Elbert Hubbard Quotes," Elbert Hubbard, *The Quotations Page,* quotationspage.com/quotes/Elbert_Hubbard/.
2. "Untitled by Blaine Hogan," Tim Schraeder, *Church Marketing Sucks,* July 27, 2011, churchmarketingsucks.com/2011/07/untitled-by-blaine-hogan/.
3. Image source: "H2Ego," Pleated-Jeans.com, stream.pleated-jeans.com/post/26833802319/h2ego.
4. Daniel Pink, *A Whole New Mind: Why Right-Brainers Will Rule the Future* (New York: The Berkley Publishing Group, 2005).

Chapter 12

1. "The Seeing/Believing Gap," Marcia Conner, *Fast Company,* February 2006, fastcompany.com/919282/seeing-believing-gap.
2. Image source: *This Is Broken,* goodexperience.com/blog/broken/images/fly.jpg.
3. "The Art of Rainmaking," Guy Kawasaki, GuyKawasaki.com, February 2006, blog.guykawasaki.com/2006/02/the_art_of_rain.html.

Chapter 13

1. Eric Schmidt and Jonathan Rosenberg, *How Google Works* (New York: Grand Central Publishing, 2014).
2. Image source: Pleated-Jeans.com, pleated-jeans.com/2012/07/30/funny-pic-dump-7-30-12/.
3. "People Don't Hate Change, They Hate How You're Trying to Change Them," Michael T. Kanazawa, *ChangeThis*, July 9, 2008, changethis.com/48.01.CorporateChange.
4. Ibid.

Chapter 14

1. "Project Annihilation: Death of an iTrip," Bard Dybwad, Engadget, March 24, 2005, engadget.com/2005/03/24/project-annihilation-death-of-an-itrip/.
2. "Harvey Samuel Firestone," Wikipedia, en.wikipedia.org/wiki/Harvey_Samuel_Firestone.

Chapter 15

1. "Why Business Leaders Should Act More like Artists," John Maeda, *Harvard Business Review*, December 1, 2009, hbr.org/2009/12/why-business-leaders-should-ac.
2. "Why Artists Should Act Like Leaders," *Accidental Creative*, accidentalcreative.com.
3. More about Christine Caine at christinecaine.com.

GIVING CREDIT WHERE CREDIT IS DUE

There are countless people who listened, inspired, encouraged, motivated, guided, assisted and challenged me to write. Here goes my best attempt at an impossible task: thanking those who deserve the thanks for helping me communicate to the communicators.

- Thanks to my main man, Mark Meyer, who brings out my best all day, every day. I love, love, love doing life with this amazing human.
- Thanks to Mom and Dad for raising me to be brave, to enjoy life's experiences and to be ignorant to what's impossible.
- Thanks to my string of bosses, June Dugan, Maggie Smith, Roger Mason, Tony Morgan and Tim Stevens for smoothing my rough edges, teaching me a ton and for becoming good friends.
- Thanks to my Meyer home team—Emmi, Easton, Mel and Bunny—for spurring me on, backing me up in every way, praying for me and going on chocolate and cereal runs.
- Thanks to my two favorite contrarians, Jason Miller and Erin Meyer, who force me to look at things from every angle and to never accept the lazy answer.
- Thanks to my former team members Jami Ruth, Lisa DeSelm, Jeanna Leitch, Daryl McMullen, Jason Powell, Justin Moore, Bonnie Moore and Brittany Jaso for years of the best work, fun, stories and snackie snacks.
- Thanks to my pastor Mark Beeson and the leadership team at Granger Community Church for your faithfulness, your example and your endless support.

- Thanks to Tim Schraeder for being that constant "you HAVE to do this" voice in my life and pushing me to update my original manuscript.
- Thanks to Peter McGowan for sharing clients, experiences, venues, Walt Disney and *Hamilton* to sharpen my worldview and communications lens.
- Thanks to Chad Cannon, Emily Lineberger, Haley Walden and Alison Kennedy for partnering with me to bring this book to a new audience facing new realities. You listened patiently as I caught up to you, instigated higher-level thinking, provided tactfully honest feedback and worked your tails off to upgrade (let's be honest) me.
- Thanks to all the generous professionals and organizations who inspired me, provided examples and graciously allowed me to mention and learn from them along the way. Much love goes to the Granger Community Church, PlainJoe Studios and Unstuck Group teams, Brad Abare, Chuck Scoggins, The Center for Church Communication, Judy Stallwitz, Hillside Church, Gerry True, Oak Hills Church, Lori Bailey, Life. Church, Evan McBroom, Fishhook, Larry Little, Phil Cooke, Haydn Shaw, Rick Bailey, Dawn Nicole-Baldwin, Aspire!One, Chris Forbes, Mark Batterson, Christine Caine, Blaine Hogan, Walt Disney, Seth Godin, Guy Kawasaki, David Armano, Andy Sernovitz, The Harvard Business Review, Basecamp, Xplane, LEGO, Google, Unum, Pepsi One, Justin Timberlake, REI, Jessica Hagy, Michelle Wegner, Laura Meyer, Steve Smith, Explosm, *Doghouse Diaries*, Eric Smith Images, Dr. Mark Goulston, Dennis Fletcher, *The Leadership Journal*, McDonald's and Starbucks (among many others).